Assessment-Driven Instruction in Physical Education

A Standards-Based Approach to Promoting and Documenting Learning

Jacalyn Lund, PhD
Georgia State University

Mary Lou Veal, EdD
Middle Tennessee State University

Human Kinetics

Library of Congress Cataloging-in-Publication Data

Lund, Jacalyn Lea, 1950-
  Assessment-driven instruction in physical education : a standards-based approach to promoting and documenting learning / Jacalyn L. Lund, PhD, Georgia State University, Mary Lou Veal, EdD.
        pages cm
  Includes bibliographical references and index.
  1. Physical education and training--Study and teaching (Secondary)--Examinations. 2. Educational tests and measurements. I. Veal, Mary Lou. II. Title.
   GV362.5.L84 2013
   372.86'044--dc23

                    2012039965

ISBN-10: 1-4504-1991-7 (print)
ISBN-13: 978-1-4504-1991-8 (print)

The web addresses cited in this text were current as of November 2012, unless otherwise noted.

Acquisitions Editor: Cheri Scott; **Developmental Editor:** Jacqueline Eaton Blakley; **Assistant Editor:** Anne Rumery; **Copyeditor:** Joy Wotherspoon; **Indexer:** Nancy Ball; **Permissions Manager:** Dalene Reeder; **Graphic Designer:** Nancy Rasmus; **Graphic Artist:** Kathleen Boudreau-Fuoss; **Cover Designer:** Keith Blomberg; **Photograph (cover):** © Human Kinetics; **Photographs (interior):** Photo on page 6 courtesy of Comstock; all others © Human Kinetics, unless otherwise noted; **Art Manager:** Kelly Hendren; **Associate Art Manager:** Alan L. Wilborn; **Illustrations:** © Human Kinetics; **Printer:** P.A. Hutchison

Printed in the United States of America   10   9   8   7   6   5   4   3   2   1

The paper in this book is certified under a sustainable forestry program.

Human Kinetics
Website: www.HumanKinetics.com

United States: Human Kinetics
P.O. Box 5076
Champaign, IL 61825-5076
800-747-4457
e-mail: humank@hkusa.com

Canada: Human Kinetics
475 Devonshire Road Unit 100
Windsor, ON N8Y 2L5
800-465-7301 (in Canada only)
e-mail: info@hkcanada.com

Europe: Human Kinetics
107 Bradford Road
Stanningley
Leeds LS28 6AT, United Kingdom
+44 (0) 113 255 5665
e-mail: hk@hkeurope.com

Australia: Human Kinetics
57A Price Avenue
Lower Mitcham, South Australia 5062
08 8372 0999
e-mail: info@hkaustralia.com

New Zealand: Human Kinetics
P.O. Box 80
Torrens Park, South Australia 5062
0800 222 062
e-mail: info@hknewzealand.com

E5589

CONTENTS

PREFACE

As university teacher educators, we share a passion for helping teacher candidates understand how to assess student learning in physical education. Because of our interest in standards-based assessment for learning, we have taught assessment courses for undergraduate teacher candidates at our respective universities. We have given numerous conference presentations on assessment for teachers using information gained from our research on assessment. For several years, we've tried out our ideas in our classes about what teacher candidates need to know about assessment, and we've experimented with a progression of learning experiences that best help teacher candidates learn key concepts about assessment. Even with all our experience, however, our students have struggled with understanding how to use assessment to improve student learning. This book is the result of many years of thinking and writing about assessment.

During our own professional preparation programs we, like other teacher candidates, took a course called "Tests and Measurement." We both recognized, even as beginning teachers, that assessment was a way to enhance both teaching and learning. To us, it seemed important to put what we learned about tests and measurement into practice—not just to measure learning, but to promote it. At the time, it was somewhat unusual for physical education teachers to collect data about student learning, but we were driven to document that learning was taking place.

For many years, assessments in physical education consisted mostly of skill tests. As young teachers, we remember using these and feeling that something was missing. Since the criteria for these skill tests were usually reported in statistical terms (something that we haven't really said much about in this book), it was difficult for us as teachers to determine what students really needed to learn and be able to do and to translate student performance into grades. In contrast, standards-based assessment uses a criterion-referenced system; student performance is compared to a standard that represents mastery. The criterion-referenced mindset is much more compatible with what teachers are trying to do in physical education.

The normative curve that many of the statistical analyses are based on assumes that student scores will fall along a normal curve, which is shown in chapter 13. However, the normal distribution of scores assumes that there is no intervention involved (Guskey 2011). Since teaching is an intervention, it disrupts the distribution of scores on a normal curve. Unfortunately, many of the skill assessments that we have in physical education are norm referenced; while they may be good assessment protocols, it is difficult to develop appropriate criteria that are based on a mastery- or criterion-referenced mindset.

Our ultimate goal is to help you learn to think like assessors, meaning that you are deliberately working toward helping students meet learning outcomes and standards. We have purposely designed this book so it could be used in a methods class, an assessment class, or for in-service education. While the primary focus of the book is assessment in the psychomotor domain, we've included chapters on assessment in the cognitive and affective domains because most physical education programs and the standards of the National Association for Sport and Physical Education (NASPE) emphasize all three domains.

This text is designed to prepare teacher candidates to meet standard 5 (Impact on Student Learning) found in the NASPE *National Standards and Guidelines for Physical Education Teacher Education* (2009). It begins with a discussion of assessment concepts that must be understood, along with an argument for why teachers must learn to think like assessors. After discussing some misconceptions that we have encountered in our classes, we explain the importance of linking assessment to intended learning outcomes. Next, teacher candidates learn to answer the key questions of who, what, when, and how assessment is used in physical education.

Part I of this book is primarily concerned with planning for assessment, both long-term plans and lesson plans. In part II, we help you fine-tune your assessment skills by teaching you how to use assessment strategically and in meaningful ways. One of the hardest things for teachers to do is to design learning outcomes with specific criteria that guide assessment. We take you through this process step by step and provide useful guidelines for setting reasonable and attainable criteria. Part II also provides samples of various assessment tools and guidelines for developing tools in all three domains. Finally, in part III, we explain how to use assessment data to improve teaching and learning.

Most methods classes are organized around management concerns. This book is focused on student learning and on using assessment to become a more effective teacher. Assessment is the focus throughout the book instead of merely appearing in one chapter as a factor to consider after the decisions about lesson organization are made. We are not saying that management and organization aren't important, but rather that *student learning* should be the first consideration. All other decisions should be made with regard to how they influence student learning. While we emphasize throughout the book that assessment is most useful to facilitate learning, we also provide a chapter on grading. The book ends with some suggestions for your further development as an assessor.

Learning to effectively design and use quality assessments in physical education requires strong knowledge of assessment concepts, which are addressed in the first chapter of this text. We tell our students that learning to be an assessor begins with learning the language of assessment. In some ways, it is like learning a new language, so this text includes a glossary that defines the terms that constitute this language of assessment. These terms appear in **bold** where they are first used in the book's text. The glossary also lists the chapters where the concepts are discussed. To further build your assessment language skills, we highlight select key concepts at the beginning of each chapter.

In addition to a strong understanding of assessment concepts, teachers need what we call *assessment PCK:* an integration of the subject matter (e.g., volleyball), knowledge of the environment and about students, and procedural knowledge about assessment and about how to manage assessments in the physical education classroom.

In this book, readers will find many examples of quality assessments, along with practice tasks to help them design their own teaching assessments. One thing that distinguishes this text from typical measurement texts is the inclusion of practice tasks, called Your Turn. We envision this book as both text and workbook, in which readers are asked to design a variety of assessment tasks and recording forms as they move through the chapters. We hope that you will read the chapters and complete the Your Turn activities as homework. You can then use class time to discuss and share the Your Turn responses, and the instructor can work on clarifying ideas and misconceptions.

In our classes, we appreciate hands-on activities, and we believe that deeper understanding results when our students actually use the assessment ideas, not just read about them. In fact, our assessment class is designed to be taught in the classroom and in the gymnasium. During the gymnasium portion of the class, our teacher candidates actually experience assessment as though they were in a physical education class. Most of the examples of assessment forms in chapter 8 were designed for our assessment classes. Because our students had experienced them as students, they were able to effectively use them or adapt them during methods and student teaching.

By definition, assessment is the gathering of information to make decisions about learning. Therefore, one of the principles emphasized in this text is that assessment always yields a written record. Although teacher observation is not assessment by itself, the *record* created from the observation is assessment. For example, teacher observations can be recorded in many ways including, but not limited to, a checklist, a rating scale, or a rubric. The key idea is that teachers must keep records of what they see as a way of monitoring learning because it is impossible for a teacher to recall from memory how individual students are progressing. Eyeballing in a class is not an effective way to document student learning. An assessment might require teachers to check off skills as individual students demonstrate them correctly, which creates a written record to show that learning is taking place. Both observing and *documenting* learning are emphasized.

Assessment research and theory published over the past three decades provides a strong rationale for the assessment practices recommended in this text. We have contributed to the body of literature that supports the use of assessment in physical education. Relevant research and theory is woven into chapters as needed to support the arguments for including assessment as part of the instructional process in addition to using it to document learning.

In a recent study, we learned that teacher candidates struggle with implementing assessment partly because they lack necessary skills to organize and implement it (Lund and Veal 2008). Chapter 12 on management of assessment represents a new approach to preparing teachers to assess learning: No existing measurement text has included this type of approach. Another way this text differs from traditional measurement texts is the inclusion of a chapter on how to use assessment data instead of a chapter on statistics. The Your Turn exercises will guide you in using assessment data to make decisions about teaching.

We know that in some teacher education programs, there is no separate assessment course, so we suggest that the text could be used in a secondary methods course. The most important tool for teacher educators will be the Your Turn exercises that ask students to design their own assessment tools for specific uses. We envision this text as an interactive tool that poses questions that require students to reflect on what they've read and then apply their knowledge to a specific teaching situation. When you purchase this text, you will have access to a valuable web resource. All of the Your Turn elements will be included, so you can download them from the web and type or write responses. Instructors who want to review or grade some of the Your Turn activities can collect them without requiring

students to tear pages out of their books. In addition, copies of assessment forms will be included in the web resource so you can easily print them out and use them during field experiences.

Before moving on to chapter 1, we strongly recommend that the reader complete an assessment *concept map* as a way of documenting the existing assessment knowledge structure. This practical exercise will help the student and the teacher educator see which concepts are understood prior to instruction. Concept mapping involves the construction of a diagram made up of assessment terms. The terms are connected with linking words that show an understanding of how a pair of concepts is related. Remember that a concept map is *hierarchical,* meaning that the more general concepts are at the top and the more specific concepts are at lower levels. Do not look up the meaning of concepts as you construct the concept map. This exercise is meant to show what you know *prior to* reading the text and completing the course. In chapter 14, we recommend that you construct a second concept map so you can visualize how your knowledge of assessment has grown. See the concept mapping exercise that follows the preface.

We hope that you will benefit from our experiences in teaching physical education teachers how to integrate assessment into instruction.

Although this book has been a labor of love, it has caused us to do much self-reflection about why we do the things that we do and why we teach assessment concepts in the manner described in the next several chapters.

We wish you the very best as you progress through this book, and we hope that it will unlock some of the assessment secrets that have eluded you in the past.

Jackie and Mary Lou

CONCEPT MAPPING EXERCISE

Directions

Follow the step-by-step directions below to create your own personal assessment concept map:

1. Go to the Cmap website: http://cmap.ihmc.us.

2. Download the Cmap program to your computer. When you click on the Cmap download information and forms, you will be asked to fill out a form. Cmap is free for educational purposes, but most universities will not allow you to download it to university-owned computers. If you use a dial-up connection, allow more time for the program to download.

3. Before you begin, study the information on the Cmap website about how to construct a concept map.

4. Once you've downloaded the program, open it and use the pull-down menu to start a new Cmap. Type the following concepts into the box on the right. After you type a concept and hit Enter, each will appear on the large mapping surface in a box. If you click on the box, you will see that each concept can be moved around. The arrows at the top of the box can be expanded to connect concepts. The question marks that appear between concepts are for linking words.

5. When you have completed your map and you are satisfied with its appearance, use the pull-down menu to export your Cmap and *save it as a jpg file* on your computer or travel drive. If you skip this step, you will not be able to view your map again.

Focus Question

How is assessment used by physical education teachers?

Parking Lot of Concepts

Type the following concepts into your concept map.

- Affective domain
- Criteria
- Culminating activity
- Effort
- Learning outcomes
- Self-assessment
- Posttest
- Product
- Skill level
- Summative assessment

- Cognitive domain
- Descriptors
- Data
- Formative assessment
- Observation
- Performance-based assessment
- Pretest
- Psychomotor domain
- Skill test
- Teacher-directed assessment

- Checklist
- Critical elements
- Diagnostic assessment
- Grading
- Participation
- Planning
- Process
- Rubric
- Statistics sheet
- Written test

Some additional terms to substitute are as follows: rating scale, projects, portfolio.

HOW TO USE THIS BOOK
AND WEB RESOURCE

This book and web resource are designed to work together in order to give instructors and students a flexible way of interacting with and responding to the concepts taught. Throughout the book, readers are periodically prompted to stop reading and do exercises called Your Turn. These exercises vary in length and complexity; some offer a few questions that call for a short written reflection, while others challenge readers to create their own rubrics and other forms. All of them are carefully written and placed with the intent of providing a meaningful personalized learning experience for each user.

All of the Your Turn exercises are available in Word format on the web resource that may be accessed at www.HumanKinetics.com/AssessmentDrivenInstructionInPhysicalEducation. In this way users may download and complete the exercises and easily email them to instructors or upload them into an LMS. Of course, the completed exercises may also be printed out and turned in as hard copies. Completed assignments may also be saved by students and compiled into an electronic portfolio that can be provided to potential employers as a professional-looking sample of what the student has learned and is able to do.

The web resource also includes select tables and forms that readers might find useful to have in Word format. These are marked with the following icon.

ACKNOWLEDGMENTS

We thank our students at Georgia State University and Middle Tennessee State University, who patiently offered suggestions and encouragement while we prepared this text. Most important, their changing concept maps showed us that their knowledge had been growing as we got better at explaining assessment concepts.

Planning for Assessment

ONE

An Introduction to Assessment

If we wish to maximize student achievement in the U.S., we must pay far greater attention to the improvement of classroom assessment. Both assessment of learning and assessment for learning are essential. But one is currently in place, and the other is not.

Stiggins, 2002, p.764

LOOK FOR THESE KEY CONCEPTS

- assessment
- assessment for learning
- assessment of learning
- domains of learning (psychomotor, affective, cognitive)
- reflection
- performance-based assessment
- standards (NASPE and state)
- thinking like an assessor

Part I of this book discusses the decisions that are required for planning the learning process and the work that must be completed before starting instruction. You will find early in your career that teaching is a lot of work! The chapters in part I guide you through the planning part of instruction, including the planning of assessments. Part II will help you learn to apply and refine the planning and assessment concepts.

This book will help you learn to **think like an assessor,** meaning that the teaching decisions you make are based on data about student learning. In this first chapter, we introduce you to some of the most important concepts in this book, and we begin to build your knowledge base so you can advance your understanding of assessment concepts. We begin with the idea of learning because the purpose of teaching physical education (PE) is to help students learn. We hope that by the time you read this textbook in an assessment or methods course, you are already committed to the idea that you are in the business of student learning. After defining the assessment process, we share our beliefs about assessment, and then we discuss common misconceptions about assessment that we have encountered among our students.

What Is Learning?

Learning in physical education is complicated. Unlike the academic subjects (e.g., history, math, science) that focus primarily on cognitive learning, physical education occurs in *three* different **domains of learning** (see table 1.1). Our primary learning domain is **psychomotor,** which involves movement skills and fitness. However, the psychomotor domain is very much influenced by the **affective domain,** largely because of the influence of student effort in learning motor skills. Many physical educators believe the affective domain is just as important as the psychomotor because our students must learn to value physical activity in order to maintain lifelong health and wellness. Last, but not least, the **cognitive domain** works hand in hand with the psychomotor domain. Research by Lee (1997) reveals that when people are learning motor skills, they learn best when they think about the movement process.

Learning in the psychomotor domain has been defined as a permanent change in behavior. Once a motor skill has been learned, it does not occur by chance or luck. This means that when a sport skill is learned, it can be repeated consistently. This doesn't mean perfectly. Think about your own experience learning to ride a bicycle. You probably fell a few times before you learned to ride, but once you learned, you could ride successfully over and over again, even if you didn't practice for a while. Some skills are much harder to learn than others because they require adjusting to conditions created by other players or moving equipment. The important thing to remember is that students in physical education *should learn motor skills*. If learning does not occur, it's hard to justify having physical education as a school subject. We maintain that you have to do more than just provide physical activity. Anyone can supervise physical activity, but not just anyone can teach teenagers how to play soccer or basketball or badminton.

As a teacher, you will go through a planning process in which you decide the **standards** that will be addressed in each unit and the student **learning outcomes** that will be the focus for each lesson. The standards define what students should know, be like, and be able to do. The learning outcomes give you a direction for teaching and learning, and they guide your assessment decisions.

What Is Assessment?

NASPE's (1995) definition of **assessment** is "the process of gathering evidence about a student's level of achievement. . . and of making inferences based on that evidence" (vii). Let's unpack that

Table 1.1   Types of Learning in Physical Education

Learning domains	Types of learning
Psychomotor	Performing motor skills, movement, physical activity (PA), physical fitness
Affective	Exhibiting positive social behaviors (e.g., team work, fair play) and personal attitudes (e.g., valuing PA)
Cognitive	Knowing and understanding tactics, problem solving, rules, skills, player positions, and key elements of performance

definition and see what the authors meant. The phrase "gathering evidence" implies that assessment involves collecting written data about student learning. Physical education teachers observe students every day, but observation, by itself, is not assessment. When observation is used in gathering assessment data, there is *always a written record* of what is observed.

The next phrase is "about a student's level of achievement." Here, we see that assessment is a process that involves looking at individual students and how much each one has achieved. This should indicate that you are obligated to assess each student fairly and individually.

The last phrase refers to "making inferences" based on the written data. When you make inferences, you come to careful conclusions after reflecting on the assessment data. This process of making inferences through **reflection** is surely one of your most difficult tasks, but it is also critical for making teaching more effective. The best professional physical educators give the task of making inferences about student learning a high priority as they gather data about students' learning and about their own teaching. They know that using a variety of assessment techniques makes them more effective teachers because they assess learning in more than one way.

All effective teachers use assessment. In academic subjects like history, math, and English, teachers focus primarily on thinking, understanding, and problem solving, so their assessments are usually written tests and written or oral projects. Physical education teachers focus primarily on movement, physical activities, and sport skills, so their assessments are different. They are a little more complicated because they involve physical performances in addition to written work.

Assessment has changed a great deal over the past several decades. This change is reflected in this NASPE (1995) statement: "The primary goal of assessment should be seen as the enhancement of learning rather than simply the documentation of learning" (vii). We now see that assess-

ment is intertwined with the teaching process and is not separate from teaching. It serves two primary purposes in all school subjects, including physical education.

1. **Assessment *for* learning:** These ongoing assessments help students learn by providing feedback that leads to goal setting and improvement. They also help you adjust instruction to meet students' needs.
2. **Assessment *of* learning:** These assessments are used for grading. They are final because there is no chance for the teacher to adjust or for learners to improve.

Assessments are a critical aspect of the teaching process because they give you an opportunity to communicate expectations to students. In all subject areas, when students see that there is assessment, they perceive that what is being assessed is important. Expectations are defined in the statement of student learning outcomes, which include the criteria for success. Let's use the high jump as an example. Assume you want students to be able to perform the high jump. Before you teach it, decide *how high* you want students to be able to jump. The question of how high determines where you set the bar for the high jump. Of course, you will tell and show your students where you set the bar, and you'll explain and demonstrate for them how to perform the high jump. After your instruction, you'll give students lots of chances to practice the high jump, starting at a lower level. Gradually, you'll raise the bar. Over the several days or weeks of practice, you will help students chart their practice by letting them assess their improvements (i.e., gradual gains in how high they can jump, improved technique or form that allows them to jump higher). As the bar is gradually moved higher and higher, and students increase the height of their jumps, they demonstrate learning. Given sufficient practice, most students will be able to jump at the criterion level if it is reasonable. Keep in mind that you can direct students'

Students can demonstrate learning by jumping increasingly higher distances.

energy and effort by telling them the target ahead of time. Knowing the target up front helps students tell how much effort they need to put forth to reach the target. Given enough practice and effort, most students can learn to high jump. But remember that it takes time and lots of practice to learn motor skills.

Just as it takes time for students to learn motor skills, it will take you time to learn how to be a good assessor. You will practice developing assessments, administering them, and then revising your initial work. Over time, you will become more proficient at developing new assessments while increasing your arsenal of assessments to use with your students. As your assessment skills increase, it will become second nature to use assessments as an integral part of teaching.

The standards-based assessment discussed in this textbook is very different from traditional forms of assessment and evaluation. Some call standards-based assessment a new *paradigm*, meaning a different way of thinking about assessment practice. In the past, the term *evaluation* was the most commonly used. It was associated with grading and testing. As you read earlier, many educators now believe that the primary function of assessment is to help students learn, rather than to assign grades. The assessment practices

we describe in this book are sometimes known as **performance-based assessment** because they let students demonstrate what they know and can do. Performance-based assessments often consist of authentic tasks. Students usually know the criteria in advance so they can use it to improve their performance. Finally, standards-based assessment is often a performance-based task that is assessed with the use of a rubric or other statements of criteria. Standardized tests are used less often now than in the past.

Assessments in physical education should:

- be developed before teaching a unit (e.g., basketball) of instruction,
- be developed for all three domains of learning,
- be focused on essential skills and concepts;
- yield a written record,
- provide evidence of student learning, and
- signal to students what is important.

Our Beliefs About Assessment

This book may challenge some of your beliefs about assessment. Our own beliefs about assessment have been challenged and shaped by our teaching experiences in physical education and in teacher education. As we share some of our perspective with you, think about how your own experiences and views compare with what we describe.

• We strongly believe in *the power of assessment for learning.* In other words, assessment should be used throughout the instructional process to enhance student learning rather than simply being done at the conclusion of an instructional unit for the purpose of determining a grade. This belief is supported by a number of research studies (e.g., Black and Wiliam, 1998b). We believe that *good assessment assists students in the learning process.*

• We believe that in a quality physical education program, *teaching is purposeful* and *learning is intentional.* When learning is expected, assessment is necessary for documenting that students have reached the desired level of competence. Physical education should be more than just providing students with physical activity; physical education should be about teaching new skills and concepts and then holding students accountable for learning. It is your responsibility as their teacher to ensure that students learn. Quality PE looks different than activity-driven programs because you must allocate sufficient time to each unit you teach. Students need adequate practice and instructional time

if they are to achieve competence in a sport or activity.

• We believe that secondary physical education students require *a substantial amount of time to practice and learn.* There is no need to assess if you aren't spending sufficient time for students to learn. Allocate ample time for each unit taught. One-week units are too short for learning because students need adequate practice and instructional time if they are to achieve competence in a sport or activity.

• We believe that in a quality program, *teaching decisions are data-driven* and *lessons are focused on learning outcomes.* If students don't accomplish a learning outcome, you are responsible for reteaching and for figuring out how to change the instruction or practice tasks to ensure student learning. This willingness to change instruction requires that you practice reflective decision making and base your teaching decisions on assessment data. Physical education classes at every educational level should be about acquiring the skills and knowledge that are vital to a long, active, and healthy life.

• We believe that *simply asking students to improve is not enough.* Teachers sometimes use improvement as a proxy for learning, but physical education programs should produce physically educated students. Particularly at the level of senior high school, when many students take their last physical education classes, it is vital

YOUR TURN 1.1

Choose three of the *misconceptions* about assessment listed below and explain why you think they are misconceptions. Be prepared to discuss each misconception.

Misconceptions About Assessment

- Pretests are always written tests.
- Assessment is the same thing as grading.
- Learning can be assessed only with a written test.
- Only the athletes can learn in physical education.
- Physical educators can accurately assess the amount of effort their students expend.
- Assessment takes unnecessary time away from teaching and activity.
- Physical education teachers don't need to write down assessment information because they can see if students are learning or not.
- It's not fair to assess motor skills because not all students are athletic.
- Observation is a type of assessment used in physical education.
- You can't assess the skill level of lower-skilled students because these students don't try.
- Accountability is always punitive.

that students graduate with a level of competence that enables them to live a physically active and healthy lifestyle.

- We believe that the future of physical education depends on your ability to show that your *students are learning important skills and knowledge* that are valued by students, parents, administrators, other teachers, and the community.

Case Study

Let's consider a hypothetical case study that will reinforce some of the concepts we've just discussed and preview the process you'll learn more about in the coming chapters.

Mr. Thomas, a physical education teacher at Green Middle School, is preparing to teach a badminton unit to his classes because it will help his students reach the state physical education standards. During a badminton unit, he can teach the tactics important to success in all net games. His students have had limited experience in net games and limited experience with striking skills that use a racket. He had thought about teaching tennis, but after a diagnostic assessment on racket striking skills, he determined that his students would have an easier time learning game-play tactics for a net game if they were using a slower object. He needs to set unit goals that match the standards he is trying to help his students meet. His goals are as follows:

1. Students will demonstrate various offensive and defensive skills needed for playing badminton.
2. Students will demonstrate the ability to combine psychomotor skills in a meaningful way in order to play a game of badminton at a recreational level.
3. Students will be able to serve strategically while playing badminton.
4. Students will know basic offensive and defensive tactics for net/wall games.
5. Students will know the rules of badminton and be able to correctly apply them during a game.
6. Students will demonstrate elements of fair play during game play.
7. Students will demonstrate the ability to work willingly with others.

The **culminating activity** for this unit will be a round robin tournament. Because of the number of students in his class, Mr. Thomas has decided that it would be best to use doubles teams (2v2) rather than singles. The round robin tournament will give him lots of opportunities to observe games and use his **game-play rubric** as he assesses his students and provides feedback to help them better use the information from his assessment of their play. The rubric will allow him to look at the descriptors and to provide feedback about performance on each descriptor. His rubric will assess all three domains: psychomotor, cognitive, and affective. The rubric has four levels so that he will be able to track improvement as students progress through the tournament. Improvement is important because if students stop getting better, it means he is not teaching new things. Note that improvement is seen as a means for getting students to reach a level of competence needed for playing the game at a level that the students will enjoy rather than the final goal of instruction.

To help Mr. Thomas focus his teaching and motivate students, he creates a graphic organizer. The purpose of a **graphic organizer** is to identify what he plans to teach—he is not trying to train students for Olympic competition!—making sure that he covers all the elements necessary for them to play. The central organizer will also ensure that skills and knowledge are presented in logical order or sequence. He also wants students to see the connections between badminton and other types of net/wall games, as well as to understand that this game is an activity that is fun to play with friends and can help increase fitness. Mr. Thomas writes **essential questions** to open up student thinking on these areas and to initiate reflection about other areas related to badminton.

Mr. Thomas begins thinking about what he will teach by determining what students will need to know and be able to do to be successful in the culminating activity: the tournament. In the psychomotor domain, students will need to do the following: serve, hit forehand and backhand shots, use the drop shot when playing offensively, and use the clear shot for defensive purposes. Those students who learn the basic shots very easily will have the opportunity to learn how to smash and hit drives, giving them a good repertoire of offensive weapons. Regarding goals in the cognitive domain, Mr. Thomas will teach students the various tactics associated with net games, the rules and how to use those rules to take advantage of scoring opportunities, what correct form (critical elements) looks like for various shots so that they can help themselves and others become better players, and some interesting history about the game. He also wants students to be able to apply the rules to the game, so he knows that he will use some type of assessment of rules to determine this knowledge. Since Mr. Thomas really wants students to learn how to work with a partner to play a game, he will emphasize cooperation during his unit. Another aspect of the affective domain is to be sure that students play fairly and don't purposely violate rules to win. Students should demonstrate respect for others during game play and be positive with comments made to others.

Mr. Thomas administered a **diagnostic assessment** on the skill of striking with a paddle, which was taught in elementary physical education classes. He found that students had knowledge of this skill, but they struggled when they had to initiate play. He found that students were able to hit the ball when a partner tossed it. When Mr. Thomas gave a diagnostic written assessment on game-play tactics for net games, he found that students had very limited knowledge of net/wall sports. He did not ask questions specific to the rules of badminton on his diagnostic assessment because when asked who had played before, few students raised their hands. Those who had played backyard badminton with family were not familiar with basic strokes or rules.

Mr. Thomas is ready to start planning his unit. The first thing he must do is identify the skills, knowledge, and dispositions that he expects his students to demonstrate during the unit. For psychomotor skills, he will teach the following: long and short serve, overhead clear, underhand clear, serve receive, and serve return. The smash and the drive will be shown, but they will not be included in the basic requirements for all students because they are more advanced.

To ensure that students have mastered the basic skills, Mr. Thomas will administer skill tests to assess each one. Students will be held accountable for those skills and will be expected to use them correctly during game play, but the skills will not be evaluated individually during game play. Students will have multiple opportunities to reach the criterion levels for the various skills because skills will be tested at the beginning or end of class or while other students are engaged in game play. Once students achieve the criterion level of performance on an assessment, they do not need to continue taking the assessment. The psychomotor assessments, including the skill tests and the assessment of game play, will constitute 60 percent of the grade in the badminton unit.

Mr. Thomas will administer a written test on badminton rules before the start of game play to ensure that everyone knows the rules. He also will require students to either announce or officiate games so that they can demonstrate their knowledge of the application of these rules. He has created rubrics for assessing knowledge as students officiate and announce games; he will share these rubrics with students before they are assessed on those items. He included a descriptor about following the rules of the game on the rubric for game play. The cognitive assessments will be counted as 20 percent of the grade.

On the game-play rubric, Mr. Thomas has added a descriptor that includes criteria for fair play. Other ways that he will assess the affective domain include willingness to complete duty team assignments during game play, participation

YOUR TURN 1.2

Carefully read the story about Mr. Thomas. It should reinforce some of the concepts we discussed in this chapter. After reading about Mr. Thomas' decision-making processes, see if you can answer the following questions about his teaching.

1. Why did Mr. Thomas decide to teach badminton?
2. Identify the various steps in the planning process and put them in order.
3. What three learning domains should be assessed in physical education?
4. Why did Mr. Thomas use a diagnostic assessment before teaching badminton?
5. How does assessment *for* learning differ from assessment *of* learning?
6. Why is physical education included in a school curriculum?
7. How will grades be determined for the badminton unit?

in sponge activities at the start of class, and journal entries and exit slips completed at the conclusion of some classes. The various assessments of the affective domain will count as 20 percent of the grade in the badminton unit.

As Mr. Thomas starts to plan his lessons, he will need to create outcomes for each lesson that can be assessed so that he will know whether students have learned the content that he presented in the lesson or if they need additional time to master it before learning the next concept. He also will need to develop quality tasks and to manage resources as he implements instruction. Student learning will be the primary element determining what he teaches and the tasks and activities for his students.

Summary

The next chapters explain how to deliver the type of instruction outlined in our discussion about Mr. Thomas. Our goal for you is that you will learn how to become a competent assessor and an effective physical education teacher.

TWO

Planning the Big Picture for Student Learning

Curricular choices made in the absence of assessment-elicited evidence about students' current status are curricular choices almost certain to be flawed.

Popham, 2010, p. 7

What do a recipe, directions for assembling a bicycle, and a sewing pattern all have in common? If you said that they all represent directions for making something, you are correct. Just as cooks, mechanics, and people who sew follow plans, you should also plan your lessons so that you can teach as effectively as possible. This chapter provides an overview of the planning process used in physical education. We also make the case for planning assessments before starting a unit. Finally, we introduce some assessment terms that will be further explored in future chapters.

Step 1: Select Unit Activity and Standards

If you stop to think about it, trying to decide what to teach as a beginning teacher is a daunting task. With so many wonderful games and activities to share with students, where do you start? Before the standards movement, many physical education teachers chose to teach units simply because they enjoyed the activity or sport and thought their students would enjoy learning how to participate in it. Teachers did not give much thought to what a physical education program should accomplish or what students were expected to know and be able to do when they graduated from high school. In fact, there was not a lot of agreement about what it meant to be a physically educated person. In 1992, the National Association for Sport and Physical Education (NASPE) published a document titled *Outcomes of Quality Physical Education Programs* that listed 20 outcomes of a quality physical education program that, if accomplished, would help students become physically educated.

From that document, a writing team convened by NASPE developed physical education **content standards** that were published in 1995 and revised in 2004 (see figure 2.1). Standards are very broad statements about the content of a subject area. The standards movement in the

United States has changed education in many ways. The advent of standards gave various subjects (e.g., math, social studies, science, reading, physical education) targets for students to reach as they progressed through the various grades. To use standards, you must unpack them and determine what students should know and be able to do when they complete their education. You can unpack standards either by grade level or by level of schooling (e.g., primary [P–2], intermediate [3–5], middle school [6–8], or high school [9–12]). You will typically do this when writing curriculum for your districts (see Lund & Tannehill, 2010, for an explanation of the curriculum development process). With that brief introduction to standards and curriculum development, let's begin the process of developing instruction that maximizes student learning.

As a teacher, you must ensure that students meet the state standards. Many states have adopted the content standards developed by the National Association for Sport and Physical Education (NASPE, 2004). Where we refer to content standards, they are talking about the NASPE physical education content standards because these standards are the most widely accepted in physical education. Your state might have its own physical education standards; be sure to refer to the physical education standards in your state when planning lessons and developing assessments.

When selecting activities for a standards-based curriculum, the units you include should be varied. It is not possible to meet the NASPE standards if you teach only fitness activities (e.g., weight training, running), invasion sports (e.g., soccer, basketball, football), or dance (e.g., social, hip hop, modern). Students in physical education classes are diverse; they have different needs and enjoy doing different things. Most school curricula suggest several different sports or activities that are acceptable for secondary physical education classes. Hopefully, the curriculum used in your school encourages you to select a variety of activities. If you offer a variety

The NASPE standards for physical education state that a physically educated person:

1. Demonstrates competency in motor skills and movement patterns needed to perform a variety of physical activities.
2. Demonstrates understanding of movement concepts, principles, strategies, and tactics as they apply to the learning and performance of physical activities.
3. Participates regularly in a physical activity.
4. Achieves and maintains a health-enhancing level of physical fitness.
5. Exhibits responsible personal and social behavior that respects self and others in physical activity settings.
6. Values physical activity for health, enjoyment, challenge, self-expression, and/or social interaction.

Figure 2.1   NASPE physical education content standards.
Reprinted from NASPE 2004.

of activities, your students will be more likely to have meaningful and enjoyable experiences in physical education classes. This enjoyment will lead to increased *approach tendencies* (Siedentop, Mand, & Taggart, 1986), meaning that students will be more likely to continue to be active for a lifetime. Although the selection of activities is a curriculum function, it is important to remember the points discussed in this paragraph when selecting what you will teach.

To meet the standards, activities are selected for the physical education curriculum. The goal of physical education is not simply to teach the various activities, but *rather* to use them to deliver the standards and teach universal concepts critical to physical education. For many years, teachers felt obligated to teach as many sports and activities as possible. This is sometimes called an *exposure curriculum* because students are simply shown numerous activities in short units. The exposure curriculum consists of lots of activities, each taught in one- or two-week units in which students learn a little about a lot of activities, but fail to learn enough to become competent at any of them. In contrast, a standards-based curriculum requires students to know how to play a type of game (e.g., invasion games, net/wall games, target games) or perform an activity (e.g., dance, gymnastics, swimming). The teacher selects a specific game or activity to teach the concepts critical to playing or performing something from that game or activity category. For example, if, according to the standards, your students were to learn the concepts of net/wall games, you could choose pickleball, volleyball, badminton, or tennis to teach those concepts. Students should learn the concepts

that will allow them to play any net/wall game successfully.

It simply is not possible to teach physical education briefly and do it well. The sports and activities taught in physical education are complex, and students need time to learn the skills and practice using them effectively in an applied setting. If a teacher fails to allocate sufficient time, students will not become competent at anything or experience the success that makes an activity enjoyable. This does not mean that students need to develop phenomenal skills or high levels of proficiency. The goal of physical education is not to develop future Olympians or even varsity sport players, but rather to teach students enough about a sport or activity so that they will be able to play a game or participate in an activity at a reasonably competent level. Being competent might include play with their friends at a social event or something more organized, such as intramural sports or recreational adult leagues. Research tells us that players who are more skilled are more likely to participate on a voluntary basis (Rink, 2000; Siedentop, 1991; Stodden et al., 2008). The ultimate outcome of a good physical education program is to help students develop a good attitude toward a healthy, active lifestyle and a desire to be physically active for a lifetime.

In a standards-based curriculum, teachers use the premise that less is more; it is better to teach fewer activities in depth (which results in greater **competence**, deeper understanding, and higher levels of thinking for students) than to teach a little bit about everything, which prevents students from gaining competence in anything. We recognize that this is a huge paradigm shift for some teachers.

YOUR TURN 2.1

Write down three different types of each of the following activities: invasion games, target games, and dance, and identify three different units to teach at least one component of health-related fitness. Suggested answers are at the end of this chapter.

	Invasion games	Target games	Dance	Health-related fitness activity
Example 1				
Example 2				
Example 3				

The paradigm shift represented by standards-based instruction requires you to select activities based on whether the content will help meet standards. Because physical activity is so complex, students can meet many standards depending on how or what you teach. For an example, think about a jump rope unit. Why would you teach it? We came up with the following reasons:

- To teach rhythmic movement
- To reach students who learn best with music and rhythm (one of Gardner's [1985] multiple intelligences)
- To teach the locomotor skill of jumping
- To increase cardiorespiratory endurance
- To give students a fitness activity they can do for a lifetime
- To teach students how to sequence several movements or skills and basic choreography skills
- To encourage creativity and innovation
- To teach students how to work together as a group
- To teach students how to work independently (stay on task without teacher guidance)
- To teach the importance of practice for improving skills

YOUR TURN 2.2

Explain three advantages to the selection of activities with standards-based instruction versus the exposure model. If possible, discuss your ideas with a partner or small group. Some suggested answers are at the end of this chapter.

You get the idea. Many concepts can be taught with a rope jumping unit. Remember that the *activity* is the means for teaching the *concept*. Trying to teach all of the ideas that were listed would not be a good idea; a rope jumping unit taught for fitness is very different from one taught as a rhythmic activity. Remember, *less is more*. Aim to provide more in-depth knowledge and skills about fewer different topics. As a teacher you must focus instruction and deliberately select instructional tasks that will allow your students to meet the learning outcomes established for the unit.

Step 2: Choose a Culminating Activity

Lots of activities can be used to teach the desired outcomes for physical education and to help students learn different parts of the standards, depending on how they are set up. While deciding what activity to teach, you must also decide how to frame it so that your students learn the concepts most valuable for them to know and be able to do. Consider the analogy of taking a trip: Without a final destination, you're just driving around. To paraphrase the words of the white rabbit in *Alice in Wonderland*, if you don't know where you are going, any path will take you there.

When planning what you want students to know at the conclusion of instruction, it's best to develop **culminating activities** that require students to use all the skills and knowledge acquired during the unit. Think about our opening statements about plans: In addition to providing the directions for completion of the desired product, a picture of what you should build or make is typically included in recipes, bicycle assembly manuals, and sewing patterns. If you had never cooked the recipe, put together a bicycle, or made a shirt, you would be trying to create something without being sure of what it would ultimately look like. In much the same way, the culminating assessment will give both you and your students a picture of what the learning will look like in its finished form.

Culminating activities are complex. The following list of characteristics will help you develop a culminating activity for your unit. A culminating activity does the following:

- Involves more than one learning domain (affective, psychomotor, cognitive)
- Provides the opportunity for students to demonstrate what they have learned during a unit
- Requires higher-level thinking (synthesis, evaluation, analysis)
- Requires several days of preparation and can take place over multiple days
- Addresses multiple standards
- Requires students to apply what they have learned during the unit
- Requires that students have adequate resources (equipment, time, space) to complete the activity

Remember Mr. Thomas at Green Middle School in chapter 1? He chose a badminton unit to help his students meet the state standards and to teach tactics important to net/wall sports. To ensure that his students have an opportunity to combine their skills and knowledge, Mr. Thomas will set up a round-robin doubles tournament, where every pair plays the other pairs in the class. Tournament play is an excellent way for students to demonstrate their psychomotor skills, knowledge about the game (rules and tactics), and respect for others. It is an appropriate culminating activity for badminton and many other sports.

If Mr. Thomas were to decide to teach a dance unit, the culminating activity might require students to create a modern dance or hip hop routine or to perform several structured folk or square dances. Mr. Thomas also could require students to perform for their peers during an in-class performance. Similar culminating performances would also be appropriate for gymnastics, rope jumping, or roller skating units.

Tournaments, dance performances, and portfolios are just a few of the culminating activities that you can design that require students to combine the skills and knowledge acquired during the unit and allow them to demonstrate their learning in a meaningful way.

The tournament will give Mr. Thomas' students the opportunity to demonstrate that they are meeting NASPE standards 1, 2, and 5. Although a lot of cardiorespiratory activity is required for playing the game, the primary focus of this unit is not NASPE standard 4, so Mr. Thomas will not include this standard when identifying what the unit will accomplish.

You might wonder how fitness education is incorporated into an activity-based unit. Some people feel that to achieve fitness, students need to participate in a unit designed specifically for one or more components of fitness. An example of this type of activity would be a unit where students run sprints or distances to increase cardiorespiratory fitness. In 2008, the AAHPERD alliance scholar cited research stating that students were more likely to exercise for longer periods of time when participating in a sport because they enjoyed playing (Berg, 2008). Because of the additional time spent playing, the students' fitness benefit was the same or even better than if a running unit had been taught. Using this logic, you should know that if students become competent players and engage in vigorous games, they will receive a fitness benefit during the game. This latter approach gives a purpose to fitness: Students increase their fitness in order to play the game, rather than just working on fitness in isolation. Younger students often fail to see the relevance of being fit. For them, old age and death are so far away that the concept of delaying them is not a motivator. People who fall off the exercise wagon typically do so because they fail to make exercise a part of their normal living pattern, which they will miss if they don't engage in fitness. If we mix a little fun with exercise, people will be more likely to continue to stay physically active.

Badminton could be something that students do outside of the physical education class, but Mr. Thomas will not assess this or hold students accountable for documenting activity outside of class. For this reason, Mr. Thomas will not list standards 3 or 6 as outcomes of the unit. When Mr. Thomas selects other units for his students, he will need to make sure that he emphasizes the standards that were not featured in his badminton unit.

At the secondary level, the primary goal should be to have students apply knowledge and skills

Make exercise as fun as possible if you want your students to choose to be physically active.

4. How can I make this culminating activity an interesting and fun learning experience that fully engages my students?

5. Should the culminating activity be a performance (as in game play or a dance composition) or a product (usually consists of written work) that students complete?

6. How does the culminating activity contribute to the student's learning?

7. Is the culminating activity designed so that students of all ability levels can complete the activity successfully?

8. How can I encourage students to use higher-order thinking skills (synthesis, evaluation, analysis)?

A single game will not give you sufficient opportunity to determine whether students have accomplished the intended goals. By observing and assessing students multiple times, you will be able to accurately and fairly assess the actual level of competence that students have achieved. Additionally, students can receive feedback based on assessments during games, further increasing their competence. Games used for the culminating activity do not need to have an official number of players. Small-sided games actually give you a better opportunity to observe students, since you have fewer players to watch at any given time. Additionally, with small-sided games, players are more likely to touch the ball because of the lower student-to-ball ratio, thus giving students more opportunity to respond.

A round-robin tournament toward the end of the unit provides students with more chances to demonstrate what they have learned. Students will have the opportunity to play several games giving you multiple occasions to observe students using the **game-play rubric** developed for the unit. Chapter 4 explains how to develop a rubric for a culminating activity.

Game play gives you the opportunity to observe skills, dispositions, and knowledge that are important for students to learn, but that are not readily observed away from game play. A game-play rubric looks at multiple aspects of the game, including student selection and use of skills during play, as well as knowledge about the application of rules, offensive tactics, defensive tactics, teamwork, and fair play toward others. It should challenge students to improve their skills and knowledge. Athletes want to improve their skills while playing a

in a meaningful game or to participate in a meaningful culminating activity. The culminating activity should require students to utilize all three domains of learning in a meaningful way. To illustrate this concept, think about game play and the constant analysis of the game context required before selecting a skill or tactic to use to gain an advantage. They also must demonstrate how they work and play responsibly with others. Similarly, dancers often work with others when they synthesize or create dances; thus, they also use three domains.

When creating a culminating activity, ask yourself the following questions:

1. What does the activity look like when performed by competent participants?

2. How can my students demonstrate that they can apply knowledge and skills authentically in this activity?

3. How can I design the activity so that it is meaningful and has real-life applications for my students?

sport, and the same is true for students in physical education classes.

The criteria of a successful culminating activity include the following:

- It will take several days to complete. Because this is a complex activity, it will take you several days to teach the skills needed for completing the culminating activity. Students will require several days of practice and work to achieve the final goal designated for the activity.

- It addresses all three domains of learning. A good culminating activity in physical education requires students to use the psychomotor, cognitive, and affective domains.

- Students will demonstrate higher levels of thinking while completing the task, including synthesis, or evaluation. (Note: This concept is explained further in chapter 9.) A good culminating activity requires students to use at least one of these higher-level thinking skills.

- The culminating activity is a task that students should find meaningful and fun.

When developing a culminating activity, you can readily see how all of the learning domains are used. Using all three domains simultaneously is typical of the complex activities that result when quality physical education classes are taught.

Table 2.1 provides several ideas for you to consider when developing your culminating activity. The list is meant to suggest some possible activities rather than being a finite list; feel free to create your own culminating activity.

Step 3: Identify Unit Goals

As you think about your activity, you must decide what students should accomplish during this unit. These statements will become the **unit goals.** When developing goals, remember that they must align with the standards that the unit will address. The verbs used in standards indicate the level of learning required for meeting the goal. Bloom's taxonomy provides guidance about the levels of learning explanation. Table 2.2 has a list of the levels of learning associated with the cognitive domain for Bloom's taxonomy. The unit goals are quite broad and should represent conceptual learning and not minutia. They contain a verb to indicate student performance and a criterion that can be used to assess whether students meet the intent of

Table 2.1   Possible Assessments for Physical Education Units

Unit	Culminating activity	Assessment and assessment tool	Data produced
Invasion games (e.g., football, soccer, basketball, lacrosse)	Round-robin tournament with small-sided games	Game-play rubric that guides teacher observation	Information (based on the descriptors) about the game (e.g., knowledge of the game, tactics, teamwork, fair play, ability to select the most appropriate skill)
		Stat sheets	Numerical product data (results) about how skills are used; effectiveness of skills used during the game
		Game performance assessment instrument (GPAI)	Knowledge about the use of tactics; information about effectiveness of decisions made during a game
Net/wall games	Round-robin tournament, either singles or doubles; could do a ladder tournament	Game-play rubric that guides teacher observation	Information (based on the descriptors) about the game (e.g., knowledge of the game, tactics, teamwork, fair play, ability to select the most appropriate skill)
		Stat sheets	Numerical product data (results) about how skills are used; effectiveness of skills used during the game
		GPAI	Decisions about tactics used in a game and the use of skills that support these tactics

(continued)

Unit	Culminating activity	Assessment and assessment tool	Data produced
Archery	Competition or meet: Do different rounds at different distances.	Score sheet: Different rounds will have different numbers of ends; end is 6 arrows.	Number of points will indicate accuracy and consistency of performance.
		Teacher observation using a quantitative rubric	Numerical data about correct form, a critical indicator of success with target games
Bowling	Bowling tournament: Bowl several games (at least 3).	Scores for bowling games (10 frames)	Score is the total number of pins, which indicates accuracy.
		Teacher observation using a quantitative rubric	Numerical data about correct form, a critical indicator of success with target games
Gymnastics	Intraclass meet: Students are required to do a floor exercise, vault, and one other apparatus event (beam and uneven parallel bars for females; rings, parallel bars for males).	Teacher observation using a qualitative rubric that differentiates by level of difficulty	Skill level, level of difficulty of skills performed, choreography, transitions between skills, and how well it is performed
	Circus—balancing on the low wire, pyramid building, unicycle riding, juggling, tumbling with others	Qualitative rubrics for different events	Information about the ability to balance, juggle, tumble, and so on consistent with the events offered
Rhythmic gymnastics	Intraclass meet: Students do balls, hoops, ribbons, clubs, and freestyle. Choose 2 events and compete; could do individual or group routines.	Teacher observation rubrics for the routines for each event	Skill level, choreography, and quality of performance
Track and field	Intraclass meet: All students compete in a relay, a running event, a jumping event, and a throwing event.	Score sheet to record time, distance, height	Numerical product data on each event
		Data sheet to keep records of event completion and completion of duties	Participation points for completion of events and serving as judges or officials; data for affective domain
		Quantitative rubric on form for field events	Data about the use of correct form
Softball	Round-robin tournament in small-sided teams	Score sheet to record data from each time at bat	Batting average; on-base percentage; number of extra base hits
		Teacher observation using a qualitative rubric	Information about tactics, fair play, base running, batting, fielding and catching, throwing
		GPAI	Information about decisions made during a game; application of tactics important to field games

Unit	Culminating activity	Assessment and assessment tool	Data produced
Golf	Play several holes and multiple rounds of golf	Teacher observation using a qualitative rubric	Data on application of rules and etiquette, choice of club, knowledge of rules
		Score sheet	Data on ability to put the skills of the game together in a meaningful way
		Teacher observation using a quantitative rubric on form	Correct form on shots
		Stat sheets	Distance for various types of shots; accuracy of putting; number of fairways hit (driving accuracy), greens in regulation percentage
Jump rope	Jump rope routine—short rope and long rope	Teacher observation using a qualitative rubric	Data on rhythm, smoothness, choreography, level of difficulty of steps used, ability to work with a group (if performance is a group performance)
	Perform each jump rope skill at least 10 times without missing.	Recording sheet to check off skills as they are performed	Data on which skills are successfully completed
Structured dance	Performing group routine to music: Use a video to score so that each student can be evaluated.	Teacher observation using a qualitative rubric	Data on rhythm, transition between steps, staying with others in the group, knowing steps, aesthetics (use of other body parts along with foot movement)
Creative dance	Create dance for a class performance or create a video.	Teacher observation using a qualitative rubric	Information about choreography, change of levels, aesthetics (involving multiple body parts to enhance quality of the performance), transitions between steps
Swim	Intraclass swim meet: Require students to choose events (distance, sprint, relay; they must do 2 different strokes).	Recording sheet for event times	Time will be an indicator of quality of performance. Use a camera at the finish line to record order. Students may be timers.
Synchronized swimming	Synchronized swim meet	Teacher observation using a qualitative rubric	Data on rhythm, choreography, difficulty level of skills
Quad skating	Obstacle course	Teacher observation using a qualitative rubric	Data on form, transition between moves,
		Time completion of the event with deductions for falls, missed gates, and so on	Proficiency of skills and ability to maneuver on skates; ability to complete the course in a certain amount of time
	Routine	Qualitative rubric	Data on form, skills, transition between moves
Wrestling	Wrestling tournament	Stat sheet	Points earned during different matches; transitions between moves; type of pin
		GPAI	Data on the ability to select the appropriate move
		Score sheet to record time to pin	Ability to combine skills

Table 2.2   Levels of Bloom's Taxonomy

Level	Examples of verbs used to write questions at this level
Knowledge: "awareness of specific facts, universals, and information; it requires remembering and the ability to recall" (McGee, 2000, p. 553)	Recognize, recall, identify, define
Comprehension: "the ability to interpret knowledge and to determine its implications, consequences, and effects" (McGee, 2000, p. 553)	Interpret, summarize, illustrate, rephrase
Application: "the ability to use knowledge and understanding in a particular concrete situation" (McGee, 2000, p. 553)	Apply, use, generalize, transfer, relate
Analysis: "the ability to identify the elements or parts of the whole, to see their relationships, and to structure them into some systematic arrangement or organization" (McGee, 2000, p. 554)	Classify, distinguish, discriminate, categorize, compare, analyze
Synthesis: "the ability to structure a whole from understanding of the relationships among specific elements or parts" (McGee, 2000, p. 554)	Design, formulate, plan, produce, synthesize, develop
Evaluation: "the ability to form judgments with respect to the value of information" (McGee, 2000, p. 555)	Judge, assess, argue, appraise

the outcomes. Typically, a unit has five to eight goals. In Mr. Thomas' case, he is addressing three standards; the unit goals are listed under each standard.

Goals for *standard 1* are:

- Students will demonstrate various offensive and defensive skills, including a strategically placed serve needed for playing badminton.
- Students will demonstrate the ability to combine psychomotor skills in a meaningful way to play a game of badminton at a recreational level.

Goals for *standard 2* are:

- Students will demonstrate knowledge of basic offensive and defensive tactics for a net/wall game by using them during game play.
- Students will demonstrate knowledge of the rules of badminton by applying them during game play.

Goals for *standard 5* are:

- Students will demonstrate the ability to work with others by willingly playing with anyone in the class.
- Students will demonstrate the disposition of wanting to play fairly by not breaking

rules to get an advantage over classmates or opponents and by being courteous to others.

Step 4: Write Assessments for Each Goal

You must have some way to assess each goal. In his badminton unit, Mr. Thomas has decided that he will use a rubric that lists the performance criteria for each goal. Mr. Thomas will use this during the tournament to guide his observations as he assesses students; he will observe each student many times during the tournament. He also plans to have his students officiate games (another indicator of their ability to apply the rules), perform a series of skill tests, and take a written test about the rules. He will also conduct other teacher-directed assessments that will help him determine whether the unit goals were met.

To ensure that he has several possible assessments, Mr. Thomas makes a table of his unit goals and then lists various ways that he could determine whether students met the goals. Some examples are shown in table 2.3. He will not use all of these assessments during his unit; he simply wants to make sure that he has several assessment options so that he will be able to

Table 2.3   Possible Assessments for Unit Goals

Unit goals	Possible ways to assess whether the goal was met
Students will demonstrate the ability to combine psychomotor skills in a meaningful way to play a game of badminton at a recreational level.	Game-play rubric used by the teacher while observing a game
Students will be able to serve strategically while playing badminton.	Skill test for the serve, game-play rubric used by the teacher while observing a game
Students will know basic offensive and defensive tactics for a net/wall game.	Written test, quiz, PowerPoint presentation explaining offensive tactics, scouting report assessment, coaching playbook, announcing games to others, video recording, and self-analysis of game play; game-play rubric used by the teacher while observing a game or while watching a video, GPAI
Students will know the rules of badminton and be able to apply them during a game.	Written test or quiz; game-play rubric used by the teacher while observing a game; PowerPoint; officiating evaluated by a rubric
Students will demonstrate elements of fair play during game play.	Game-play rubric used by the teacher while observing a game
Students will demonstrate the ability to work willingly with others.	Game-play rubric, teacher evaluation using disposition rubric during skill practice

accurately assess whether his students have met his unit goals.

Setting the Criteria for Student Learning

As you begin the process of **planning** and writing assessments, you may ask yourself many questions:

- What level of competence is needed for reaching this unit goal? How good is good enough?
- What do my students already know? Where will I start?
- How do I narrow the content and teach for competence in the time allocated?
- How can I get students to see the big picture of what I want to teach?
- What knowledge and skills are critical for my students to learn?

These questions will be answered as you identify topics for the unit and determine the criteria used to establish the desired level of competence.

Setting the level of competence is often difficult for a beginning teacher. A general rule of thumb is that students should have enough competence so that they can perform a skill fairly

automatically in the applied setting (i.e., an **open environment** such as gameplay, not when the skill is put in a **closed environment,** as for a skill test) and that they are able to transition from one skill or movement to another with little or no hesitation. The level of competence will be further defined when the rubric for the culminating assessment is fully developed. When using skill-test assessments, you must determine the level of competence for discrete skills. Chapter 6 contains a discussion about knowing where to set the bar for psychomotor assessments.

Some teachers think that the criteria of an assessment should be determined after the skill is assessed. Others feel that if you take a mastery approach to teaching a unit, then the criteria must be set at a level where students have sufficient competence to be successful when participating in the sport or activity. Both ideas have support, and they are discussed further in chapter 6.

The decision about the time allocated to teach a unit rests in the nature of the game, sport, or activity. Some units are much simpler and require less time to deliver, while others are much more complex. At the very least, allocate sufficient time so that students can learn the activity or game well enough to enjoy participating. Several things will affect how much depth is required for teaching a unit. Recognizing that there is a minimal level of learning below which it is useless to even consider offering the unit, several other factors influence how high teachers can set the bar for learning. Some things to consider include resources, students' ability and attitude, and teacher expertise. These ideas are summarized in the following table.

YOUR TURN 2.3

Can you explain what effect each of the factors listed in the following table has on how much students learn?

Factors	Potential influence
Resources	
Time	
Space	
Equipment	
Number of students in the class	
Student ability and attitude	
Level of fitness	
Previous experience in a sport or activity	
Age and developmental skill level	
Culture for learning	
Teacher expertise	
Teacher has taught the unit before	
Teacher knowledge of the unit	
Certifications involving safety (applicable for adventure activities, swimming, and so on)	

YOUR TURN 2.4

Our goal for this chapter is to introduce you to a standards-based planning process. To review the important concepts taught in this chapter, you are asked to demonstrate your understanding of the planning process. Let's see what you learned. Please feel free to refer back to the chapter when completing this exercise.

Step 1

Identify one activity that you want to teach and the standards that you will target when you teach it.

Step 2

Summarize a possible culminating activity. At this point, you just need to give a broad description of your culminating activity. Chapters 3 and 4 provide additional information to help you fully develop your culminating activity and choose the rubric to use with it.

Step 3

List five to eight goals for the unit (in the left-hand column of the table).

Step 4

List several possible assessments for each goal (in the right-hand column of the table).

Unit goal	Possible assessments

Summary

If you were able to complete the four steps outlined in this review, you have mastered the content in this chapter. This chapter provides an overview of the process used to plan your unit of instruction. You were asked to begin think- ing about goal setting to match standards. The next chapter explains how to develop a graphic organizer to give a visualization of the content that you will teach in your unit. It also explains how to write essential questions that will help you challenge students to greater understanding about the content of your unit.

Answers to the Your Turn Activities

YOUR TURN 2.1

Examples of Game and Activity Categories

Invasion games: soccer, flag football, basket- ball, floor hockey

Target games: bowling, archery, golf

Dance: line, folk, ballroom, square

Fitness: gymnastics for flexibility, track and field for cardiorespiratory, weight training for strength

YOUR TURN 2.2

Explain three advantages of selecting activities with standards-based instruction versus the exposure model.

1. Students learn concepts that can be used in several games.
2. Students develop competence in a game or activity.
3. Students are more likely to enjoy the game because of their enhanced skill.

THREE

Focusing the Content of a Unit

We set students up for success when we show them the target, provide practice in shooting at it, and provide an assessment forum for them to see themselves demonstrating increasingly higher levels of proficiency.

Stiggins, 1997, p. 38

LOOK FOR THESE KEY CONCEPTS

- backward design
- block plan
- culminating activity
- essential questions
- graphic organizer
- pace

In chapter 2 you learned how to begin the planning process for developing a standards-based unit of study. This chapter helps you continue that process by explaining how to develop a graphic organizer, essential questions, and a block plan to optimize student learning. All three further define the content you intend to teach by helping you focus on the most important concepts.

Backward Design

The process used to develop a unit of study is called **backward design** (Wiggins & McTighe, 1998). When using this approach, begin with the end in mind by asking this question: What should students know and be able to do at the end of instruction? In chapter 2, you learned how to create a **culminating activity** that allows students to demonstrate their expertise in a unit based on your instruction. Additionally, you wrote learning goals for that unit and identified possible assessments.

The next step in the planning process is to identify the skills, knowledge, and affective domain behaviors that students will need to successfully participate in the activity. For example, if you select volleyball for a certain unit, you will need to make sure your students know the tactics necessary to play net/wall games. To execute offensive tactics, students will need to be able to pass the volleyball (overhead and forearm) and spike the ball. Because a tactic for net/wall games is to deceive the opponent, students will also need to learn the dink so that opponents won't be able to anticipate a spike. Critical defensive skills are blocking and the forearm pass to receive a hard hit ball (e.g., serve or spike). The serve is another offensive skill needed for putting the ball into play. Students will need to know not only the skills, but also when to use them and how to move into position to use them in an applied setting (e.g., game play). In addition to knowing skills and tactics, students will also need to know the rules for the game. Emphasize some affective domain traits, such as cooperation and fair play.

Graphic Organizers

The culminating activity is a way to visualize what students will ultimately be expected to know and do. After you determine the content of the unit, use the **graphic organizer** to diagram the relationships among the various types of knowledge, skills, and affective domain traits that you intend to teach. Additionally, graphic organizers can indicate the sequence in which you will present concepts and skills.

 YOUR TURN 3.1

Using the game or activity unit that you began developing in chapter 2, identify the skills, knowledge, and affective domain traits that you will need to teach during the unit.

Psychomotor skills	Cognitive knowledge	Affective domain traits

Teachers often use a graphic organizer to paint the big picture for students. Graphic organizers are visual representations of the content and concepts taught during the unit and the relationships between them. Instead of merely listing the knowledge and skills taught during a unit, the graphic organizer allows you to arrange the concepts you intend to teach in a meaningful representation of the unit. According to the San Diego County Office of Education (http://kms.sdcoe.net/differ/21-DSY/55-DSY.html), graphic organizers help you do the following:

- See the relationships between various concepts.
- Help students understand sequence and interrelationships.
- Provide second-language learners with a visual image for new vocabulary and concepts.
- Review materials as a postreading activity.
- Evaluate student understanding.

Figure 3.1 is a graphic organizer used for a team handball unit. In physical education, the sequence of instruction is often critical. Creating a graphic organizer will require you to think about the sequence you intend to use for teaching the content of the unit. With this graphic organizer, the slanted lines mean that the skills are taught in that order. If the boxes are attached to a straight line, the order of teaching does not matter. The graphic organizer template shown can be used for most physical education units. It organizes content around the three domains and fitness. The directions for creating this template are found at the end of the chapter. Figure 3.2 is another example of a graphic organizer that we have developed for Mr. Thomas' badminton unit. By listing all the concepts, you can ensure that your instruction is thorough and deliberate and that you address or include important concepts.

Essential Questions

Children ask a lot of questions. They don't want just the answer, they want to know why, and one question often leads to the next. It is this type of curiosity that essential questions (EQ) try to spark: not just the *what*, but the *how* and *why* parts of learning.

A big push in education today is getting students to think critically. All teachers, physical educators included, should embrace this notion.

YOUR TURN 3.2

Look at the knowledge, skills, and affective domain traits that you have identified as necessary for student success in your culminating activity. Create a graphic organizer template using the directions for the template given at the end of chapter 3. Remember that if the content is on a straight line, the material can be presented in any order. To create a sequence of instruction, place the content on a slanted line. If you prefer a different format for a graphic organizer, do an Internet search for "graphic organizer" and look at some of the other designs. Remember that the purpose of this organizer is to make you think about what needs to be included in your unit and the sequence of instruction.

Lower levels of learning, such as knowledge (when students learn or memorize facts) and comprehension (students are able to restate information using their own words), are quite basic types of learning; if this is all that you aspire to teach, students often become bored. One way to challenge students is by asking questions. A broad educational goal is to encourage students to think and to ask questions, thus developing lifelong learners who continually work to answer relevant questions while, at the same time, learn to think critically about various topics. You should contribute to this educational goal when you teach.

Essential questions are the concepts of the unit or lesson phrased in the form of a question. These help you focus or limit instruction while simultaneously encouraging students to think and ask questions about how the information being taught relates to the world around them. Essential questions typically focus on the big ideas of the unit, address important understandings, and help organize the content of the lesson. Essential questions are just like the name implies: They represent the *essential* content that students should learn. Teachers often write essential questions on a white board or poster paper for students to look at during the lesson, and then refer back to this question as they present new knowledge. The content of the lesson should enable students to answer the lesson's essential question. In addition to writing essential questions for a unit, teachers typically write new questions for each lesson.

When teaching your students, standard 2 of the NASPE physical education standards is an excellent source of material for essential questions,

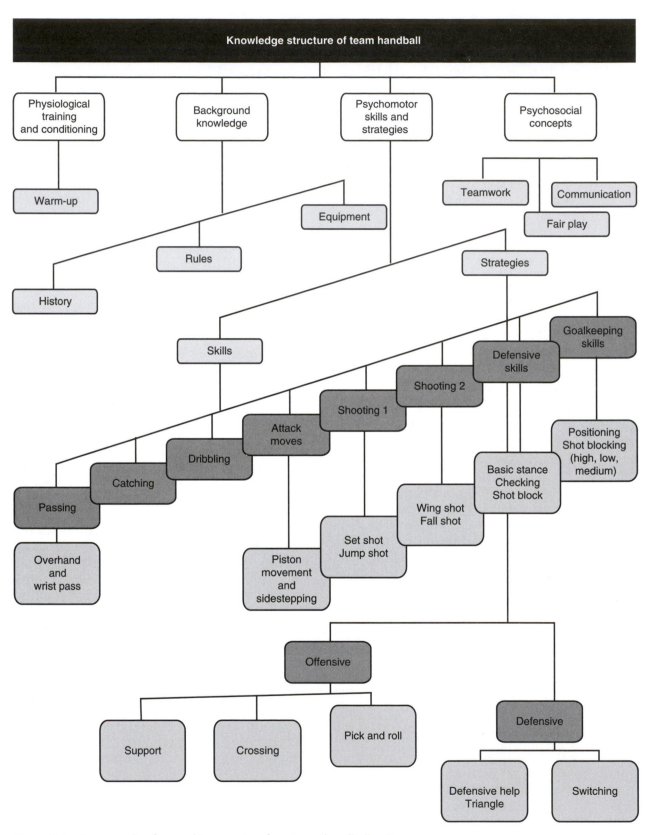

Figure 3.1 An example of a graphic organizer for a team handball unit.

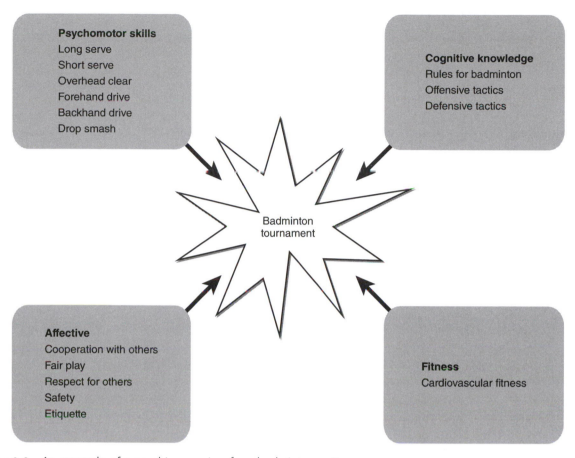

Figure 3.2 An example of a graphic organizer for a badminton unit.

since it represents concepts important to the content area. Essential questions should lead students to ask additional questions, and help them understand the material you are trying to teach and transfer their learning to other activities and sports. It is not enough to provide students with information; they should be able to apply this information and see how it relates to other ideas. Schools today want instruction to set the stage for students as they make sense of the world around them. Additionally, students should begin to wonder about other related ideas and to develop their own questions (constructivist learning theory).

Content Addressed by Essential Questions

Essential questions address the concepts (from the cognitive domain) that will be taught in the unit rather than focusing on the skills that students will demonstrate to show **competence** for the unit. Units are taught so that students can learn essential knowledge about sport and activities. For example, one focus of instruction is to teach invasion-game

concepts. A variety of sports can be used to teach these concepts: soccer, basketball, team handball, ultimate, and so on. Some of the questions for an invasion-game unit will be on the tactics essential for effectively playing an invasion game rather than those specific to, for example, soccer.

Similarly, dance is used to teach locomotor skills (e.g., leap, hop, skip), nonlocomotor skills (e.g., balance, twist, roll), and movement concepts that are essential to movement (moving in different pathways, at different levels, with varying amounts of force, and so on). Rhythm is typically involved with dance activities. The focus of the essential questions written for a dance unit will be on movement concepts that can be taught using dance. Gymnastics activities also require students to apply movement concepts while performing various locomotor and nonlocomotor skills and combinations of the two. Several activities are associated with components of health-related fitness, such as aerobic dance, inline skating, swimming, and track and field. If the intent of teaching these units is to improve fitness, essential questions written for these units should include fitness concepts.

In addition to the concepts associated with the various types of movement and fitness, other types of cognitive learning can be taught using activities. History, biomechanical principles of performance, principles of exercise physiology, and motor learning are examples of cognitive learning that are important to physical education. There are lots of potential essential questions. However, when writing essential questions, focus on the indispensable content that you will emphasize in the unit of study and limit your questions to those topics. Essential questions are designed to help the learner, not to impress an administrator or course instructor. Essential questions should not be too universal (e.g., written so broadly that several answers are correct). For example, a broad essential question might be "Why should I become fit?" A focused essential question would be "How does fitness affect the quality of play for a game of badminton?"

Characteristics of Essential Questions

The following is a list of five characteristics of essential questions from Wiggins (1998) that relate to physical education units. Other authors have slightly different variations of these, but the same general ideas apply.

1. *Essential questions (EQs) don't have an obvious answer.* They are designed to be open-ended, but not vague. When developing an essential question, as a rule of thumb, the word *what* typically yields a listing or a finite response, whereas questions that ask *how* or *why* are more open. They encourage students to think critically.

   Compare these two questions:

   ◦ What are the critical elements of a tennis forehand?

   ◦ How will using the critical elements of a tennis forehand contribute to generating more force?

   The first question has a definite answer. The second addresses the concept of force generation and the contribution that the various critical elements make toward a powerful serve. It isn't that you wouldn't teach the critical elements of a skill, but you want your essential questions to encourage students to think about why the critical elements are important rather than just testing to see if students know what they are.

2. *EQs are intended to raise the possibilities of other questions, often crossing subject areas.* When talking about crossing over different subject areas, you could be thinking about math or social studies, or if you are focusing on physical education content, you might think about motor learning concepts, exercise physiology concepts, biomechanical concepts, and so on. In the previous essential questions, the second question touches on biomechanics as well as motor learning, thus crossing subject areas.

3. *EQs address the philosophical or conceptual foundations of a discipline.* Both basic fundamental principles and concepts that apply across various types of games are important in the disciplines. Some concepts are important to teach with rhythms, body control, and gymnastics. This foundational knowledge is part of the enduring understanding you are trying to teach. If you teach some basic fundamental concepts, students will be able to apply them to other activities and to successfully participate in these activities as an adult.

   ◦ EQ: Which tactics used in badminton are similar to those found in other net sports?

   ◦ EQ: How does the angle of the racket face during contact affect the direction that the shuttle will go after it is no longer in contact with the racket?

4. *EQs recur naturally.* Some questions are appropriate for any invasion game. Some questions concerning biomechanical principles are important for similar skills (e.g., serve in tennis, spike in volleyball, overhand throw). Questions concerning teamwork are important for many activities. When you have a naturally recurring question, use or modify it so that it is important for what you want to teach. Don't let the ease of rewording limit the quality of the essential question that you write for your unit. Typically, you write additional EQs specific to the unit. When writing questions about the conceptual aspect of a game, you will have the opportunity to get students thinking about the similarities between games, and thus reinforce previous learning. In the following examples, the sport-specific term is italicized. Note that depending on the sport,

YOUR TURN 3.3

Here are some examples of essential questions. Identify the conceptual knowledge addressed in each. Answers are available at the end of the chapter.

Essential question	Conceptual knowledge
How do I increase the effectiveness of the smash?	
How does the up and back formation in doubles make a team more effective?	
How do I correct a serve that consistently lands short of the target?	
How are badminton strokes used to create an offensive advantage?	
Why is base position important in game play?	
How does health-related fitness affect the quality of my game play?	

this is an essential question that you could apply for a variety of sports.

- ○ EQ: How can I generate more force to increase the effectiveness of the *badminton serve*?
- ○ EQ: How can I use the *drop shot* effectively, given the skills of my team?

5. *EQs are framed to provoke student interest in a topic.* Essential questions often raise the *what if* ideas and questions. Essential questions can motivate students because they want to discover the answer to the question. This information leads to additional curiosity and more questions from the students themselves. Learning is no longer linear—the possibilities are endless.

- ○ EQ: How can I change the way that I practice in order to use the spike most effectively?
- ○ EQ: How can I use spin to make my serve more effective?

Writing Essential Questions

Don't be worried about writing the perfect essential question the first time that you attempt it. When learning skills, there is a learning curve. A learning curve also exists for writing essential questions. The important part is to start writing them. With more practice, your skills for writing questions will improve. Here are some suggestions for writing your essential questions:

- • Begin by defining what you want to teach during the unit. Why did you select this activity or content and what does it teach (think standards)? What are your goals? What will your students know and what will they be able to do when they have successfully completed this unit?

- • After you have defined why you are teaching the unit and what you hope to accomplish, what are the key ideas that you will teach? Remember, part of this will come from the intent of the unit—what you are trying to accomplish.

- • Develop essential questions for a conceptual level. Too often, beginners write essential questions just to have them for a unit (many schools require teachers to write essential questions each day) or course requirements (e.g., the instructor requires them for a class). Essential questions should be designed around the most important concepts that you want to achieve. Good questions emphasize the most important content presented in the unit. Essential questions should require students to do something meaningful with the information to answer the question. The ultimate goal of instruction should always be that students are able to use the information presented in a meaningful way.

YOUR TURN 3.4

Write an essential question that could be used for multiple sports or activities.

- Students should be able to answer essential questions by the completion of the unit. The answer to an essential question should not be immediately obvious to students. Students will receive new information during the unit or lesson and will use it to help them answer the question. Essential questions should require new thought; they should not be answered by restating facts.

- Three key words are used when developing essential questions:

  ○ *Why:* Why do things happen the way they do? This requires an analysis of cause and effect.

  ○ *How:* How could things be better? The question is the basis for problem solving and synthesis (creating something).

  ○ *Which:* Which do I select? This requires decision making based on clearly stated criteria and evidence.

Although essential questions can also begin with other words, these three words are helpful to beginners as they learn to write essential questions. Table 3.1 shows Mr. Thomas' essential questions. Note that Mr. Thomas used his **unit goals** as a basis for writing essential questions for his unit.

Table 3.1   Mr. Thomas' Essential Questions

Unit goal	Essential questions
Students will demonstrate various offensive and defensive skills needed to play badminton.	How can I use my skills to create space in my opponent's court to set up an attack?
	How can my team effectively defend the smash?
Students will demonstrate the ability to combine psychomotor skills in a meaningful way to play a game of badminton at a recreational level.	How can my team gain an offensive advantage in badminton and score?
	How do I keep my drop shot from landing too deep in the opponent's court?
Students will be able to serve strategically while playing badminton.	How can I use my serve to set up an attack?
	How can I correct a serve that consistently lands short of the intended target?
Students will know basic offensive tactics for a net/wall game.	How can I support my teammate on offense when I am not making the hit?
	How can my doubles team make our offensive play more aggressive? What strategies can we develop to play effectively during a game?
Students will know basic defensive tactics for a net/wall game.	How do I defend space on my side of the net?
	How can my doubles team effectively defend against the smash?
	Why is it important to develop a game-play strategy with my partner in badminton?
Students will know the rules of badminton and be able to correctly apply them during a game.	How do the rules of badminton make the game different from other net games?
	How do the scoring rules in badminton affect my team's offensive strategy?
Students will demonstrate elements of fair play during game play.	Why is it important to play fairly during a badminton game?
	Which elements of fair play make badminton most enjoyable?
Students will demonstrate the ability to work willingly with others.	Why is it important to work with my partner to play a more effective game of badminton?
	How can I effectively communicate with my partner to implement offensive and defensive strategies?

YOUR TURN 3.5

Follow these steps to write essential questions for your unit.

- Step 1: Identify the unit goals that will be taught in the unit. Since you developed unit goals in chapter 2, you can use them for this exercise. If you wish to develop new unit goals, feel free to do so.
- Step 2: If you have any goals that cover similar topics, place them next to each other. Look closely: Can you combine any of your unit goals, or is each a distinct, separate goal?
- Step 3: Using the recording sheet, write at least one essential question for each of your goals. The essential question should require students to think, analyze, and apply information taught during the unit.

Recording Sheet for Step 3

Unit goals	Essential questions

- Step 4: Check for the following:
  - _____ Is each unit goal addressed with an essential question?
  - _____ Do you have 5 to 7 questions?
  - _____ Do the questions embrace the scope of the unit?
  - _____ Do the questions limit the scope of the unit?
  - _____ Will the questions spark interest in learning?
  - _____ Does each question require more than a yes or no answer?
  - _____ Do the questions address some of the essential concepts related to the skill or activity?
  - _____ Do the questions lead students to ask additional questions about the topic?
  - _____ Does each question require more than facts for an answer?
  - _____ Does each question require new thought rather than facts to answer?
  - _____ Does each question require the use of a higher level of thinking to respond? Which type of higher-level thinking is required?
    - Analysis (taking apart the known: compare and contrast, classify)
    - Synthesis (putting together the new: create, write, design)
    - Evaluation (judge the outcome: justify, decide, recommend)
- Step 5: After writing your essential questions, have a colleague or peer review them and give you feedback. The following checklist can be used for this feedback.
  - _____ The question cannot be answered with a simple yes or no.
  - _____ The question cannot be answered with facts alone.

(continued)

(continued)

_____ The question requires the use of a higher level of thinking to respond.
- Analysis (taking apart the known: compare and contrast, classify)
- Synthesis (putting together the new: create, write, design)
- Evaluation (judge the outcome: justify, decide, recommend)

_____ The question requires new thought rather than a collection of facts.

_____ The question is designed to spark student interest in the topic.

Overall comments and suggestions for improving the questions:

Creating a Block Plan

After you have developed your goals for instruction, identified the culminating activity, determined the content students need to participate in the culminating activity, pictured it using your graphic organizer, and written essential questions, you will want to arrange the content into a logical sequence of instruction and distribute this content over the time frame of the unit to ensure that students will be able to reach your final goals. Chapter 5 helps you develop the actual content of a lesson.

The **block plan** is a way to briefly indicate what you are going to teach every day. Sometimes when teachers see 15 or 20 days of instruction, they think that they have a lot of time, so they end up spending too much time at the beginning of a unit teaching a few things and then running out of time at the end. When we were beginning teachers, our students would grumble about spending a lot of time learning the skills but never using them during game play. Conversely, some teachers teach all the skills and knowledge during the first few days of a unit (unfortunately, we have seen this done in as little as one day) and then let students play games or in a tournament without doing additional instruction as game play progresses. In other cases, teachers ambitiously plan to teach a lot about a sport or activity and then realize that there simply is too much material to cover. These are just some of our reasons for developing a block plan. Note: A block plan does not require you to develop a complex description about the sequence of instruction. Rather, you can use a block plan to map the big picture of the content that you will teach and to estimate the amount of time that you will allocate to each major section or skill of the unit.

When planning a unit, learning needs to occur in portions small enough that students will be able to process the information; additionally, some student learning needs to take place every day. Instructional models have different approaches about how student learning is packaged: With the tactical model, you can use game play to teach content with skills taught as needed; if you use direct instruction, you teach skills first and then move to game play. A block plan provides a way for you to map learning, spreading it out over the unit.

Developing a block plan allows you to **pace** instruction and make sure that you teach something new each day. You do not need to include a lot of detail on the block plan, since its purpose is to distribute instruction over the allocated time. Eventually, you will have a specific learning outcome for every day (chapter 5). For now, it will be sufficient to just list general ideas and topics that you will cover on each day of the unit.

Table 3.2 shows Mr. Thomas' block plan for his badminton unit. Note, this unit will last only three weeks because the content of badminton, the students' level of skill, and the final desired level of play can be reached in that time frame.

Table 3.2   Mr. Thomas' Block Plan for Badminton Unit

	Day 1	Day 2	Day 3	Day 4	Day 5
Week 1	Diagnostic assessment on the serve	Short serve and serve return	Backhand drive Long serve and serve return	Overhead clear Introduction to basic rules for doubles	Mini-tournament using serves and clears Skill testing
Week 2	Mini-tournament continued Focus on offensive positioning Skill testing	Drop shot Skill testing	Doubles player positions Defensive tactics Skill testing	Transitioning from defense to offense Skill testing	Forcing the opponent to move Skill testing Written test
Week 3	Tournament play emphasizing net shots tactics Game-play rubric	Tournament play emphasizing hitting to the open space Rubric or GPAI	Tournament play emphasizing communication with partner about covering the court Game-play rubric	Tournament play emphasizing fair play Game-play rubric	Tournament play emphasizing moving the opponent to create open space Rubric or GPAI

►YOUR TURN 3.6

Now it is your turn to divide the content of your unit over the time allocated for instruction. Here is a template for your unit. Note: We have added an extra week for those who wish to have a 20-day unit. Please feel free to add additional time if you need.

Activity:			Grade level:		
	Day 1	Day 2	Day 3	Day 4	Day 5
Week 1					
Week 2					
Week 3					
Week 4					

Summary

Congratulations! After completing all the exercises in chapters 2 and 3, you should now have a basic idea of what you intend to teach in your unit. Chapters 4 through 7 help you fill in the details by explaining more about assessment, content development, and managing instruction.

Answers to the Your Turn Activities

⦿ YOUR TURN 3.1

Here are some examples of essential questions. Identify the conceptual knowledge addressed in each.

Essential question	Conceptual knowledge
How do I increase the effectiveness of a smash?	Biomechanics of the effect of force on the speed of the implement hit
How does the up and back formation in doubles make a team more effective?	Game-play tactics: offensive and defensive strategies
How do I correct a serve that consistently lands short of the intended target?	Biomechanics: kinematics of projectile motion
How are badminton strokes used to create an offensive advantage?	Game-play tactics: Creating space; hitting to open space; moving the opponent
Why is base position important in game play?	Game-play tactics
How does health-related fitness affect the quality of my game play?	Health-related fitness components

Directions for Creating a Graphic Organizer in Microsoft Word

How to Make Pretty Boxes

1. In Microsoft Word, select **Insert > Shapes**. Select a box from the shapes toolbar.
2. After you have created a box, select the box by clicking it.
3. Copy the box (**Ctrl + C** or **right click on mouse > Copy**).
4. Paste the box anywhere on the page and as many times as you'd like.

How to Write in the Boxes

5. Select the box you desire to write inside of.
6. **Right click on the box** and click **Add text**.
7. Type in what you want. Edit or format the text as you wish.

How to Make Pretty Lines

8. Click on the **Line** in the shapes toolbox (between the Textbox and line with an arrowhead).
9. Move your mouse onto the page and click and drag the line to the desired location and length. (Clicking and letting go will not give you a line. Hold down the left mouse button and drag.)

10. An easy way to align the box and line is to click on the outside of your box and drag it straight down or across.
11. An easy way to make sure your line is exactly vertical or horizontal is to hold the **Shift** key down *while dragging* the line.

How to Keep Everything Together After Connecting Lines and Boxes

12. After you have made and connected your boxes and lines, select each element of that group (i.e., the main box on top, the lines down from it, and the ascending boxes attached). You can do this by holding the Shift key and clicking on each box or line.
13. When everything is selected (you'll see many little white boxes), right click with the mouse inside all of these white boxes.
14. Select **Group**. This will make all the boxes into one box.
15. You can do the same steps and select **Ungroup** in order to break the image down into individual pieces again.

***The best thing to do with all of this is to just try. If you're not sure of something, try it! You can always undo a mistake (**Ctrl + Z**).

FOUR

Writing Rubrics

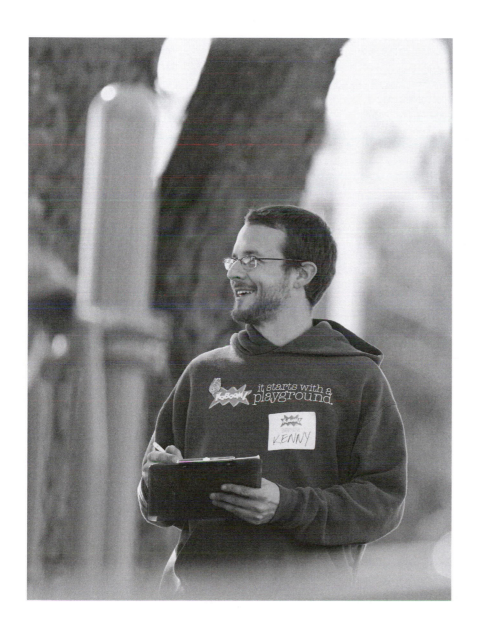

Many educational targets are in fact far more complex than we had previously realized.

Stiggins, 1997, p. 48

LOOK FOR THESE KEY CONCEPTS

- ❯ accountable
- ❯ competent performance
- ❯ descriptor
- ❯ open and closed environment
- ❯ qualitative rubric
- ❯ quantitative rubric

Teachers know that they should assess students, but sometimes their assessments fail to align with what they are trying to teach. We both remember doing skill assessments in volleyball as beginning teachers to ensure that our students had learned the skills needed for playing the game. Additionally, we gave written tests to make sure that students understood the rules. Yet, when we watched game play and observed students' lack of ability to use all of these skills and knowledge together, many of the games were of the serve-and-drop variety, and they really weren't much fun to play. Twenty-twenty hindsight tells us that our assessments were not aligned with our final goal; rather, they were measuring intermediate goals for what we ultimately wanted our students to be able to do at the conclusion of the unit. We were not holding students **accountable** (requiring them to complete a task or learn skills) for the entire body of knowledge and skills that they needed to achieve our final outcome. Although this statement seems like common sense now, given the many ways that we currently use to assess students, remember that times have changed. In the past, teacher candidates were taught to only use skill tests, written tests, and fitness tests. If we had looked at the desired outcome of our teaching, it would have immediately been obvious that we were failing to assess what we really wanted students to know and be able to do. Unfortunately, we were concentrating on the smaller pieces of the puzzle, rather than trying to look at the big picture that we really wanted to assemble.

Our ultimate goal for a volleyball unit was for students to be able to play volleyball games and demonstrate **competent performance**. In short, we wanted students to enjoy playing the game using the skills they learned and to work as a team applying various tactics as they tried to defeat an opponent.

In chapter 2 we discussed the concept of creating a culminating activity, and you learned about writing goals and focusing instruction in chapter 3. The next step is to decide which assessment you will use to hold students accountable for what you have taught. When designing the assessment, consider the following implementation questions:

1. What factors must I consider to make the assessment feasible to administer?

2. How can I assess all three educational domains: psychomotor, cognitive, and affective?

3. Should the assessment focus on group or individual efforts, or both?

4. What criteria should students achieve when completing the culminating assessment?

5. How much time do I need to allocate to complete the culminating assessment?

A good assessment allows teachers to make valid inferences about what students have learned. If your goal is for students to play a volleyball game, then assessing students while they are actually playing allows you to make a valid assessment of that ability. However, making that valid inference of the ability will occur only if you are using the right elements or **descriptors** as a basis for your judgment and then using good criteria to evaluate each of those descriptors. For example, a volleyball game would not be a good place to evaluate flexibility or strength, but it would be an excellent setting to determine whether students could move on the court and get into position to play a ball.

Similarly, game-play assessment should consider skill, but it is not a good setting to assess each discrete skill. Game play occurs in an **open environment.** This means that the events on the court are unpredictable because they depend on things that cannot be controlled, such as the setup by another player or the position of one's opponents on the court. In an open environment, variables are constantly changing, thus requiring constant adjustment to the events that are happening on the court. Although your descriptor might include the use of correct form on skills to hold students accountable for a reasonable level of good form, it is best to assess discrete individual skills away from game play in a **closed environment** that is somewhat controlled. You want to encourage the use of correct form during play, but you will realize that players often break form while playing a ball that is difficult to reach. A second reason for an assessment of skills outside of the game is that it is possible that a player will not be able to demonstrate the skill during game play due to lack of opportunity. For example, a player might never have a chance to spike during the volleyball game because of being in the wrong position or not receiving a good setup from teammates.

The assessment criteria for culminating activities are usually put together into a document called a **rubric.** Two types of rubrics are commonly used in education: an **analytic rubric** (allows discrete analysis of the various elements necessary to the performance or product) and a **holistic rubric** (used to give a single score or rating for the overall performance). Because you need to give feedback about performance to students, we recommend using an analytic rubric. Holistic rubrics are most commonly used for large-scale assessments where students are not given feedback (e.g., a state-level assessment). See Lund and Kirk (2010) for a more complete explanation of holistic rubrics.

The two types of analytic rubrics are quantitative and qualitative. A **quantitative rubric** has a list of statements germane to the performance. Assessors rate the performance by assigning a number that is anchored to a statement that describes the level of performance. Figure 4.1 is an example of a quantitative rubric and recording sheet. Although we have used quantitative rubrics for game play assessments in the past, we feel that qualitative rubrics are the better choice for complex assessments. We do see a use for quantitative rubrics for assessing activities that have a multistaged performance, like those found, for example, in the delivery of a bowling ball (four-step approach), field events in track and field (long jump, discus throw, high jump), or diving. The focus of these sports is on a single skill rather than on a combination of multiple attributes that are observed simultaneously.

Qualitative analytic rubrics provide written descriptions of the levels of performance. Figure

4.2 is an example of a **qualitative rubric,** which is used for complex performances that involve multiple skills or supporting actions and other aspects that are important considerations for the overall performance during the game. These aspects typically involve all three learning domains.

YOUR TURN 4.1

Look at the two example rubrics in figures 4.1 and 4.2 and identify three ways in which the two types of rubrics differ. Suggested answers are at the end of this chapter.

Quantitative Rubrics

Quantitative analytic rubrics are best used with activities and sports in which the performance involves a sequential movement. Target games are good examples of this type of movement, as are gymnastics skills, diving, rope jumping tricks, and field events for track and field units. Because of the activities for which they are written, quantitative rubrics are content specific. They are written for use only with that unit. They are fairly easy to develop and administer, since they simply identify the phases of performance and then require the user to make a rating about whether the performer demonstrates them. With single-skill events or sports, the quality of performance is usually judged by the number of consecutive repetitions or a percentage of successful performances (e.g., 3 out of 4). Optimal performance is generally defined by the ability to perform consistently (consecutive correct performance as in three in a row or a high percentage of successful performance as in 4 out of 6 attempts).

When writing a quantitative rubric, focus on the key items. Too often, teachers include extraneous items that are not of primary importance to the performance. This results in a rubric that diminishes the weight of the primary elements by including those of less importance. Typically, the essence of a performance can be captured with four to six descriptors.

If you use quantitative rubrics, anchor the number with a phrase that gives a sense of what the number means. The levels of the rubric will be tied to consistency of performance. Some people might wish to use words like *rarely, sometimes, often,* or *always.* These words are somewhat subjective, and they can cause problems with consistency if they are not defined for the person using the rubric or if people using the rubric are not trained about the level of performance that the word represents. If using a single word to describe a level, an alternative is to anchor the level to either a percentage (e.g., 0–25 percent, 26–50 percent, 51–75 percent) or to use numbers to indicate consistency, as was done in figure 4.1.

Refer to the discussion about consistency found in chapter 6.

At first glance, a quantitative rubric seems pretty complex. The steps shown in figure 4.3 and discussed in the next section will provide you with a process to follow when creating your own quantitative rubric.

Archery Rubric

Directions

Observe each archer shooting an end and rate each of the steps on a scale of 4 to 0 using the following definitions:

    4 = Exhibits the behaviors consistently or almost always (3 or more times in a row)

    3 = Usually exhibits the behaviors (4 out of 6 trials)

    2 = Behaviors are exhibited sometimes or about half the time

    1 = Behaviors are exhibited occasionally (2 or fewer out of 6 trials)

    0 = Nonparticipant or student does not complete the assessment

Name	Ready position	Nock	Draw	Anchor	Release and hold
	Straddle line; bow held down at side; side to target weight balanced	Bow raised; arrow placed on top, nock in string, arrow on rest	Turn bow to perpendicular; slowly pull string back w/3 fingers; rotate bow elbow down; draw elbow back.	Anchor thumb under chin; adjust aim based on previous shots; look at target.	Count to 3 before fingers release string; maintain anchor position; keep bow arm up.

Critical elements adapted from Haywood and Lewis (1989).

Figure 4.1   Example of a quantitative rubric for archery.

Adapted from Haywood and Lewis (1989).

Descriptors	Level 1	Level 2	Level 3	Level 4
Shot execution	Student relies on one or two shots during a game. Incorrect form causes shots to be misplaced or ineffective. Reaches for the shuttle, rather than moving into position.	Student uses all shots taught, but not necessarily at the appropriate time. Shots have some form breaks. Student is sometimes out of position. Attempts to return to home base, but does not always get there.	Student executes all shots taught, usually with correct form and at appropriate times. Frequently in position to play shots. Can anticipate opponents' shots. Player arrives in position with enough time to play the shuttle.	Student executes all shots taught with correct form, using them at appropriate times. Anticipates shots, moving into position and playing the shuttle in an unhurried manner. Often uses shots to gain a tactical advantage.
Serve	Serve is usually not effective; player relies on one type of serve.	Serves are adequate and usually cross the net, but they are weak.	Student uses both long and short serves, resulting in strong, well-placed shots.	Student varies long and short serves. Opponent is often on the defensive when returning serves.
Knowledge of rules	Student is unfamiliar with rules and depends on opponents or partner for help.	Student shows evidence of knowing many rules, but may make errors. Knows serving order and rotation.	Student shows evidence of knowing most rules and applies them appropriately.	Student clearly knows all rules and applies them during game play consistently and correctly.
Use of strategy	Hits shots directly back to opponents. Little communication and teamwork with partner, resulting in both players going after the shuttle at the same time.	At times, student attempts to hit the shuttle to open spaces to move opponents. Communicates with partner as they work together to cover the court.	Student uses strategy to defeat an opponent, hitting shots to open spaces on the court to gain an advantage. Works well and communicates with partner and does not try to play alone.	Student utilizes strategy to win points by forcing opponents to move. Uses clear and drop shots to gain an offensive advantage. Consistently works well with partner to cover the entire court.
Fair play and etiquette	Complains consistently about line calls made by the opponent. Makes incorrect calls in own favor. Behavior may be ill-mannered.	Occasionally recognizes good play of partner and opponents. May try to play the entire court, taking partner's shots. Sometimes calls shots honestly and fairly.	Usually recognizes good play by opponents and partner. Shares play with partner. Shots are usually called honestly and fairly.	Consistently recognizes good play by opponents and partner. Consistently calls all shots honestly and fairly and is known as a fair player.
Effort	Stops practicing or talks to friends during practice times.	Attempts to improve skills and knowledge during practice times.	Usually works hard to improve skills and knowledge.	Takes full advantage of practice times to improve knowledge and skills.
Cooperates with others	Works only with friends or is sometimes rude when forced to play with others.	Will work with those who are not close friends when asked to do so by the teacher.	Willingly works with any member of class for partner work.	Works well with any member of class and is sought by others for partner work. Seeks to help others during practice.

Figure 4.2 Example of a qualitative rubric for badminton.

1. Identify the content.
2. Decide on the phases or elements needed for performing the skill.
3. Identify the critical elements of each phase.
4. Determine how many levels you will use.
5. Define what the levels mean.
6. Develop a recording sheet.
7. Pilot the rubric.
8. Refine the assessment.

Figure 4.3 Steps to creating a quantitative rubric.

Step 1: Identify the Content

In this step, you will identify the skill that is being assessed and then obtain resources for gathering information about teaching the skill. Whereas you might think that you know how to perform the skill and can write the rubric without further consultation, it is always better to find resources to inform the process. Different resources or books will have different ways of describing the phases of performance and may use language that is more clear or easier to understand than your own descriptions. After gathering several resources—try to find at least three different sources written by experts—read their descriptions for performing the skill and look for similarities and differences in the way that the skill is described.

Step 2: Decide on the Phases or Elements Needed for Performing the Skill

The sports or activities being assessed using the quantitative rubric tend to be skills that will be performed in a closed or reasonably stable environment. The quality of performance or form depends on performing various elements in a certain sequence or order. In step 2, you will decide on the major elements that you want to observe to ensure correct performance. For example, the major phases or elements in archery are as follows:

- Straddle the line with bow in nondominant hand
- Nock the arrow
- Draw and aim
- Anchor
- Release

In target sports (e.g., archery, bowling, golf) aiming at the target will always be one of the elements. Whereas the form involved with getting the implement to the target stays consistent, the accuracy of the performance depends on making sure that the implement is released to the target. Therefore, all target sports will include some type of adjustment to target, or aiming, phase. In the case of bowling, aiming occurs before the start of the action as the bowler decides where to begin the approach and what spots on the lane to use for aiming. In archery, the aiming occurs during the drawing of the bow. Even though the aiming phase may not appear to be part of the form, it is a crucial part of the accuracy with which the object arrives to the target.

YOUR TURN 4.2

Identify the phases or elements needed during the approach and release of the ball in bowling.

Step 3: Identify the Critical Elements of Each Phase

Step 2 identifies the major phases of the skill. Step 3 further defines those phases by adding the critical elements of the skill associated with each phase. Although the rubric will list only the phase, the phase will be evaluated using the various critical elements important to the performance. For example, the critical elements of the first phase, straddle the line, would be as follows:

- Feet straddle the line
- Bow held down at the side
- Side to target, weight balanced

YOUR TURN 4.3

Now identify the critical elements for each of the bowling phases you listed in Your Turn 4.2.

Step 4: Determine How Many Levels You Will Use

During step 4, you will decide how many levels to write. As previously stated, there are a variety of philosophies about how many levels to use. We prefer four levels, with a fifth level of "does not participate."

Step 5: Define What the Levels Mean

Because consistency is related to performance, we have used numbers to help us define the levels. An archery end consists of six arrows so we have used 6 as a basis for defining consistency.

Here is how we define the levels:

Level 4 = Exhibits the behaviors consistently or almost always (3 or more times in a row)

Level 3 = Usually exhibits the behaviors (4 out of 6 trials)

Level 2 = Behaviors are exhibited sometimes or about half the time

Level 1 = Behaviors are exhibited occasionally (2 or fewer out of 6 trials)

Level 0 = Nonparticipant or student does not complete the assessment

With other sports, fewer trials may be sufficient to establish consistency of performance. Refer to chapter 7 for a discussion of process assessment and criteria.

Step 6: Develop a Recording Sheet

The quantitative rubric will have a score sheet for recording the results of the assessment. Numbers are used for recording results. Think of them as a sort of shorthand so that multiple students can be recorded on a single sheet.

An easy way to develop a recording sheet is to use the table function in Microsoft Word. You may want to sketch out your table first with paper and pencil to decide how many columns and rows are needed. We recommend putting the roster of students in a column on the left-hand side of the sheet and the phases critical to performance across the top.

YOUR TURN 4.4

Use a computer to design a rubric and the recording sheet for a bowling quantitative rubric. Bring the rubric and the recording sheet to the next class to share with a peer for feedback.

Step 7: Pilot the Rubric

As with all rubrics, you will need to pilot it to see if you have correctly identified the phases important for performance and the accompanying critical elements. In some cases, you may want to combine some of the phases, or you may need to create additional phases. When looking at the results from using the assessment, the students with the best performances should have the best scores. If the rubric does not allow you to make a valid inference about the results (e.g., the best students should receive the best scores), then the rubric needs revision.

Step 8: Refine the Assessment

After doing a pilot test of the assessment, make refinements and corrections. If you need major revisions, consider another pilot. If few changes are made, the rubric is probably ready for use.

Qualitative Rubrics

A qualitative analytic rubric is used for complex performances that involve multiple skills or supporting actions and other aspects that are important considerations for the overall performance during the game. These complex performances typically involve the simultaneous assessment of all three domains.

The qualitative rubric provides written descriptions of the levels of performance for each of the descriptors used on the rubric. The descriptions capture those elements of performance or product that distinguish the performance from that of other levels. See figures 4.2 and 4.4 for an example of a qualitative rubric and recording sheet. When writing the rubric, ask yourself what level of performance you expect of your students. The descriptions for the various levels should designate characteristics that are unique to that level of performance. With practice, you can learn to use a qualitative rubric with good accuracy.

The number of levels that you use for the assessment depends on the rubric you use. At the

Badminton Recording Sheet

Directions

For each descriptor of the badminton rubric (see figure 4.2), record the level observed for each student.

Name	Shots	Serve	Rules	Strategy	Fair play	Effort	Cooperation
1. Yoshie	2	3	3	2	3	2	3
2. Nicholas	1	2	1	1	2	2	3
3.							
4.							
5.							
6.							
7.							
8.							
9.							
10.							
11.							
12.							
13.							
14.							
15.							
16.							
17.							
18.							
19.							
20.							

Figure 4.4   Sample badminton recording sheet.

very least, three levels are required, whether or not the descriptor being observed is present and one additional level. With fewer than three levels, the rubric cannot discriminate a level of quality. It would actually be a performance checklist; the trait is either present or not.

The more levels used, the smaller the difference between them. This will influence accuracy when using the rubric, since there is less difference between adjacent cells. Four and six levels are commonly seen on quantitative rubrics. It is suggested that you use a zero score for a non-participation. Use an even number of levels (not counting the zero) to avoid a tendency to give a middle score, as with five levels. For example, level 1 would be an unacceptable performance,

level 2=passing, level 3=ideal, and level 4=beyond expectations.

Remember that the numbers are indicators of a performance for recording purposes; they do not represent an ordinal score. Students scoring a 3 are not three times as good as those scoring a 1. Also remember that some descriptors might have greater importance than others. Translation: The scores of the different descriptors should not be added to calculate a grade.

When novices write rubrics, they often struggle with writing the unsatisfactory level. Some teachers make the mistake of just stating that the person did not demonstrate the behavior that is indicative of the descriptor. For example, if the descriptor was court movement, a poorly written rubric would simply state that "the player failed to move around the court." This really isn't very helpful. When writing the unsatisfactory level, be sure to describe what you observe that is unsatisfactory. Unsatisfactory performance might include doing random movements or failing to get into position to play the ball. Another type of unsatisfactory movement would describe a ball hog consistently playing all the court positions. A good description will let students know which types of behaviors you would like to discourage. It can help students improve their performances.

Every once in a while, you will have a student who is truly remarkable, and you would like to recognize the student's level of excellence. If you set the top level of performance as something that all students can readily achieve, the outstanding students might not be motivated to learn anything or try to improve. Wiggins (1998) recommends reserving that top score for exceptional work. It gives the top students something to strive for, but this is reserved for the very, very best. Reserving a higher level and awarding it only on rare occasions gives you an opportunity to recognize outstanding performance, something that you don't always have the chance to do. Others have a different perspective about the top score because of its implications for grading. Chapter 13 covers this topic in more detail in the discussion on grading issues.

If you decide that the top level on the rubric should be reserved for exceptional students, then the target level, or the level below exceptional, will describe the A-student performance. Those being evaluated with the rubric must be informed of this, or they will be frustrated that they are not receiving the highest score.

You need to let students know how good their skills must be to meet the *cut score*, the score below which students fail. On written work, 70 percent is often considered the cut score. Performance below 70 percent is failing (e.g., 69 percent), or unacceptable. Passing is the level that a state-mandated test would aim for all students to minimally achieve. In other words, the passing level is the minimal performance that a student would need to meet the standard. The target performance describes the level you strive to help all students reach. However, you know realistically that some students will not reach this level due to insufficient allocated time for this unit or lack of prior experience in the activity. Think of getting all students to the target

level as a personal challenge to your teaching ability!

If the quantitative rubrics seemed complex, qualitative rubrics can seem even more daunting. With practice, however, you can learn to develop rubrics. Once again, a step-by-step process is offered to help you develop your own qualitative rubrics (see figure 4.5).

Step 1: Visualize the Final Product

After identifying the culminating activity for the sport or unit that you are going to teach, the first step in developing the rubric is to determine the outcomes that you wish to achieve when the instruction for the unit is complete. Throughout the following explanation of the steps, we're going to ask you to complete practice tasks for an invasion game (e.g., basketball, soccer). Begin here by identifying your invasion game.

Step 2: Brainstorm Behaviors That Represent What Students Should Achieve

When developing a rubric, think of various student behaviors that represent things that you *would or would not* like students to demonstrate when they are completing the culminating assessment. The *would not like to see* list is often a great resource when it is time to write the unsatisfactory level of the rubric. As stated previously, errors or omissions are excellent sources of verbiage for the unacceptable level. It helps to brainstorm with others to develop this list of positive and undesirable behaviors or to use expert resources and references for the sport or activity to generate ideas. To generate this list of items or phrases, think about the things that distinguish good play

---

1. Visualize the final product.
2. Brainstorm ideas for the behaviors representative of what you are trying to achieve.
3. Identify descriptors.
4. Write the levels.
5. Pilot the rubric.
6. Revise the rubric based on your pilot use.

Figure 4.5   Steps to creating a qualitative rubric.

or participation from mediocre or unacceptable performance. By generating a list of the things that distinguish good play from that of other levels, you will have a good start on developing an analytic qualitative rubric for your culminating activity.

Write a list of things that distinguish good play from mediocre play in the invasion game that you selected.

Step 3: Identify Descriptors

A descriptor is the name given to the characteristic or trait that is one of the major elements that will be assessed on the rubric. When developing a rubric, always go back to what you want to assess (e.g., the outcomes developed in the first step) so that the rubric aligns with the assessment. Because you will want to limit the number of items that are assessed (and do a really thorough job of assessing those things that matter most), rubrics should look at the most important items and use those as descriptors. For a qualitative rubric, you will probably have 6 to 8 descriptors. If you will use the rubric to assess performance on only a single occasion (e.g., a dance performance), you can include even fewer items. If you have the opportunity to use the rubric multiple times for the same students, consider using only a few of the descriptors instead of trying to give students a score on the entire rubric. The other descriptors can be assessed at a later time.

By looking at student learning from a conceptual perspective, you can use rubrics for multiple assessment tasks (e.g., a rubric for different types of structured dance or rhythms, an invasion game rubric). Another point to remember is that the rubric should focus on things that can best be assessed during game play or during the culminating performance. Look at the list of items developed in step 2; if several are about the same thing, group them and then develop a single descriptor to represent them.

Go back to your list and group the like items so that you identify the descriptors for your rubric.

When writing a **game-play rubric,** begin by looking at the unique features of the game and then include those items in the rubric. For example, the offensive tactics for invasion games involve moving the ball or object down the field or court by either passing or dribbling and then putting it into the goal to score. The rubric should assess students' ability to move the ball or object to an open space (passing), the ability to maintain possession when on offense, and the knowledge of when to pass and when to keep the ball or object. The defensive tactics used for an invasion game involve positioning players between the ball or object and the goal and working with others on the team to regain possession. Additionally, you will be able to assess students' ability to apply rules to the game situation and use those rules fairly to gain an advantage. Teamwork and fair play are affective domain traits that are important to the game, so students should be held accountable for those characteristics as well.

When working on the descriptors, ask yourself if the list of behaviors generated in step 2 can fit under all of these categories. If not, you may want to rewrite your descriptors. If you have no items that fit with one of the descriptors that you generate, consider deleting that item from your rubric, since it might not be important.

Write the descriptors for an invasion game rubric. In our example (see figure 4.2), the descriptors appear in the left-hand column.

Step 4: Write the Levels

The next step involves writing the levels of performance. For this rubric, we are going to suggest writing four levels: unacceptable, passing, target, and superstar. The number of levels depends on a variety of things: Some states require a six-level rubric; some people like to write a level for each letter grade assigned (e.g., A, B, and so on). Remember that the more levels that you write, the smaller the difference between levels.

When writing the levels, some people prefer to start writing the target level of performance since it is easiest to visualize. Others like to think about the errors that people make during performance. Typically, these are the two levels that teachers usually write first. It really doesn't matter where you start. Write the level that is easiest for you to do first and then continue to write the others.

To get ideas for the written descriptions of the levels, go back to the list generated in step 2 of good and not-so-good behaviors or knowledge, and sort them into levels. Use these phrases to start writing your levels. When you finish, read all the levels that you've written and make sure that there is a clear difference between the levels. Remember that your goal is to describe each level of performance; simply stating that students don't do something is not a good description.

YOUR TURN 4.8

Working with a partner, develop a qualitative rubric for an invasion game using table 4.1. You have already completed steps 1 through 3; use this information to write the levels of the rubric. Choose only three of your descriptors for this rubric. Complete sentences are not necessary.

Step 5: Pilot the Rubric

Because it is difficult to write a really good rubric, the next step is to pilot the rubric, using it to assess a group of students for the selected activity. When using a rubric for the first time, you must not use it to assign a significant portion of students' grades, since there are probably errors in the rubric. Be sure to pilot the rubric and make sure that it is valid before using it for a high-stakes assessment.

Step 6: Revise the Rubric Based on Your Pilot Use

A good rubric is not easy to develop. Allow sufficient administrations or uses to fine-tune it. We have found that it typically takes about three administrations of a rubric to smooth out the rough edges. Administration and revision are important parts of the fine-tuning process that occurs when you develop rubrics. Some teachers share their rubrics with an assessment buddy (someone with whom you talk about assessment and share work) and allow this person to provide feedback. Be sure that the person you ask for feedback has good content knowledge about the sport or activity for which you are developing the rubric.

YOUR TURN 4.9

Write another rubric by yourself and choose your own sport. Using table 4.1 as a guide, practice writing levels for a qualitative rubric with three descriptors. Use an expert source to help develop descriptions of each level. Don't rely on your own content knowledge alone.

YOUR TURN 4.10

Exchange your rubric with a partner and provide written comments and feedback on your partner's rubric.

Summary

If you've made it this far and you understand the concepts we've discussed, you have come a long way toward becoming an assessor. Using the steps outlined in this chapter, you should be able to write quantitative rubrics for those activities best assessed with that type of rubric and a qualitative rubric for culminating activities used for assessing your classes.

YOUR TURN 4.11

On a scale of 1 to 3, rate your level of confidence in your ability to do the following:

    1 = Unsure

    2 = A little confident

    3 = Very confident

    ___ Develop a culminating activity for a physical education unit.

    ___ Explain the difference between a quantitative and a qualitative rubric to a peer.

    ___ Develop a quantitative rubric for a physical education unit.

    ___ Develop a qualitative rubric for a physical education unit.

    ___ Justify the selection of either a qualitative or quantitative rubric for a given physical education rubric.

Sharing the culminating activity and the rubric with students early in the unit will help them understand what is expected. Most students exhibit greater effort and on-task behavior when they have an explicit goal that guides their practice each day. The next section of this book guides you in fine-tuning your ability to plan your teaching and assess students' learning

Table 4.1   Rubric Template

Descriptors	Unacceptable	Passing	Target	Superstar

Answers to the Your Turn Activities

YOUR TURN 4.1

How do the two types of rubrics in figures 4.1 and 4.2 differ?

1. Numerical ratings are used in quantitative rubrics; narrative descriptions are used for levels in qualitative rubrics.
2. Quantitative rubrics are used in activities that involve sequential movements.
3. Qualitative rubrics are used in more complex activities, such as invasion and net/wall sports.
4. Descriptors in quantitative rubrics are the execution steps; descriptors in qualitative rubrics fall into the three domains.

PART II

Fine-Tuning Your Assessments

FIVE

Using Assessments Strategically

In a meta-analysis on formative assessment, the majority of studies found that improved formative assessment helps low achievers more than other students, and so reduces the range of achievement while raising achievement overall.

Black & Wiliam, 1998b, p. 141

This chapter focuses on some important ideas about when and how assessment is used. First, assessment can take place at any time during a unit of instruction, and it can occur at any time during a lesson. Second, a variety of purposes can be served depending on when and how assessment is used during a unit. Third, you can either direct assessments or allow students to do it. It's likely that you have only experienced teacher-directed assessment, such as a fitness test or a written test composed by the teacher. However, in several studies conducted in a variety of subject areas, researchers have found that when students are involved in assessing their own work and that of others, they learn more (e.g., Black et al., 2004; Stiggins, 1997; Zimmerman & Bamdura, 1994).

Chapter 2 suggests that you begin your planning with the end product in mind. A high school teacher planning to teach a tennis unit will decide how students will be graded before lesson one is taught. If the psychomotor unit goal requires students to be able to play a doubles tennis match, you know you will need to use a tool that can assess students' game play ability. Let's imagine that you allot 20 lessons to the tennis unit and you plan to teach the following psychomotor skills: serve, forehand and backhand drives, volley, and lob strokes. After 20 lessons, students should be able to *(a)* play a doubles match using all four strokes appropriately and at a competent level, *(b)* understand rules, tactics, and scoring, *(c)* officiate their games, and *(d)* work cooperatively and fairly with a partner as well as with opponents. Once the goals of the tennis unit and the culminating activity have been determined, you're ready to plan other types of assessments that will prepare the learners to meet the unit goals. The next sections describe how to use assessments strategically throughout a unit of instruction. We include a sample assessment block plan as an illustration.

Different types of assessment can be used at different times during the unit:

- **Diagnostic assessment** (also known as a pretest) occurs before instruction begins.
- **Formative assessment** (also known as monitoring assessment) occurs while learning and improvement is taking place.
- **Summative assessment** (summing up for a grade) occurs near the end of a unit of instruction.

Summative Assessment

Obviously, the primary purpose of assessment near the end of an instructional unit is to determine a fair grade for each learner. We call this assessment *of* learning because summative assessment is used after students have experienced all the instructional lessons and after they have had ample opportunities to practice. Summative assessments are used for accountability, and they contribute to the grade. Students should be informed of these summative assessments at the beginning of a unit of instruction. When students know how they will be graded at the end of a unit, they are more motivated during practice to strive for success (Lund & Shanklin, 2011).

Remember that if assessments are used for a grade, they must be teacher directed because it would not be fair to ask students to grade each other. In a **teacher-directed assessment,** you record and supervise the **assessment task.** Table 5.1 shows a list of examples that can serve as summative assessments.

Think about the kinds of assessments you experienced in high school physical education. If you're like most teachers today, you took a written test in physical education that counted toward a small percentage of your grade. It's possible that you never experienced some of the assessments that we will explain in this book. Maybe you took a tennis skill test that consisted of serving the ball 10 times, with points awarded for hitting certain areas of the court. Skill tests are

Table 5.1   Examples of Summative Assessments

Learning domain	Examples of summative assessments
Psychomotor	Assessment during tournament play, skill tests, personal best scores in target sports
Cognitive	Portfolio, referee a game, written exam, history project, sport commentator
Affective	Individual and team points for fair-play behaviors and teamwork, points for task completion

the most common type of psychomotor assessments. They are tests of motor ability that have been developed to assess specific sport skills, either standardized (i.e., validated by measurement experts) or made by teachers. Over several decades, AAHPERD scholars and measurement experts developed dozens of skill tests that were recommended to physical education teachers (e.g., Strand & Wilson, 1993).

More recently, experts have looked at assessment of game play from a different perspective, recognizing that skill test batteries were often poor predictors of game-play ability in physical education and that skill tests are better used in skill development rather than as a culminating assessment. Many teachers now recognize that assessing game play requires a more holistic record based on multiple observations of modified game-play tasks or multiple observations of each student during tournament play. While there is a place for skill testing as part of the grade, most scholars recommend the addition of culminating assessment tasks to supplement data about student performance. We suggest that summative assessment should be framed around a culminating project or activity, which could consist of a tournament, a portfolio, a final project, or a performance. The culminating activity often takes several days to complete, and it consists of several tasks used in real-world application tasks that allow students to demonstrate their learning in all three domains. Chapter 4 discusses culminating assessments and rubrics in some detail. Chapters 9 and 10 discuss assessment of learning in the cognitive and affective domains, respectively.

Formative Assessment

Formative assessments are used *while learning is forming*. In contrast to summative assessment, which is *of* learning, formative assessments are *informative* because they are intended *for* learning and they are *not* used to determine a grade. Teachers use formative assessments to help students review skills or concepts that were previously

YOUR TURN 5.1

Think about a unit that you plan to teach. What are some summative assessments that you could use to reveal whether your students have mastered the skills and achieved the learning goals you set for the unit? List these summative assessments.

taught and practiced. They are always planned to help students perform successfully in the culminating activity, and they are indicators of progress toward the final learning goals established for the unit. Since formative assessments are not graded, they are typically directed by students, either as **self-assessments** or **peer assessments**, and they can occur at any time during a lesson or unit. The key to using formative assessment to improve learning is to embed feedback about progress in meeting learning outcomes within the assessment.

Formative assessment also functions as a type of accountability, meaning that students tend to be more motivated and on task when they are engaged in an assessment task. In addition, formative assessments communicate your expectations to students and provide information so that both you and the students know how they are progressing toward the culminating activity. While students are participating in formative assessment tasks, you are free to monitor and give extra help to students who need it. You can also conduct your own formative assessment of students during these self- and peer assessments.

Peer Assessment

Chapter 8 includes many sample forms for peer assessment and presents some advice to help you develop your own recording forms. Here's an example. In lesson 2 of a softball unit, Ms. Robins teaches her sixth-graders how to perform an overhand throw to get the ball from the outfield to the infield. The students practice the throw in a series of tasks that gradually help them apply the skill while playing a modified game. In lesson 3, to reinforce correct form, Ms. Robins designs an assessment task that requires learners to observe and make a record of a partner's overhand throwing technique. She knows that when performers practice the correct movement technique, the distance for the throw will improve. The assessment helps students focus on two critical elements: bringing the ball back behind the head and taking a long contralateral step (i.e., stepping in opposition). When students observe a partner's form and make a written record of what they observe, they learn cognitively because they focus on the critical elements of the skill. An added benefit of peer assessment is the opportunity to practice positive social skills while coaching and providing feedback to a partner. Of course, the final aspect of this formative assessment process is that performers must use the data to set new goals for their own performances. One way to make this explicit is to ask learners to write a new performance goal after each assessment task. Black and Wiliam (1998a) explain that "assessment is formative only when comparison of actual and reference levels yields information which is then used to alter the gap" (p. 53). In other words, students must use the data to figure out what they must do to reach competence. If assessment data are just recorded and then handed in, students will not benefit from the process; students must use the data to reflect on and design ways to improve their skills.

Figure 5.1 shows important guidelines to follow when you use peer assessments.

Self-Assessments

Self-assessments can also be used as part of the formative assessment process. One type of self-assessment is to use a simple skill assessment as an **instant activity** that begins when students enter the gymnasium from the locker room. For example, in a badminton unit, after students have been taught the key skills of short serve and long serve, they should practice those skills every day. As students enter the gym, they pick up a log sheet and pencil. The teacher instructs students to take 10 trials of each type of serve and record how many out of 10 serves hit a specific target area. The goal for students is to improve their score each day. Logs do not need a space to set regular improvement goals as part of the self-assessment. Figure 5.2 is an example of a log used for middle-school basketball. When a student uses a basketball log like the one in figure 5.2, a score will be recorded on the first day the log is kept. The next time the log is used, the student should look at the previous score and try to improve it. For example, on the first day, the student made 1 out of 5 right-side layups and hit the rim on another shot, so the score was 3. The student decides that on day 2, the goal will be to make 2 out of 5 baskets and hit the rim once for a score of 5.

Logs can also be used for self-assessment and to track progress in activities such as weight training (to record the amount of weight lifted and number of repetitions) and jogging (number of laps and time elapsed). Other activities that logically incorporate self-assessment are target

1. The teacher designs the assessment task and a recording form.
2. The teacher explains and demonstrates how to give and receive feedback during peer assessment.
3. Peer assessments are focused on key psychomotor skills or other important outcomes.
4. Students work in pairs; one is a performer and the other is an observer, assessor, and coach. Some tasks require a third person to set up the performer.
5. While the performer is practicing, the peer assessor observes carefully and makes a written record using the assessment recording sheet.
6. The observer/assessor uses assessment results to give feedback and coach a partner's improvement.
7. The teacher monitors the observers to be sure they are correctly observing critical components and giving helpful feedback.
8. Students use the results of peer assessment to set personal improvement goals.
9. Results are not used for grading.

Figure 5.1   Guidelines for using peer assessment.

sports like bowling, golf, and archery. When students record their scores, they are able to track improvement, see their progress over time, and set goals to improve. See chapter 8 for examples of logs in physical education and guidelines for developing them. Figure 5.3 summarizes the key points of self-assessment.

Teacher-Directed Formative Assessments

Formative assessment has the most powerful effect on learning when students are involved in the assessment process, but there are times when teacher assessment proves to be the best way to improve learning. Remember that when teachers simply monitor, observe, and give feedback, they are engaging in important teacher behaviors, but they are *not* assessing. However, when a teacher makes a written record of the observations, assessment has occurred. Occasionally, teachers collect formative assessment data while they monitor students' practice. If the results of the assessment are used by the teacher to make instructional decisions or if the results are communicated to students to improve learning, formative assessment has occurred.

Administer formative assessments to acquire data needed for planning future instruction. For example, during lesson 5 of a volleyball unit, you

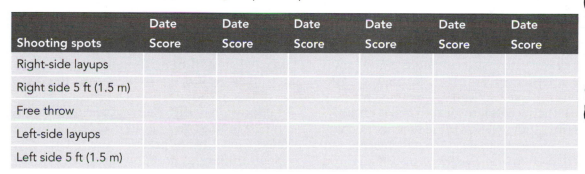

Basketball Shooting Log

Directions

When you enter the gym, pick up your log, a pencil, and a basketball. Go to a basket where there are fewer than five other students and begin working. Take five shots from each spot and record a score for each. Give yourself 2 points if you make the basket and 1 point if you hit the rim. For each mark, you can get up to 10 points.

Shooting spots	Date Score	Date Score	Date Score	Date Score	Date Score	Date Score
Right-side layups						
Right side 5 ft (1.5 m)						
Free throw						
Left-side layups						
Left side 5 ft (1.5 m)						

Figure 5.2   Middle-school basketball log.

1. The teacher designs the assessment task and recording form.
2. The teacher emphasizes the value of assessment for goal setting and improvement, which encourages honesty.
3. The teacher explains and demonstrates how the self-assessment is done and how to use the recording form.
4. Data obtained from the recording form are for monitoring and goal setting, not for grading.
5. Students are more likely to keep accurate records of their performance if they are used *for learning and not for grading*.
6. During the assessment task, the teacher monitors, gives feedback to learners, and spot-checks student records for accurate recording.
7. These self-assessments could be used as artifacts in a portfolio when the intent is to show growth or improvement over time.

Figure 5.3   The key points of self-assessment.

YOUR TURN 5.2

In net/wall games, after students have been taught the serve and have had ample opportunities to practice, look for a success rate of about 75 to 80 percent. **Can you compute the success rate in this example?** Students on one court served 21 times. Of those, 14 crossed the net and landed in bounds. Their success rate is _____ percent.

YOUR TURN 5.3

If the success rate is too low, what are two changes you can make in your teaching?

1. _____

2. _____

might observe students during the application task and make a record of how many serves are missed versus how many serves cross the net and land in bounds. In this assessment, you would be looking at a sample of students in the class, not at individual success rates. (Note: When sampling, you should use different students each day so that, eventually, you will observe every student in class.) By dividing the number of successful serves by the total number of serves (# successful serves ÷ total serves), you can compute a success rate as a percentage. A high success rate is a good indicator of whether students have learned to serve, and a strong serve can lead to greater game play success. If the success rate for the class is under 75 percent, the students need more practice and you must use the results to decide what the students will need to do to improve their success rate. You may simply need to provide more practice time. The problem could also be that the instructional cues were unclear to students or that they simply did not understand your instruction. It could be that students just need to see more good serves in order to understand how to perform. Once you identify the most feasible answer, you can plan an instructional change.

In the preceding example, you would have directed the assessment, but data collection could have also been completed by a student who was not able to actively participate. If all students can participate, you just have to decide whether students will benefit from collecting game statistics more than by participating in the application task. If the answer is that the students will benefit from the practice, then you will record the data.

Look at Your Turn 5.2. Did you get 66 percent as the success rate? If you don't know what you should do when the success rate is below 75 percent, go back to the previous discussion.

Using Formative Assessments to Improve Student Learning

Since formative assessments are for improving learning, let's consider other ways you might use the written records. After reviewing the recording sheets, make a list of several students who are not progressing and give them extra help during the next class. If more than half of the students are unsuccessful on their serves, reteach the serve lesson to the whole class, using some task modification or different verbal cues to improve understanding. You could decide that students simply need more practice and set up several opportunities and situations to practice the serve.

In the preceding example, be aware of how many different students are represented in those 21 serves. The advantage of using peer assessments or peers to gather statistics is that more students have data gathered on their performances. When a greater number of students are represented by the data, you will be more likely to make an accurate assessment about the needs of the class.

Once students understand that the assessments are to help them learn, they will be less tempted to cheat or inflate their scores. We also have found that some students cheat when they don't know how to assess. We remember a class of physical education majors who had misrepresented assessment results on assists during a basketball unit. A few questions about the data quickly revealed that many of them didn't know what an assist was. Clear criteria, clear directions, and clear expectations for learning are often the key to accurate assessing.

Remember the following guidelines about using formative assessment data to help students perform better.

- The key is to use data to help students reflect on how they are doing. Be ready to adjust your teaching to help students learn.
- When collecting formative assessment data, do not use it for grading.
- Remember to analyze assessment data carefully and keep in mind the context in which data were collected.

Getting Started With Formative Assessment

At this point, you may be asking how you can decide what formative assessments are needed in a unit. Remember that we advised you to start with the end product and work backwards. In the example of summative assessment at the beginning of the chapter, we suggest that our high school teacher has decided her students should be able to play a doubles tennis game. The psychomotor skills she teaches will logically become the focus of formative assessments. Since tennis is a net/wall game that begins with a serve, she will teach the serve in lesson 1 and give students a daily log to complete in the next eight lessons, right up to the time their tournament play begins. Students will practice the serve every day because it is so critical to successful game play. (Note: You might choose a different essential skill as the daily focus.) Next she thinks about other skills that students need for successful game play. Our teacher knows that correct technique is essential for execut-ing the forehand drive, so she decides to use peer assessments in several lessons. If our teacher has access to video or flip cameras, or tablets, she could let students self-assess their technique from a video. This idea might even be a good rainy day activity.

Because the teacher is leading up to a predetermined culminating activity, the formative assessments are all aimed at helping students be successful by the end of the unit. If a skill test is used as part of the grade, students will practice that skill test on a regular basis during the unit. Ms. Robins is a perfect example of how this should be done. Because her students practiced the skills they would be graded on, they were much more successful than students in other classes (Lund, 1992). Formative assessments are excellent ways to teach protocols for skill assessments. If a rubric will be used to obtain a game-play rating, then students should be familiar with the rubric and should use parts of the rubric during formative self- or peer assessments.

In the previous situation, the skill assessments for the serve and forehand drive were used to motivate students; if students can see their scores on skill assessments improve, they will have concrete proof that their hard work is paying off. Additionally, some teachers reward students for improvement by placing colorful stickers on the logs or by giving positive written feedback. By giving positive reinforcements, many students will work harder and improve even more.

Diagnostic Assessment

Now that you have decided which skills will be the focus of formative assessments, you are ready to think about what you need to know about

YOUR TURN 5.4

For each of the following activities, identify the two psychomotor skills you think are most important for successful game play. For each skill you selected, write an example of a formative assessment you'd like to use.

Activity	Key psychomotor skills	Formative assessments
Basketball	1. 2.	1. 2.
Volleyball	1. 2.	1. 2.
Badminton	1. 2.	1. 2.

students' skills, knowledge, and attitude before teaching. If you want to help your students learn, you need to determine what students know and can do before starting instructional lessons. The students' attitudes toward the activity should also be considered during planning.

Students in ninth grade have had eight years or more of previous instruction in physical education classes. Many have participated in sport, dance, swimming, and gymnastics in community recreation programs or at home. Even in middle school, students come to physical education classes with lots of experiences in sport and physical activities. Part of the planning process for physical education teachers is to find out what students already know and can do so that they can aim instruction at an appropriate level for each student. High school teachers who decide to teach tennis can assume that students have been taught striking skills in previous grades. It's safe to assume that some students watch tennis on television, while others play on community teams. All of these factors mean that you need to administer some type of diagnostic assessment to learn more about students before beginning instruction. Typically, you should conduct diagnostic assessment during the first days of a unit.

The first and most important rule about using a diagnostic psychomotor assessment is that you must not pretest psychomotor skills when students lack experience in the activity. This requires that you know something about the curriculum in the prior schools your students attended. Let's say, for example, Mrs. Clark wants to include golf in her high school curriculum. She knows that golf is not taught in the middle school, and she has learned that there are no community golf programs. Mrs. Clark should not administer a psychomotor assessment of golf. She might choose to administer an affective or cognitive pretest to see what, if anything, students already know about golf.

Another important rule is that a diagnostic psychomotor assessment is not used when safety risks outweigh the benefits of the assessment. For example, it would not be prudent to diagnose students' skills in gymnastics because safety is such an important consideration in conducting a gymnastics unit. Likewise, you would not use a diagnostic psychomotor assessment in an archery unit because safety rules need to be taught and practiced before students engage in archery. Given these two cautions, let's consider when and how you can use diagnostic assessments. Figure 5.4 lists several suggestions for using diagnostic assessment.

Purposes of Diagnostic Assessment

One purpose for using a diagnostic assessment is to identify a **baseline** (or beginning) score in order to plan lessons at appropriate levels of difficulty. Too often, our teacher candidates start teaching a unit as though students have never participated in a sport or activity. We cringe when we see candidates start a soccer unit by teaching a basic dribble. In some cases, students might not have actually played the sport but may have already developed the skills they need for success. For example, although many students have never heard of team handball, several skills used to play basketball are also used in team handball. If a student has acquired the skill in basketball, there is no need to reteach it for team handball. A caution is offered here: Sometimes students have participated in units but have never perfected the skills. You need a good diagnostic assessment so that you can find that just right starting point that challenges students, instead of boring them, yet allows them to experience some success after a bit of practice. If you want to report on program effectiveness, a baseline score is essential. We discuss ways to use data to compute improvement in chapter 11.

You may also use a diagnostic assessment to identify students' **skill levels** so you can form even teams and aim instruction at the correct level. Mr. Wilson, a high school physical educator, conducts several different badminton tournaments

---

1. Do not pretest when students lack experience in a psychomotor skill.
2. Do not pretest when safety risks outweigh the assessment benefits.
3. Use diagnostic assessment when you're unsure of students' present level of skill.
4. Use teacher-directed diagnostic assessment if improvement will be figured into a grade.
5. Use diagnostic assessment when even teams need to be formed based on skill level.

Figure 5.4 Guidelines for using diagnostic assessment.

based on students' skill levels. He knows that students participate in a badminton unit during seventh grade, so during the first week of his ninth-grade unit, he observes students during diagnostic doubles scrimmages and records a rating for each student using a game-play rubric. His rubric consists of three well-defined levels to assess the use of strokes, as well as knowledge of rules and tactics. He groups students by skill level for instruction so he can better match his teaching to the needs of students. He also uses the scores from the assessment using the rubric to place students into the correct tournament so the level of competition is appropriate for each student.

If a middle school teacher plans to conclude a basketball unit with a tournament in a sport education season, then students should be placed on teams during the first week. A diagnostic assessment will help ensure that teams have a combination of more- and less-skilled students; this will result in a more enjoyable tournament for students because each team has a reasonable chance to win the tournament.

Choosing Diagnostic Assessments

Table 5.2 shows that you can diagnose students' current level of skill, attitudes, and knowledge using a variety of assessments. Diagnostic assessments can be conducted either by you or by students who use self- or peer assessments. Given these broad parameters, how should you decide what to assess? In general, if you don't have sufficient information about students' skills, knowledge, and attitudes to plan a unit of instruction, then diagnostic assessment is required. Chapters 9 and 10 address the assessment of knowledge and attitudes in more detail; in this section, let's think about what diagnostic assessments are needed in the psychomotor domain.

First, recall that we recommend a backward design planning process, starting with the end product in mind. Think about what students should be able to do by the end of the unit. If game play is going to be the culminating activity, then unpack game play to think about the skills

students need for success. Then ask yourself this question: What skills are absolutely essential for successful game play? It's not feasible to preassess all the psychomotor skills, so you will need to prioritize. In most cases, you will select only one or two key skills for diagnostic assessment. Choose a skill for diagnostic assessment that most players use in the game or activity, or choose one that is likely to predict successful game play. Again, keep in mind that you should not give a diagnostic assessment when students have no prior experience; this will eliminate some skills right away. Most likely, a diagnostic skill assessment will be needed for teaching major sports that are most popular in the United States. You might start by thinking about the skill themes (Graham, Holt-Hale, & Parker, 2010) taught in elementary schools, such as throwing, kicking, striking, or catching. The skill themes are the foundation for sport skills that students likely have the most experience with, so they are good selections for diagnostic assessment. For example, the skill theme of throwing in basketball takes the form of various passes used to set up an offensive play. In flag football, the quarterback throws a pass to a receiver; that type of throw resembles an overhand throwing pattern used in several sports.

The next consideration in deciding which diagnostic assessment to use is to block out your unit of instruction and think about how much time you're willing to spend on the diagnostic assessment. The time spent diagnosing is determined by what you need to know and how you will use the assessment data. Each practice task, instructional demonstration, assessment, and application task takes time.

If you plan to administer a diagnostic assessment at the beginning of a class and then begin instruction on that skill that same day, it is best to have tasks planned for students of different abilities. After the assessments, assign students to go to the appropriate station and practice the skill, where they will acquire increased control when performing the shot and the ability to use it in an applied setting. The skilled physical educator must prioritize each part of the lesson and unit

Table 5.2   Diagnosing Skill, Attitude, and Knowledge Through Assessment

Learning domain	Possible diagnostic assessments
Psychomotor domain	Skill test, rating scale, self-rating, observation rating using a rubric
Affective domain	Written test on etiquette, questionnaire
Cognitive domain	Written test on strokes, rules, scoring and tactics

List the specific sport skills that apply to each skill theme outlined in the following table.

Elementary skill themes	Secondary sports	Sport-specific skills
Throwing	Softball	
Catching	Ultimate Frisbee	
Striking	Volleyball	
Kicking	Soccer	

YOUR TURN 5.6

Study the sample assessment block plan for ninth-grade tennis. In the spaces below the block plan, fill in the names of the specific assessments in the block plan for each type of assessment (summative, formative, and diagnostic).

Monday	Tuesday	Wednesday	Thursday	Friday
1 Diagnostic assessment of serve	2 Teach serve	3 Teach drives Student serve logs	4 Student serve logs Peer-assess drives	5 Student serve logs
6 Student serve logs Self-assess drives	7 Student serve logs Peer-assess serve	8 Student serve logs Teach volley	9 Student serve logs Peer-assess volley	10 Student serve logs Practice games
11 Teach scoring Practice games	12 Practice games with peer collection of statistics	13 Practice games with peer collection of statistics	14 Practice games with peer collection of statistics	15 Practice games with peer collection of statistics
16 Tournament and teacher-directed assessment of game play	17 Tournament and teacher-directed assessment of game play	18 Written exam	19 Tournament and teacher-directed assessment of game play	20 Tournament and teacher-directed assessment of game play

Provide the names of the specific assessments used in the block plan for each type of assessment.

1. Summative assessments:
   a. _____
   b. _____
2. Formative assessments:
   a. _____
   b. _____
   c. _____
3. Diagnostic assessment:

   _____

YOUR TURN 5.7

Referring to the blank table that follows, work individually or in pairs to develop your own assessment block plan for a sport or physical activity that you know well. Choose an activity that could realistically be taught in a middle school or senior high school. In this block plan, choose a summative assessment, at least three formative assessments, and one diagnostic assessment. Write a rationale for each type of assessment you included in your plan.

Monday	Tuesday	Wednesday	Thursday	Friday

Summative assessment: _____

Formative assessments: _____

_____

_____

Diagnostic assessment: _____

to get the maximum benefit for students. At this point, you may be thinking that this planning process is hard. Yes, it is difficult, but if it were easy, anyone could teach.

Summary

Good assessments are used strategically throughout instruction. By using a backward mapping strategy, you can look at final learning goals and develop assessments to enhance the learning process. Diagnostic formative and summative assessments all play a critical role in improving student learning. Learn how to use them strategically to maximize student learning.

SIX

Choosing Meaningful and Purposeful Assessments

To be effective, assessment must be much more than a data-gathering process; it must be a process of making meaning and providing meaningful feedback to the learner to guide his or her actions toward improvement and continuing learning.

Lambert, 2007, p. 15

LOOK FOR THESE KEY CONCEPTS

❭ developmentally
  appropriate
❭ feasible
❭ fairness
❭ meaningful

❭ objectivity
❭ stable results
❭ subjective
❭ valid inferences

In previous chapters, we talked about the planning process in some detail. You have begun to think about the big picture in terms of what to teach and how to assess the key concepts included in your curriculum. Before we get into the details about assessment techniques and strategies, you need to understand some general concepts about what makes a good assessment. The guidelines that follow are primarily directed toward teacher-designed assessments, but we also include information about what to look for when selecting a standardized test. The following questions are addressed in this chapter as they relate to both teacher-designed assessments and standardized tests.

- What kinds of assessments are most meaningful to my students and me?
- How can I determine if the assessment is providing credible information?
- How can I ensure that the assessment process is fair to students?
- What assessment choices should I give to students?
- What factors should I consider that determine if an assessment is doable?
- How can I minimize my own **subjective** bias when conducting an assessment?
- How can I ensure that assessments are developmentally appropriate?

Before we move on, readers should be aware that our approach to this chapter is based on pedagogically sound, standards-based assessment. We are not measurement specialists and we do not pretend to be experts in psychometrics. We are, however, experienced teacher educators and we believe that approaching the question of meaningful assessments from a psychometric perspective does not serve our students well. We refer skeptics to Lambert's (2007) excellent discussion of what she calls "two contradictory schools of thought about assessment" (p. 12). Her discussion of the confusion that has resulted from the side-by-side use of behaviorist theory and cognitive conceptions of learning was very helpful to our understanding of why physical educators have rejected traditional approaches toward measurement and evaluation. Lambert states, "the former emphasizes discrete outcomes, measurable in traditional ways; the latter places more credence on the processes of learning and on holistic learning outcomes that require knowledge to be demonstrated and applied in action" (p. 12).

Qualities of a Meaningful Assessment

The best way to begin thinking about what makes a good assessment is to decide that the assessments you choose to use in your classes should be **meaningful** and purposeful to you and your students. As Wiggins (1998) notes, a good assessment actually teaches and improves learning. We would add that a good assessment is aligned with predetermined learning outcomes, goals, and standards. **Alignment** means that the assessments you choose give you information about the learning outcomes; in other words, you assess what you teach. The alignment of standards, goals, outcomes, and assessment is essential for a quality program.

As chapter 2 discusses, the goals and outcomes you select for your program should meet the physical education standards for your state. If you compare your state standards with the NASPE physical education standards, you will probably find that the two sets of standards are very similar or even identical. Figure 6.1 shows some qualities of a good assessment.

Many teachers in academic subjects are under enormous pressure to ensure that their students are learning and making progress each year. Although most physical educators are not yet under a mandate to administer standardized tests, schools do seem to be moving in the direction of increased testing and accountability for all

- A good assessment is fair but honest in letting students know their level of achievement.
- Good assessments are feasible given the available amount of equipment, space, and time.
- Good assessments provide accurate feedback to students about their progress toward success on the culminating activity.
- A good assessment is easy for both students and teachers to use.
- A good assessment allows teachers and students to make valid inferences about whether or not learning has occurred.
- Good assessment practices require teachers to use a variety of assessment tasks that engage students in worthwhile performances and experiences.
- Good assessments do not give an advantage to one group of students over another.
- The results of a good assessment are trustworthy and free from the teacher's purely subjective opinions and biases.

Figure 6.1   Summary of the characteristics of good assessment.

teachers. In some states, the results of standardized tests are being used to make decisions about tenure and salaries. Even if your state mandates a certain type of test in physical education, you can implement other meaningful assessments that enhance student learning. If you do use an assessment, make it mean something and use the results. Choose assessments that give you vital information that will help you teach better and help students learn or improve their skills. An example of times when this does not happen is when teachers give fitness tests and then do not use the results to change curriculum or the types of units taught.

You should develop a wide array of assessment options to align with your learning outcomes. Select assessments purposefully to match your personal goals and to align with the instructional process. No cookbook or formula exists for developing universal assessments; this is part of the artistry of teaching.

Making Time for Assessment

In chapter 5, we make the case for the value of formative assessments (self- and peer directed) that involve students in their own learning. We want to reiterate here that ample research evidence exists that assessment *for* learning is the most critical in terms of helping students learn (Stiggins, 2001). Formative assessments also have enormous potential for helping you improve. If your only goal is to improve teaching or to make decisions about lesson development, you may assess a few representative students or groups (called *sampling*) rather than every individual

student. Complete sampling while students are applying skills, usually during the application task in a lesson. For example, during a unit of flag football, Mrs. Black has the following question: Are the teams using a variety of offensive plays and do the plays result in gained yardage? While the teams are scrimmaging and self-officiating, she keeps a tally of the running and passing plays along with information about the success of each play. During the closure, she will be able to give the teams feedback about play selection and success rate. If this teacher had simply observed the scrimmages without keeping a written record, her feedback would be less effective, and she would not know the answer to her original question. She can also use the information gathered in future lessons to decide what skills, if any, need to be retaught or be given more practice time. Using assessment in this way takes no time away from teaching and practice, but it can yield important information to help students meet the learning outcomes.

Although summative assessments are necessary to help you arrive at a fair grade for each student, they don't improve either learning or teaching. Summative assessments only document whether or not learning has occurred. Likewise, while most diagnostic assessments are of value

YOUR TURN 6.1

Think back to when you were in high school. Can you recall a meaningful assessment (in any subject) that was helpful to you? Briefly describe that experience and be ready to share it in class.

to teachers, they are not going to improve learning. The key is to use assessments that are helpful to you and your students. If you take the time to assess, use the results to improve teaching, improve learning, or assign a fair grade.

Reflection

Whether you are a teacher candidate or an experienced teacher, it is important to continuously improve teaching skills. Perhaps, in your teacher preparation program, you've heard of or been asked to write reflections after a teaching experience. Taking time to think about what worked and what didn't work in a lesson will make you a better teacher. We believe that your reflections should be *based on assessment data* if they are to be useful. Instead of thinking about a lesson in the abstract, you are more likely to get better at teaching if you think about the intended learning outcomes and how well students met them, both individually and by class.

We suggest answering these two questions when writing reflections:

1. Did my students achieve the student learning outcomes established for the lesson?
2. What data do I have to back up the conclusion reached about whether learning outcomes were met?

Using assessment data to guide your reflections makes it more likely that you will actually accomplish something, because your reflections are based on evidence about student learning. Study a book that analyzes teaching (Veal & Anderson, 2011) if you need some ideas about how to improve your reflections and profit from your teaching experiences.

Credible Assessments

If you've taken the time to plan and administer an assessment, the information gained should inform and improve teaching and learning. We have watched student teachers struggle to design an assessment task, teach their students how to gather some data, collect the forms, and then toss them aside without looking at the results. This scenario happens when teacher candidates do the assessment just because they were supposed to, rather than using it to gain information about teaching and learning. You must align assessments with the learning outcomes for the day,

and then use the results. So how can you decide if assessment data are **credible?**

First, you should ensure that the **inferences** you make about the results of an assessment are valid (Popham, 2010). When you can make **valid inferences,** the assessment results are consistent with the level of student ability; in other words, the best students in the class end up with the best scores. For example, if Sandra and Jose are the best servers in pickleball, they should be in the top level on a serving assessment. If, on the other hand, Jose and Sandra's scores are not at the top, you have a problem with the assessment tool.

One thing you can do to be sure assessment tools will produce valid inferences is to ask a colleague to review the assessment to see if it appears to be clearly defined and aligned with the learning outcomes. If the tool is a teacher-designed assessment, you may need to make several revisions before you feel confident that it will give you the information you need. If the assessment tool is a **standardized test,** you should find information about the tool's validity with the instructions for using the test. When using a standardized test to make inferences about student achievement, look at the correlation coefficient for that test. If a test perfectly predicts student performance, the correlation coefficient is 1.00. Since no test is perfect, measurement experts generally agree that the higher the correlation coefficient, the better the test. So, a standardized test with a correlation coefficient of .70 or better is usually acceptable. You can find standardized psychomotor skill tests in measurement books (e.g., Lacy & Hastad, 2006; Strand & Wilson, 1993; Tritschler, 2000).

Another factor that should be considered is the stability of results. You don't want to use an assessment that produces results by chance or luck. **Stable results** come from having sufficient trials so that the results give an accurate picture of what students can do. The number of trials depends on the activity. However, on graded product assessments, it is generally recommended that students be given two or three sets of 10 trials each. Stability of results will be enhanced if students have a chance to practice assessments that will eventually be used for grading. If students have practiced and are familiar with how the assessment is conducted, they will be more likely to accurately demonstrate their learning.

One more consideration in determining whether an assessment should be used is called **objectivity**, meaning the instructor does not have any influence over the results. Objectivity is attained when the criteria are clear enough in an assessment tool so that two different teachers could use the tool and get similar results. Any assessment that relies on teacher observation needs to be carefully designed with clear criteria and directions. If you want to use an assessment in multiple classes, it is important to follow the directions in the same way so the results are credible and trustworthy in each class.

Fairness

When you administer any type of assessment, whether it is *for* learning or *of* learning, you want to be sure that the results are an accurate and true representation of students' learning. Unfortunately, sometimes factors other than student skill level account for variability in student performance. If you think about your own experiences in school, it will become quite clear that many external factors can affect how students perform. For example, the temperature in the room can influence students. It's hard for students to give their best motor performance when they are too hot or too cold. They are also susceptible to external noises, which may present a problem when conducting assessments outside. Obviously, you will try to ensure that the environment does not have an adverse effect on students' performance. The

primary thing we want you to think about in this chapter is how to select an assessment that will produce results that accurately represent student learning. We focus primarily on the psychomotor domain in this section.

When we talk to teachers and teacher candidates, we are always struck by the value they place on fairness. Let's unpack this idea of fairness and try to uncover its meaning. First, we think that fairness means that assessments result in an accurate appraisal of students' learning. Most of us have experienced unfair assessments in which teachers gave written tests that did not cover the material discussed in class. So, a fair assessment is one that is aligned with the content. Second, fairness implies that students have had ample opportunities to learn the content that is being assessed. Teachers who give fair assessments provide lots of opportunities to learn, accompanied by clear instruction, understandable examples, and plenty of practice. Fair assessments also imply that you do everything possible to help students learn before grading.

When you use any type of performance-based assessment, ensure that all students can demonstrate what they learned. The results of the assessment should not be dependent on other students. If you decide to use a group project to assess learning, clearly assign roles within the group so that students can demonstrate what they have

Clear instruction is a vital part of creating fair assessments.

learned, both individually and as a group. This applies to game-play assessment and skill tests, as well as group projects. In a game, students must have an opportunity to demonstrate what they have learned relative to each component of the rubric being used to assess game play. That's why small-sided games are often used for assessment purposes.

Psychomotor assessments seem to be viewed a little differently by teachers and teacher candidates. We think this is because physical education teachers typically have successful sport backgrounds. We have encountered many teachers who do not believe it is fair to assess in the psychomotor domain, since they perceive that many students in physical education do not have the ability to be successful. We strongly disagree with that idea. Just as academic teachers must believe that all students can cognitively learn the subject matter, physical education teachers must believe that all students can become competent and successful in the psychomotor domain. Simply put, it is your job as a physical education teacher to find ways to help students become competent in a variety of sports or activities. How is this possible if a teenager is not athletic? Think carefully about the meaning of competence. As we have stated previously, competence does not mean that students leave your class ready for professional sports. Competence does imply enjoyment and successful participation. Competent sport participants will choose to be physically active. Isn't this a worthy goal?

If you agree that physical education teachers should help students become competent in physical activities, let's think about how we can make that a reality. It is a well-accepted principle that motor learning results from lots and lots of practice. This means that instructional units need to be long enough to provide students lots of practice opportunities with clear instruction, appropriate practice tasks, and opportunities to assess *for* learning to support self-improvement. We have seen high school programs that are structured around very short units of instruction, sometimes with as few as 5 lessons. Clearly, this is not enough time for instruction, practice, and assessment. We argue for instructional units of 15 to 20 lessons in high school so students have sufficient time to practice and learn. We also recognize that since some activities are complex, teachers actually require more than 20 lessons to help students to experience success. Allowing ample practice and using formative assessment

YOUR TURN 6.2

What are two things that you can do to ensure that all your students will become competent in a variety of sports and activities? Write down your response.

makes it more likely that your students will learn, and you can feel confident that you are using fair assessment practices. We suspect that teachers who do not want to assess the psychomotor domain are really thinking about grading, so we further address fairness in grading in chapter 13.

One more issue about fairness has to do with equitable assessment. Since students come in all sizes, shapes, and abilities, consider the idea that assessments might need to be flexible to some extent. Rather than just treating all students exactly the same, it makes sense, in some cases, to treat them equitably. By this, we mean that sometimes students in physical education ought to be given the opportunity to demonstrate their skills in performances of their own choosing. For example, on a basketball team, some players are better at defense than at shooting. Yet, in physical education classes, all students are expected to learn and perform all of the skills. On a football team, players specialize and learn to play a certain position. In softball, all players bat, but they don't all play the same position on defense. In a physical education class, is it really important that students learn to perform all positions, or would it be beneficial for them to practice a few positions and become competent at those? If students are allowed to focus their practice on just a few skills, shouldn't the assessment also be focused and flexible? What do you think? Should you always dictate how you assess students, or should secondary students have a say in assessment decisions?

YOUR TURN 6.3

What does **fairness** mean to you when you think about assessment in physical education? Write down your ideas about fairness and be prepared to discuss this idea in class.

Feasibility

When something is **feasible**, it's very doable. Wiggins (1998) states that feasibility implies that the assessment is "user friendly," meaning that it is easy to use. In the context of physical education, feasibility refers to *time, space, and equipment*. Remember: *If an assessment task is not feasible, don't use it. Choose a different assessment.*

The implication of the value of time is that you have to be sure that an assessment is worth the time it takes to administer. Time is something we never have enough of as teachers; we always wish for more. It seems that no matter how many lessons you plan for a unit, you could always use a little more time. As you gain more experience and try different approaches, you will develop a better sense of how much time each instructional function takes, and you will become better and more efficient at giving information, distributing equipment, and assessing students.

You make hundreds of teaching decisions every day as you weigh the pros and cons of your actions. Always evaluate decisions about what to include in each lesson based on the benefits versus the time allotted. Mr. Rodriguez, a first-year teacher, decides to administer the Fitnessgram test to his seventh-graders. He sees them for only one semester during that year, but he is committed to helping his students learn the value of physical fitness. He believes that taking a fitness test is an important step toward developing a pattern of healthy, active living. Mr. Rodriguez learned about Fitnessgram during his professional preparation program, and he had an opportunity to practice giving the tests during student teaching under the supervision of his cooperating teacher. He is confident in his ability to administer the test, and he believes his students can complete the test in three class periods. Unfortunately, Mr. Rodriguez failed to consider that students in his school had never taken a fitness test before, so everything took longer than expected. It actually took five class periods to complete the test.

You need to be realistic about the time required for administering assessments, and you should expect that teaching students the protocols of the assessment and to learn how to use it efficiently

YOUR TURN 6.4

Do you think it was worth the time it took to administer the Fitnessgram test? Was it feasible? Explain why or why not. What could Mr. Rodriguez have done to decrease the time it took to administer the fitness test?

will take a while the first time you use a new assessment tool. In most cases, both you and the students will get better with experience. Larger classes with more students typically require more time to administer a test to each student. For example, the sit-and-reach test is a commonly used fitness test, but schools often have only one sit-and-reach box. If it takes 2 minutes to assess each student, it will take 60 minutes to test a class of 30 students. Clearly, the school needs to either purchase more sit-and-reach boxes or use a different test.

Another factor to consider when deciding whether an assessment is feasible is space. Obviously, classes with more students require more space. When considering an assessment, it might be a good idea to try it first in a smaller class just to see how students will react. Carefully consider how much space you need for each group of students. Groups need to be only as large as necessary to administer the assessment. Groups of three often work well because there is a recorder, a performer, and an assistant to retrieve balls or provide setups. The rule of thumb about space is that if you have insufficient space for a certain assessment, you must make a different assessment choice.

The last factor related to feasibility is equipment. In most cases, you should have enough equipment to allow students to work in pairs or small groups to safely complete the assessment task. If groups are larger, the task will take more time, making the assessment less feasible. As always, consider the pros and cons of the value of the assessment versus the time you need to administer it. Ultimately, the question of feasibility will often help you decide whether or not the assessment is good enough.

Developmental Appropriateness

When an assessment is **developmentally appropriate,** the assessment task is one that most students can accomplish with a reasonable level of success after being taught and given sufficient practice. Consider the fitness level of students if the test involves a level of strength or cardiorespiratory endurance. In addition, the skill level of students should be appropriate for the assessment task. You may run into difficulties if you try to administer an assessment that is just too hard for students. In net/wall games, for example, many skills require a setup from a partner in order to assess the skill. Let's assume you have taught the overhead clear in badminton. You observed that students had difficulty getting the shuttle to the back of the opponent's court. In the next class, you want students to peer assess correct form for the overhead clear in order to emphasize the components of good form. While planning the peer-assessment task, you realize that your students will not be able to do a good setup because they have difficulty with the long underhand serve. To make the assessment developmentally appropriate, you will need to modify the setup. By tossing the shuttle from the side to give the performer a good setup, the clear can be practiced and assessed. Likewise, the forehand drive in tennis may best be assessed by tossing the ball to the performer instead of wasting time trying to set up the drive with a racket hit. Our advice is to know what your students are able to do and then be prepared to modify the skill practice and assessment tasks so students can successfully meet the learning outcomes.

In addition to the psychomotor demands of an assessment task, the words on the recording form used for self- and peer assessment must be at a level the students can understand. This is not easy, since a wide range of abilities exist within every grade level. Just be sure that students can understand the vocabulary on the recording form and that the reading level required is appropriate for the majority of students. Oftentimes, students are asked to assess a partner by observing several critical elements of a skill. The critical elements are written as *cues,* defined as a word or short phrase that represents the movement in terms that students can understand. It should be understood that cues for middle school students will be different than cues for high school students. Sometimes, popular culture can be incorporated into the cues to make them more meaningful for students. For example, when seventh-graders are learning to use a pancake catch for a disc game such as ultimate, you might cue students to put their hands in the shape of a gator and have them catch the disc in the gator's mouth. You should be familiar with the vocabulary of students in their classes. Try to hit a medium level of difficulty on cues. Using pictures along with the written and verbal cues can also be helpful to learners.

Finally, a key part of the recording form is the instruction given to students. Written instructions should be at the reading level of the majority of students. This may or may not be age-related. The important thing is that students can understand your instructions and follow them. Of course, if you have special-needs or ESL students in your classes, other accommodations will need to be made, such as asking peers to read the instructions aloud.

 YOUR TURN 6.5

Let's try writing some instructions for sixth-graders (ages 10 and 11) and ninth-graders (ages 14 and 15) so you can try out the idea of making the vocabulary age appropriate. Badminton might be taught to both age groups, so pretend you are going to explain the short serve. How would you make your instructions age appropriate? Some suggested answers are at the back of the chapter.

Explanation of short serve for sixth-graders	Explanation of short serve for ninth-graders

Summary

The majority of assessments you use during your teaching career will be teacher-designed assessments that are aligned with your curriculum and learning outcomes. We hope that you will keep these concepts handy as you move forward. The most important idea is that you must be able to make valid inferences about student learning after you administer an assessment. The second major idea in this chapter is that when you select an assessment, think about the feasibility issues of time, space, and equipment as you plan. Finally, choose your assessments carefully so that they provide meaningful information to you and your students.

⟳ YOUR TURN 6.5

Let's try writing some instructions for sixth-graders (ages 10 and 11) and ninth-graders (ages 14 and 15) so you can try out the idea of making the vocabulary age appropriate. Badminton might be taught to both age groups, so pretend you are going to explain the short serve. How would you make your instructions age appropriate?

Explanation of short serve for sixth-graders	Explanation of short serve for ninth-graders
We're going to start our badminton unit with an underhand serve. How many of you have done a beanbag toss underhanded? Have you ever bowled? OK, the badminton serve is like those movements. (Demonstrate movement and ask students to follow along with their rackets.)	[Students are sitting along sidelines of a court and teacher demonstrates. Teacher is in position to serve on the court with a student on the other side of the net to retrieve.]
We're going to start with rackets touching the floor in front of our left foot. (Demonstrate and ask students to take that position.)	The most important stroke in badminton is the serve because it's how the game begins. It can also be a great offensive weapon if the serve is very close to the net because it's hard to return.
Next, drop the shuttle and gently bring the racket up to meet it like this. (Demonstrate.)	Your cues are "staggered stance," "racket back," "drop and swing," and "follow to the net." Here's what a low serve looks like.
The cues I want you to remember are *drop* and *swing*.	(Demonstrate at least 3 times, showing a low serve and gentle swing. Emphasize the cues as you demonstrate.)

SEVEN

Writing Learning Outcomes

Regardless of the subject or level of education, only those with sharp visions of valued achievement expectations can effectively and efficiently assess student attainment of those expectations.

Stiggins, 2001, p. 57

LOOK FOR THESE KEY CONCEPTS

- assessable
- condition
- criterion
- learning outcomes
- performance
- process criterion
- product criterion

Have you ever watched a mason build a brick wall? By setting one brick at a time in place, eventually the mason ends up with a nice end product: an attractive wall. The bricklayer must methodically put the bricks in place and make them fit. If a brick is too large or too small, it doesn't work very well. When bricks are uniform in size, the wall is much easier to build. Teaching students to play a sport or activity is something like the brick mason's task: Physical educators teach students something every day, and eventually the students have sufficient skills and knowledge to play and participate in various sports and activities. Learning is focused on those key concepts and skills that are essential to the content of the unit. The pieces of learning can't be too big or too small; if too big, the students will struggle, and if too small, students will get bored. Csikszentmihalyi (1997) talked about the importance of flow. For a lesson to have flow, it must challenge students, but allow them to achieve success while accomplishing the goal for the lesson.

Learning must be paced—something new needs to be learned in each lesson, but teachers must be careful not to put so much into the lesson that students are not realistically able to accomplish the intended outcome. Each day should move students closer to reaching the goals set for the unit. The outcomes need to be just right, requiring students to learn something new. They should be neither too easy nor too hard. If the majority of the students can accomplish the outcome before the lesson, then you are wasting the students' time. On the other hand, the stated outcome should be realistic for students to accomplish in the time allocated for a lesson. Pacing a lesson is one of those arts of teaching that is learned with experience.

Think of daily goals as a challenge to your teaching skills. If you are an effective teacher, how much can your students learn each day? Some teachers are reluctant to challenge their students; they plan very easy goals that are readily achieved with minimal effort. This practice actually does students a disservice because it limits their learning. The purpose of this chapter is to provide the knowledge you need to write learning outcomes that will help you maximize student learning. Secondary physical educators have a duty to help their students become **competent** in the activities that are taught. This means that students leave your program able to use skills and concepts sufficiently to enjoy being physically active for a lifetime.

What Is a Learning Outcome?

A **learning outcome** is a statement written by a teacher that defines a learner's performance through the use of an action verb (behavior), a condition under which the performance will occur, and the criteria for successful performance. Several of you who are reading this will think, "Hmmm, they used to be called lesson objectives or behavioral objectives." You are correct. In standards-based instruction, the terminology has changed from *objectives* to *learning outcomes*. Educators are now focusing on the outcomes of learning—the skills, attitudes, and knowledge that students should obtain as the result of instruction. The focus has changed to what students are accomplishing rather than your objectives for the students. When you share learning outcomes with students, they have a target to aim for while participating in the lesson. Learning outcomes direct students' attention and effort; they help students understand what is expected of them when they participate in the lesson.

Student learning outcomes are always stated in terms of what the student can do. They do not focus on what you teach, but rather on what students should learn as the result of instruction. Similarly, they do not describe the process that you will use for student learning (e.g., explain ways to move the ball down the court). Simply put, the learning outcome makes you identify what students should learn; once written, you can communicate to students what they should do by sharing the outcome with them. In addition, the outcomes let students know when they are successful. Good student-learning outcomes require you to identify the final goal for the lesson, a target that students are trying to reach. Most importantly, well-written learning outcomes guide the assessment of student performance.

A good learning outcome specifies a behavior called a performance, the condition under which the student is expected to perform the task and the criterion for success. The next section explains how to write good learning outcomes. We begin with teaching you how to write learning outcomes for the psychomotor domain first, and then move to writing them for the cognitive and affective domains.

The **performance** is simply what the student will do. It typically contains a verb that describes the outcome of learning. In the psychomotor domain, we have lots of verbs to use for student learning. For example, we are trying to teach students to do the following:

- Throw
- Catch
- Run
- Jump
- Serve
- Dance

YOUR TURN 7.1

List at least five verbs that you would use for the unit that you began developing in chapter 2 of this text.

The second part of a student learning outcome is the condition under which the task is performed. **Conditions** talk about the context in which the performance will occur. Many times, the condition affects the difficulty of the performance, so it is an important part of the student learning outcome. For example, receiving a beach ball is a different task than receiving a regulation volleyball. Serving a volleyball from behind the service line is a different task than playing from anywhere on the court. The following list shows some of the factors that change conditions. See Rink (2010) for more factors.

- Equipment (e.g., size, weight, type)
- Changing the space (e.g., size of the playing area; distance from target)

- Rules
- Purpose of the task (e.g., hitting a large target and then hitting a smaller one; practice and game play)
- Number of players or people
- Number of skills done in sequence

The final part of the outcome is the **criterion** (**criteria** is the plural form), which states the expected level of performance. In other words, how good is good enough? When performing an assessment of the learning outcome, the criterion is used to interpret the assessment results: Did the student reach the expected level of performance? The criterion level describes what a performance must either look like or accomplish to be successful. Two types of criteria exist for the psychomotor domain: process criteria and product criteria.

Process criteria focus on the use of correct form to perform the skill. As shown in figure 7.1, process criteria are almost always used when accuracy is critical, when learners are beginners, or in activities that depend on aesthetic elements for success (e.g., dance, gymnastics, diving). In physical education, when introducing new activities, focus on teaching correct form first. When learners are able to use correct form consistently, then you can focus on the outcome of the movement. Since correct form often disappears in competitive situations, it is best to avoid competition until learners are comfortable with the movement. We suggest that process criteria be used regularly in middle school physical education because learners tend to be inconsistent movers, especially if they did not learn the activities in elementary grades. When assessing students for process criteria, these are best observed in a closed environment, and not in games or competitive environments.

In chapter 6 you learned that a meaningful assessment allows a teacher to make a valid inference about students' learning. To make a valid inference about correct form (process), you must observe the motor performance multiple times. Ideally, the more times you observe students' performances, the more confident you will feel in judging competence. The goal of an assessment is to make the correct inference about student competence with a practical number of observations, given the limited amount of time available to observe each student. For closed skills (e.g., volleyball serve, forward roll, golf putting), if students can perform the skill with correct form three times in a row, we suggest that they have achieved competence. Because students might need some leeway in more complex skills (e.g., front walkover, volleyball spike, tennis backhand), the criterion level could be correct form on three out of five trials, which is enough to ensure stable results and demonstrate competence.

Product criteria focus on the outcome or result of the movement. Products can be timed, counted, or measured, as shown in figure 7.2. Product criteria might specify that students are expected to do something a certain number of times, such rally a shuttle back and forth with a partner 10 times in a row. The product could be to hit a golf ball 25 yards, or swim the length of the pool in a certain length of time. To help you understand the concept of product criteria, think of the learning outcome as a blank archery target. The criteria are represented by the circles on the archery target; the circles provide specific criteria that help students know where to aim. If the performance is simply to hit the target, an arrow that lands anywhere on the target face would count toward meeting the learning outcome. Because of the large range of passing performances, there would be no way to judge the best shot from a poor shot. By giving more points for arrows that land closest to the center, you will have a way to distinguish better performances. Of course, students should demonstrate correct form along with meeting the product criteria, so outcomes with a product criteria also require students to use correct form.

Product criteria are typically stated in terms of a length of time (e.g., jog a mile in less than 10 minutes), a distance (e.g., hit a golf ball 50 yards), or a number of correct repetitions (e.g., serve the volleyball into the opponent's court landing in bounds 8 out of 10 times). Competence is often associated with a criterion level of 80 percent, which is the equivalent of 8 correct out of 10 trials. The 80 percent threshold is for skills done in a testing or closed environment but not for skills used during game play.

To make valid inferences about student performance, you need to ensure that the outcome is not due to luck. This means that in most product assessments, 10 or more trials in a relatively closed environment are needed. Providing 10 trials allows you and your students to conveniently estimate the percentage of correct trials (simply add a "0" to the correct number of trials) and 10 practice trials is a feasible number for most practice tasks. You would not use a criterion of 8 out of 10 trials for game play because it would be difficult to arrange a game that would allow a specific number of trials for each player.

The criterion portion of a learning outcome indicates where the arrows must land on that target and how many must land there to qualify as an acceptable level of performance (product criterion). Although process criteria are preferable when students are first learning a new skill, we argue that, at the secondary level, it is not sufficient to use only process criteria. In short, competence at the secondary level should be defined by a combination of process and product criteria.

Process: The focus is on the form of the movement and the critical elements. Assessment is done in a closed environment when performance is not affected by others.

Who assesses	When to use	Examples	Criteria
Peer Self (could assess a video) Teacher	When accuracy is an important part of the performance (focus on critical elements first)	Target games • Golf • Archery • Bowling	Correct form is consistently demonstrated and typically defined as: • 3 times in a row Or • 3 out of 5 trials
	When teaching beginners	• Almost always used in elementary school • Used most often in middle school when introducing new units	
	When aesthetic elements are a critical part of success	• Diving • Gymnastics • Dance	

Figure 7.1   Process criteria for psychomotor assessments.

Product: The focus is on the outcome or result of the movement. Competence is indicated by the quantity, distance, or speed with which something can be completed. Assessment is done in a closed environment when performance is not affected by others.

Who assesses	What to assess	Sample criteria (Note: Teacher must adjust for grade level)
Self Peer Teacher	Quantity: Count it The number of times you can do a skill which indicates a percentage of success (e.g., 8 out of 10); the time in combination with number of repetitions or a score in a target game as an indicator of accuracy	• Place 8 out of 10 volleyball serves into the opponent's court • Hit badminton overhead clear against the wall at least 25 times in 10 seconds • Score 100 points in a 10-frame bowling game
Self Peer Teacher	Distance: Measure it How far or high you can do a skill or activity when power and force are required	• Throw a discus 25 feet • Clear the high jump bar at a height of 3 feet 8 inches
Self Peer Teacher	Speed or time: Time it How fast or how long you can do something to show control or competence	• Swim the length of a pool in 60 seconds or under • Hold a handstand 3 seconds to show balance

Figure 7.2   Product criteria for psychomotor assessments.

YOUR TURN 7.2

Distinguish each of the following criteria as either process or product (refer to the left-hand column of the table). Remember that the presence of a number in the criterion does not automatically make it a product criterion.

Process or product	Throw a softball a distance of 75 yards or more.
Process or product	Demonstrate correct form (step, contact on hand heel, follow through toward net) three times in a row.
Process or product	During the shot put, demonstrate the 3 critical elements of a correct spin at least 3 times out of 5 trials.
Process or product	On a soccer penalty kick, hit the target area at least 8 out of 10 trials.
Process or product	Take off from the left foot 3 times in a row when performing a layup shot from the right side.

Writing Effective Learning Outcomes for the Psychomotor Domain

Consider the following learning outcome for Mr. Thomas' badminton unit: *While standing behind the end line, the student will use correct form while executing a legal serve diagonally into the opponent's court and hit the target area 8 out of 10 times.*

As we noted earlier, the criterion portion of the student learning outcome is closely related to the assessment because the criterion defines a successful performance. By stating a clear criterion, such as 3 in a row or 8 out of 10 trials, the learning outcome is **assessable.**

To ensure that the learning outcome is assessed, we suggest that teacher candidates include the assessment with the student learning outcome when planning a lesson. For example:

Performance: while executing a legal serve diagonally into the opponent's court

Condition: while standing behind the end line

Criterion: Using correct form. . . hit the target area 8 out of 10 times.

Assessment: Peer assessment using a product recording form during guided practice.

If the learning outcome will be assessed in a future lesson (e.g., several cognitive outcomes might be assessed on a written test), this should also be noted.

Information needed about the assessment includes *who* will conduct the assessment (self-assessment, peer assessment, or teacher-directed),

what the assessment will be (checklist, log, rubric, project, score sheet, test), and *when* the assessment will be administered (instant activity, guided practice, game, end of class). The form that will be used to record the assessment results should be included with the lesson plan. We mention including the assessment here because a well-written outcome will point to the assessment. In chapters 8, 9, and 10, you will learn about different assessments for the psychomotor, cognitive, and affective domains. In chapter 11 we will discuss linking assessments with learning outcomes.

YOUR TURN 7.3

Let's see if you understand the parts of an effective learning outcome. For the following learning outcome, identify the performance (what the student will do), the condition, and the criterion.

While accompanied by the music, students will correctly perform the Virginia reel with no more than three breaks in rhythm.

YOUR TURN 7.4

Now it is time for you to see what you have learned about recognizing well-written learning outcomes, The following table lists psychomotor learning outcomes. Identify the performance, the condition, and the criterion. Indicate whether the criterion is process or product. Answers are at the end of the chapter.

Psychomotor learning outcome	Performance	Condition	Criterion	Process or product?
1. The student will be able to dribble a basketball, without looking down, three times in a row, keeping it under control while weaving in and out of cones.				
2. The student will score at least 100 points while bowling a 10-frame game on a commercial bowling lane.				
3. The student will be able to score on a penalty kick 8 out of 10 times when a goalie is playing light defense during a practice task.				

Psychomotor learning outcome	Performance	Condition	Criterion	Process or product?
4. The student will use correct form while receiving a baton pass at least 3 out of 5 attempts while maintaining running speed during a 4 x 100 relay.				
5. The student will be able to hit the target 8 out of 10 times from 15 yards while practicing shooting skills in disc golf.				
6. The student will be able to putt the golf ball into the cup using correct form from a distance of 5 feet (1.5 m) in at least 8 out of 10 attempts.				
7. The student will use correct form (short backswing and low contact point) three times in a row when practicing the badminton short serve during the peer-assessment task.				

Writing Effective Learning Outcomes for the Cognitive Domain

Writing learning outcomes for the cognitive domain is a little harder than those for the psychomotor domain. Why do you think that this is true? Write your answer before reading further.

If you answered that it is difficult to see student learning when it's cognitive, you are absolutely correct. With the psychomotor domain the learning outcome was always **overt** (easily observable). With the cognitive domain, sometimes the learning outcome is **covert,** or not readily observable. To write a learning outcome for the cognitive domain, you need to think about a behavior that the student can demonstrate that would be indicative of cognitive learning. For example, students could demonstrate knowledge of the rules by taking a written test or using them during game play. In the latter instance, you would observe whether students knew the rules using a game-play rubric. Chapter 9 contains additional ways to assess cognitive learning.

As with the psychomotor learning outcome, you will need to specify a performance. The criterion for cognitive learning outcomes usually represents the passing score, so if you use a written test, you would set the bar for example at 70 or 80 percent. The conditions for a cognitive

YOUR TURN 7.5

Learning outcome: *Students will demonstrate knowledge of the critical elements of the smash by correctly labeling at least 4 of the 5 critical elements on an action photo.*

Identify the performance task, the condition, and the criterion in this learning outcome. For example, you could represent this visually by drawing a single line under the performance task, a dotted line under the condition, and a circle around the criterion.

YOUR TURN 7.6

Now let's see how well you can identify a good cognitive learning outcome. Here is a list of cognitive learning outcomes. Identify the elements of performance, condition, and criterion for each. Compare your results with a peer, and be sure you can recognize the performance, condition, and criterion in the cognitive domain.

Cognitive learning outcome	Performance	Condition	Criterion
1. Students will demonstrate their knowledge of badminton rules by scoring 70 percent or better on a multiple choice test.			
2. Students will demonstrate knowledge about the tactics of hitting to an open space by identifying that maneuver on a video clip of class play.			
3. Students will demonstrate knowledge of rules by creating a PowerPoint presentation written in their own words (not copied from a rule book) with no errors.			
4. Students will demonstrate knowledge of an offensive tactic by correctly explaining it on a YouTube video.			
5. Students will demonstrate knowledge of the rules of a game by receiving a 2 or better on the game-play rubric while you observe.			
6. The student will demonstrate knowledge of defensive tactics by writing on an exit slip a correct way to cover the court.			

learning outcome explain the context in which the expected learning will occur.

Going back to Mr. Thomas' badminton unit, he has decided to use an action picture as a way to document student knowledge of the critical elements of the smash. The learning outcome is in the box that follows.

Writing Effective Learning Outcomes for the Affective Domain

Student-learning outcomes for the affective domain are probably the most difficult to write because many affective domain traits represent different behaviors to different people. For example, write your definition of the term *fair play*.

Share your definition with a colleague or classmate. Which ideas were the same? How were your responses different?

Fair play, also called *sportsmanship*, is a term that has a wide range of meanings. For some, the term means that students will follow the rules of the game and will not try to win by cheating. For others, the term means that students will not play in an aggressive manner or that they will accept the referee's decisions. All of these definitions are legitimate, but unless the term is defined for others, it might mean different things to different people. When writing

a learning outcome for the affective domain, you must specify the behaviors that you expect from students. By defining what you expect to see, you will help students understand the expectations and minimize confusion. To write an outcome for fair play, you might state, *"The students will demonstrate fair play by calling shots correctly and encouraging others during the game."* (Note: In this learning outcome, the criterion is unstated, but it is assumed to be occurring consistently or at all times.) Other terms commonly used in the affective domain include *effort*, *teamwork*, and *cooperation*; all of these terms must be defined by specifying the behaviors expected by students.

To develop a student learning outcome for the affective domain, think of the attitude or character trait that you want students to display and then identify the observable behaviors that will be used to represent that disposition. For example, safety is important, so the student learning outcome for the affective domain might state: *While playing badminton, the student will demonstrate safe and responsible play by following the safety rules given by the teacher with no more than one reminder per class.* As with the learning outcomes for the other domains, there should be a performance and a criterion. In the preceding example, the performance is "demonstrate safe and responsible play by following the safety rules given by the teacher." The criterion is "with no more than one reminder per class."

YOUR TURN 7.7

Let's see how well you understand affective domain outcomes. For each of the following affective outcomes, identify the performance, the condition, and the criterion.

Affective learning outcome	Performance	Condition	Criterion
1. The students will demonstrate responsible behavior toward others by not dropping them when serving as a spotter during gymnastics.			
2. The student will demonstrate willingness to help others by consistently volunteering to help others during free skate time.			

(continued)

(continued)

Affective learning outcome	Performance	Condition	Criterion
3. Students will demonstrate safety by skating under control (being able to stop when asked or when necessary) during the free skate time.			
4. During practice, the student will demonstrate support for teammates by consistently giving encouraging comments to each person on the team.			
5. Students will demonstrate personal responsibility by picking up equipment after every class without being asked.			
6. Students will demonstrate cooperation with a partner by equally sharing opportunities to return the ball.			
7. Students will demonstrate fair play by consistently accepting the decisions of an official without arguments.			

Things to Avoid When Writing Learning Outcomes

There are some potholes to avoid when writing learning outcomes. Here are some common errors that we have observed from our students. The following examples were all written by teacher candidates.

1. No condition or a pseudo condition is used.

   Example: Following teacher instruction, the student will be able to describe the four cues for hitting a serve in tennis.

2. Criteria can't be assessed.

   Example: The students will successfully demonstrate the rules during the game 90 percent of the time.

3. The process criterion leads to poor performance.

   Example: The student will be able to demonstrate 2 of the 4 critical elements on an overhand throw.

4. The performance verb can't be assessed.

   Example: The student will understand how to lead the pass to a partner.

5. There is no written documentation of assessment.

   Example: When asked by the teacher during class closure, the students will be able to explain the pivot 100 percent of the time.

6. The product is specified alone; no criteria for process is stated.

   Example: The student will be able to serve the ball into the service court 5 out of 7 times.

7. Implied assessments are cumbersome and are not feasible.

Example: The student will be able to demonstrate correct form on 18 out of 20 volleyball sets.

8. Multiple behaviors are included in the same outcome.

   Example: The student will identify how to throw to a moving target and judge where the disc will land during the lesson 3 times.

9. A specific number of occurrences are specified for game play.

   Example: During the game, the student will demonstrate 4 out of 5 drop shots.

10. A task, rather than a student learning outcome, is written.

    Example: Students will be working on throwing, hitting, fielding grounders and pop flies.

11. The response of one student is used to indicate that a learning outcome is met.

    Example: At the end of the class, students will indicate knowledge of the rules by answering teacher questions during lesson closure.

12. The same learning outcomes are used day after day after day.

We sincerely hope that you can avoid these potholes.

YOUR TURN 7.8

Identify the problem that the faulty outcomes illustrate above and what you could do to correct it. If possible, discuss these with a partner to see if your answers are the same.

Practice Writing Learning Outcomes

Now you will have a chance to practice writing your own learning outcomes. We will start with the psychomotor domain. We are going to help Mr. Thomas write his learning outcomes for his badminton unit. Since we looked at his learning outcome for the serve earlier in the chapter, the next learning outcome he writes will be for his lesson on clear shots. It reads: *While standing within 5 feet (1.5 m) of the end line, the student will be able to clear a badminton bird, using correct form, into the opponent's court so that it lands in the back half of the court in 8 out of 10 trials.* Can you identify the performance? Condition? Criterion?

In short, the learning outcome looks pretty good, but there is something missing. It does not discuss whether the bird was tossed by a partner, whether it occurred during game play, or whether a partner was on the opposite side of the net feeding the bird to the student using a setup shot. Since the setup for the shot will affect how the skill is performed, the condition needs to be stated. We will add to the condition by stating that the partner will set up the clear shot with by softly tossing the bird. The learning outcome now reads: *Standing within 5 feet (1.5 m) of the end line, the student, using correct form, will be able to clear a badminton bird, delivered with a soft toss from a partner, into the opponent's court so that in 8 out of 10 trials, it lands in the back half of the court.*

Rather than writing a single sentence, it may be easier at first to write each component separately to ensure that the outcome is complete. For the following practice activities, we suggest that you write the three components separately:

Performance: *Hit an overhead drop shot.*

Criterion: *Using correct form... into the opponent's court so that in 8 out of 10 trials it lands in the front half of the court.*

Condition: *Standing behind the short service line... delivered with a clear shot from a partner.*

Next, let's try to write a learning outcome for the cognitive domain. Mr. Thomas plans to give his students a written test using multiple-choice and short-answer questions to find out if they know the key rules needed for playing badminton.

Let's try another cognitive learning outcome. This time, Mr. Thomas wants his students to demonstrate knowledge of net/wall game tactics. He has developed a rubric to see whether they can use these tactics during game play. His goal is that every student will perform at the passing level or better according to the rubric. Write an appropriate learning outcome.

Now, let's see if you can write a student learning outcome for the affective domain. Mr. Thomas wants his students to work with a partner during peer assessments and to provide honest and accurate feedback. Write down the learning outcome.

Now you should be able to write your own learning outcomes and assessments for a unit of your choice. Remember starting to develop a unit plan for a unit of your choosing from chapter 2?

YOUR TURN 7.9

Write a psychomotor learning outcome for the overhead clear in badminton with a product criterion.

Performance: _____

Condition: _____

Criterion: _____

Use the checklist in figure 7.3 to check your work.

YOUR TURN 7.10

Write a cognitive learning outcome for badminton rules.

Performance: _____

Condition: _____

Criterion: _____

Use the checklist found in figure 7.3 to check your work.

YOUR TURN 7.11

Write a cognitive learning outcome for badminton tactics.

Performance: _____

Condition: _____

Criterion: _____

Use the checklist found in figure 7.3 to check your work.

YOUR TURN 7.12

Write an affective learning outcome.

Performance: _____

Condition: _____

Criterion: _____

Use the checklist found in figure 7.3 to check your work.

Write two student learning outcomes for each of the domains: psychomotor, cognitive, and affective. After you complete the assignment, give it to a peer or friend, who will assess your work using the checklist in figure 7.3. After receiving their feedback, go back and make the improvements, and then self-assess.

Learning Outcomes for a Unit on _____

Psychomotor 1

    Performance: _____

    Condition: _____

    Criterion: _____

Psychomotor 2

    Performance: _____

    Condition: _____

    Criterion: _____

Cognitive 1

    Performance: _____

    Condition: _____

    Criterion: _____

Cognitive 2

    Performance: _____

    Condition: _____

    Criterion: _____

Affective 1

    Performance: _____

    Condition: _____

    Criterion: _____

Affective 2

    Performance: _____

    Condition: _____

    Criterion: _____

_____ Is there a performance?

_____ Is a condition stated?

_____ Does the learning outcome state how good the performance must be for the student to pass?

_____ Does the product criterion use speed or time, accuracy, quality, or an outside standard? Does it describe the correct form expected?

_____ Does the performance use a verb that can be pictured?

_____ Can the performance be assessed?

_____ Is the outcome written in terms of what the student will be able to do?

_____ Is correct grammar used?

_____ Is the spelling correct?

_____ Could some words be omitted to make the learning outcome more clear?

_____ Are additional words needed to clarify the learning outcome?

Figure 7.3   Checklist to check work in Your Turns 7.9-7.13.

We suggest that you go back to that unit, since you have already completed some work on it. However, if you want to switch to another unit, that is fine.

Summary

In this chapter, you learned how to write student learning outcomes for the psychomotor, cogni-tive, and affective domains. You have begun to think about how to assess learning outcomes, but you need more information about different types of assessments for the psychomotor domain. In the next chapter, you'll get to practice creating different types of assessments and recording forms for psychomotor domain assessments.

Answers to the Your Turn Activities

YOUR TURN 7.3

If you indicated the performance as "perform the Virginia reel," you are right. "While accompanied by the music" is the condition specified for this learning outcome. This condition affects the difficulty of the task because it is easier for students to do the steps of a dance without the music. You should have circled the criterion "correctly. . . with no more than three breaks in rhythm." Remember we stated that students who can perform correctly most of the time have demonstrated competence. This criterion would be easy to observe and assess, even by a peer observer, so it is feasible and assessable.

Psychomotor learning outcome	Performance	Condition	Criterion	Process or product?
1. The student will be able to dribble a basketball, without looking down, three times in a row, keeping it under control while weaving in and out of cones.	dribble a basketball, without looking down	while weaving in and out of cones	three times in a row, keeping it under control	Process
2. The student will score at least 100 points while bowling a 10-frame game on a commercial bowling lane.	while bowling a 10-frame game	on a commercial bowling lane	score at least 100 points	Product
3. The student will be able to score on a penalty kick 8 out of 10 times when a goalie is playing light defense during a practice task.	score on a penalty kick	when a goalie is playing light defense during a practice task	8 out of 10 times	Product
4. The student will use correct form while receiving a baton pass at least 3 out of 5 attempts while maintaining running speed during a 4 × 100 relay.	while receiving a baton pass	while maintaining running speed during a 4 × 100 relay	use correct form . . . 3 out of 5 attempts	Process
5. The student will be able to hit the target 8 out of 10 times from 15 yards while practicing shooting skills in disc golf.	hit the target	from 15 yards while practicing shooting skills in disc golf	8 out of 10 times	Product
6. The student will be able to putt the golf ball into the cup using correct form from a distance of 5 feet (1.5 m) in at least 8 out of 10 attempts.	putt the golf ball into the cup using correct form	from a distance of 5 feet (1.5 m)	at least 8 out of 10 attempts	Product
7. The student will use correct form (short backswing and low contact point) three times in a row when practicing the badminton short serve during the peer-assessment task.	practicing the badminton short serve	during the peer-assessment task	correct form (short backswing and low contact point) three times in a row	Process

YOUR TURN 7.5

If you chose "demonstrate knowledge of the critical elements" for the performance task, you were correct. The condition is "on an action photo." The criterion in this learning outcome is "correctly labeling at least 4 of the 5 critical elements." When specifying the performance, you need to make sure that your outcome states the main purpose of learning. On this learning outcome, the observable student behavior is labeling. As a teacher, your intent is not that students can label something, but rather that they know the correct critical elements. Knowing the correct critical elements is a covert behavior that needs to be indicated by another behavior (in this case, labeling the action photo), which is the overt behavior. When writing outcomes for the cognitive domain, we suggest using a format that identifies the knowledge for which we are holding students accountable so that the intent of the learning outcome is clearly indicated to others.

YOUR TURN 7.6

Cognitive learning outcome	Performance	Condition	Criterion
1. Students will demonstrate their knowledge of badminton rules by scoring 70 percent or better on a multiple choice test.	demonstrate their knowledge of badminton rules	on a multiple-choice test	scoring 70 percent or better
2. Students will demonstrate knowledge about the tactics of hitting to an open space by identifying that maneuver on a video clip of class play.	demonstrate knowledge about the tactics of hitting to an open space	on a video clip of class play	identifying that maneuver
3. Students will demonstrate knowledge of rules by creating a PowerPoint presentation written in their own words (not copied from a rule book) with no errors.	demonstrate knowledge of rules by creating a PowerPoint presentation	written in the student's own words	with no errors
4. Students will demonstrate knowledge of an offensive tactic by correctly explaining it on a YouTube video.	demonstrate knowledge of an offensive tactic	on a YouTube video	correctly explaining it
5. Students will demonstrate knowledge of the rules of a game by receiving a 2 or better on the game-play rubric while you observe.	demonstrate knowledge of the rules of a game	on the game-play rubric	receiving a 2 or better
6. The student will demonstrate knowledge of defensive tactics by writing on an exit slip a correct way to cover the court.	demonstrate knowledge of defensive tactics	writing on an exit slip	correct way to cover the court

Affective learning outcome	Performance	Condition	Criterion
1. The students will demonstrate responsible behavior toward others by not dropping them when serving as a spotter during gymnastics.	demonstrate responsible behavior toward others	when serving as a spotter during gymnastics	not dropping them
2. The student will demonstrate willingness to help others by consistently volunteering to help others during free skate time.	demonstrate willingness to help others	during free skate time	consistently volunteering to help others
3. Students will demonstrate safety by skating under control (being able to stop when asked or when necessary) during the free skate time.	demonstrate safety	during the free skate time	skating under control
4. During practice, the student will demonstrate support for teammates by consistently giving encouraging comments to each person on the team.	demonstrate support for teammates	during practice	consistently giving encouraging comments to each person on the team
5. Students will demonstrate personal responsibility by picking up equipment after every class without being asked.	demonstrate personal responsibility by picking up equipment	after every class	without being asked by the teacher
6. Students will demonstrate cooperation with a partner by equally sharing opportunities to return the ball.	demonstrate cooperation with a partner	opportunities to return the ball	equally sharing
7. Students will demonstrate fair play by consistently accepting the decisions of an official without arguments.	demonstrate fair play by accepting the decisions of an official	without arguments	consistently

EIGHT

Choosing and Designing Psychomotor Assessment Tools

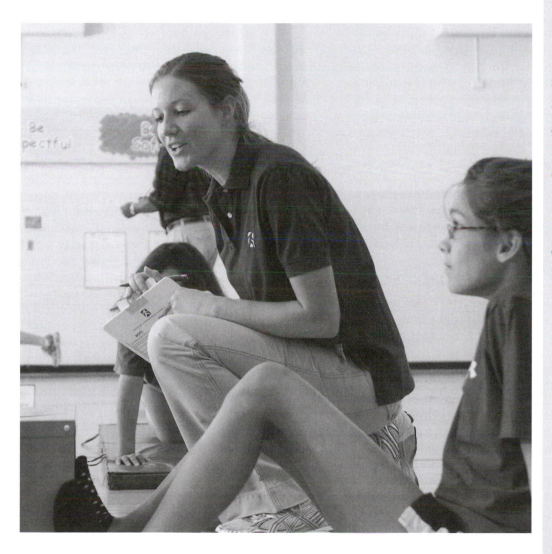

It is of course important to praise students because it often satisfies and encourages them, but it cannot help them improve their performance. Praise keeps you in the game; real feedback helps you get better.

Wiggins, 1998, p. 46

LOOK FOR THESE KEY CONCEPTS

> checklist
> critical elements
> log
> observation record

> recording sheet
> statistics sheet
> score sheet

One of the most important ideas we presented early in this book is that assessment always results in a written record. Maybe when you read that, you thought, "OK, but what kind of recording forms should I use and where do I get them?" In this chapter, we discuss and illustrate six different types of psychomotor assessment tools that are used to provide helpful feedback to students about their performances. The forms include checklists, logs, statistics sheets, rating scales, skill tests, and score sheets. Samples of each type of tool are provided, but it will be important for you to develop your own tools that meet the needs of your students. While forms developed by other teachers may give you good ideas, you'll find that designing your own recording forms is best because you will write them for a specific purpose. Use the examples in this chapter to stimulate your own creative ideas. Remember that it takes practice to learn how to design assessment forms. As you complete the chapter, you will have an opportunity to practice designing your own assessment forms.

Checklists

A **checklist,** used to assess process criteria (correct form), contains a list of critical elements that should be present in competent performance of a psychomotor skill. The **critical elements** are the aspects of movement that should be observed when the skill is performed correctly. Since they promote the use of correct form, checklists are used while learners are practicing the skill in the early phases of the unit, after you have provided instruction, demonstration, and practice tasks. Using a checklist helps students cognitively learn the elements of correct form. In peer assessment, students learn two ways: by performing and by watching. Once they have consistently achieved correct form, students will be ready to focus on the product of skill performance and to apply skills to competitive games. In other

words, checklists are a means to an end, not the final product (e.g., a formative assessment). Since checklists are used *for* learning, you should build them in a way to help students set goals for improvement based on critical elements that are not consistently exhibited.

Throughout this chapter, we encourage students to look at the data and set goals. We view improvement goals as a step toward reaching the final learning outcome. When teaching goal setting, you must help students look realistically at their current level of performance and then add a little to that performance as a goal for the next step. If the step is too small, it will take them forever to reach their final goal. If the step is too large, they run the risk of getting discouraged and giving up before they are successful. The actual goal will depend on the amount of practice time that they will have until the next assessment. Given a reasonable amount of time to practice, we recommend that, for product assessments, you teach students to add about 5 to 10 percent to their performance each time they complete the assessment to help them progress to their final goal for performance (see chapter 11 for examples).

By asking the learner to use the results to set improvement goals, you are helping students become responsible for their learning. For example, after watching a video of their performance on the volleyball set, one student noticed that her wrist was moving forward on the follow-through, causing the set to be ineffective. The student's improvement goal was to focus on this critical element and to eliminate the error on the wrist movement through practice. So, for process assessments, students should set goals to improve specific critical elements of form that are not used consistently.

Identifying Critical Elements

Although many elements can be used to refine a skill, the critical elements represent *the most important components* that are absolutely necessary for correct performance. The number of critical elements on a checklist depends on the age and ability of your students. As a general rule, we suggest that high school students can work with 3 or 4 critical elements and middle school children can work with 2 or 3 critical elements. When designing checklists for your own classes, it will be easier for you to determine the appropriate number of critical elements, since you know your students. Observers must be able to observe each critical element, so you don't want to overwhelm them with too many. It is preferable to err on the side of fewer elements. When students conduct a peer assessment, they use the checklist to guide them in filling out their **observation record** of a partner's performance. Checklists can also be used in self-assessment if a video of the performance is available.

When you design a checklist, you need to consult expert sources to determine the critical elements for performing a skill so that the most important elements of correct form are used. In most cases, teachers are not considered expert sources except, perhaps, if they coach a sport. When developing a checklist for critical elements, refer to a book written by an expert in the activity (e.g., *Steps to Success* series). Look at a section on common errors to see which critical elements are usually problematic for learners. The book by Fronske (1997) has critical elements for most sports. Websites that are constructed by experts may also be consulted for critical elements (e.g., United States Tennis Association).

Designing Checklists

A checklist can be designed to fit on a half sheet of paper, so each full sheet contains two copies of the checklist. When the assessment is done in groups, each person in the group or team should be able to record results on a single sheet of paper. Principals will appreciate the fact that you are not wasting paper, so make good use of space on the paper. Font size can be 12 points for high school students, but should be *larger for younger students*.

Figure 8.1 contains a summary list of the important parts of a checklist. In addition to guidelines for creating checklists, we've provided four sample checklists in this chapter to demonstrate both the necessary components of a well-designed checklist and the variety of forms a checklist can take to suit a number of purposes. Figure 8.2 shows a sample checklist for high school students that can be used to self-assess bowling performance. Figure 8.3 is designed for middle school peer assessment of jump rope performance. Figure 8.4 is a sample checklist for a group of three high school students who are practicing the badminton overhead clear. Sometimes a peer assessment requires the use of more than two students so that someone is present to set up or partner with the performer. When a group or team is conducting the assessment, the form should be designed so that all members of the group can record on a single sheet of paper. This helps students understand what to do and how to do it. Finally, figure 8.5 illustrates another way to design a peer assessment checklist for middle school students.

1. Title of the assessment
2. A line to record the date and class period
3. A line for the name of the performer or observer
4. Directions for using the form indicating number of trials
5. An appropriate diagram or clip art is attractive and motivating for students.
6. A list of no more than four critical elements, written as cues, that define good form
7. A place to check (√) or mark yes or no for up to four critical elements
8. A space to record results (line or a box)
9. Space and prompt to write an improvement goal
10. Correct spelling and grammar

Figure 8.1 Important parts of a checklist.

Bowling Self-Assessment

Name _____ Date _____ Class period _____

Directions

Carefully observe your performance on the video as you approach the foul line and release the ball. Look for the four critical elements listed in the table and, for each trial, circle yes if you see the element and no if the element is missing. After you watch the three trials, write a goal that will help you improve your form. When you finish, turn in the completed checklist and move to the practice area.

Critical elements	Trial 1		Trial 2		Trial 3	
1. Ball ready at waist	Yes	No	Yes	No	Yes	No
2. Push away on first step	Yes	No	Yes	No	Yes	No
3. Full pendulum swing	Yes	No	Yes	No	Yes	No
4. Balanced on release	Yes	No	Yes	No	Yes	No
Improvement goal based on the critical elements listed above:						

Figure 8.2 Sample checklist for high school students: bowling self-assessment.

YOUR TURN 8.1

Use these questions to analyze figure 8.2 and see if it is complete. Feel free to add explanations for your responses.

1. What is the title of this recording form? _____
2. Is there a place for the student's name?   Yes   No
3. Is there a place for the date?   Yes   No
4. Did the directions clearly explain what students needed to do?   Yes   No
5. Does the clip art correctly illustrate an important aspect of the form?   Yes   No
6. Do the four critical elements represent the most important form points?   Yes   No
7. Will it be easy for students to use this form to record their results?   Yes   No
8. Is there sufficient space for the student to write an improvement goal?   Yes   No
9. Did you find any grammar or spelling errors on this form?   Yes   No

Jump Rope Peer Assessment

Jumper's name _____ Observer's name _____

Directions

Watch your partner jump rope 10 times for each of the jumps. Check (√) the critical elements you see consistently (at least three times in a row). If you don't see the element, leave it blank.

Forward jump (single bounce)	Backward jump (single bounce)
_____ Head up	_____ Head up
_____ Elbows in	_____ Elbows in
_____ Feet stay close to the floor	_____ Feet stay close to the floor
_____ Number of jumps with no miss	_____ Number of jumps with no miss
Jumper's improvement goal:	Jumper's improvement goal:

Figure 8.3 Sample checklist for middle school students: jump rope peer assessment.

 YOUR TURN 8.2

Figure 8.3 is a peer assessment form for middle school students (grades 6–8). Can you find three ways that this form for middle school differs from the high school example (figure 8.2)? Write down your answers. Our answers are provided at the end of the chapter.

Overhead Forehand Clear Assessment

Directions

In groups of three, provide each person with helpful feedback on the overhead forehand clear. Player 1 is the hitter, player 2 delivers a setup, and player 3 observes and records. After five good setups, rotate positions and continue until everyone has been the hitter. The setup should be a high, long serve to the hitter's forehand side. For each trial, the observer and recorder checks (√) in the column if the three critical components are observed. After five trials, help the hitter set a specific improvement goal. If your group finishes before time is called, practice your overhead clears and work on your personal goal.

Hitter name: _____ Observer and recorder name: _____

Critical elements	Trials				
	1	2	3	4	5
Racket back, side to target					
Contact high, arm extended					
Weight shifts back to front					
Improvement goal:					

Hitter name: _____ Observer and recorder name: _____

Critical elements	Trials				
	1	2	3	4	5
Racket back, side to target					
Contact high, arm extended					
Weight shifts back to front					
Improvement goal:					

Hitter name: _____ Observer and recorder name: _____

Critical elements	Trials				
	1	2	3	4	5
Racket back, side to target					
Contact high, arm extended					
Weight shifts back to front					
Improvement goal:					

Figure 8.4 Sample checklist for high school students: overhead forehand clear assessment.

The purpose of this assessment is to help your partner improve the short serve. You can help your partner improve only by providing honest feedback. This assessment is not for a grade.

Directions

Work in pairs to complete the following assessments. Observe your partner's performance on **5 trials** of the short serve. Place a **check** (√) beside each element of the serve if your partner demonstrated that component on at least 3 of the trials. After you complete the assessment, sit down with your partner and write a specific technique goal to improve your performance.

Performer name: _____

Observer name: _____

Doubles service · Server

Singles service · Server

	√	
Short backswing		Write an improvement goal here.
Drop the shuttle and contact below the waist.		
Serve travels low over the net.		

Performer name: _____ Observer name: _____

	√	
Short backswing		Write an improvement goal here.
Drop the shuttle and contact below the waist.		
Serve travels low over the net.		

Figure 8.5 Sample checklist for middle school students: peer assessment for badminton short serve.

YOUR TURN 8.3

Compare figures 8.4 (high school) and 8.5 (middle school). Notice that the middle school assessment uses a larger font size than the high school assessment. Can you find three other differences between the two checklists? Suggested answers are at the end of the chapter, but try to identify the differences yourself before checking the answers.

YOUR TURN 8.4

Now, it's your turn to design a checklist. Use the following template to design a peer assessment checklist for middle school students. Remember to use an expert source to determine the critical elements and to follow the guidelines in figure 8.1.

Peer Assessment for _____

The purpose of this assessment is to help your partner improve the _____.

You can help your partner improve only by providing honest feedback. This assessment is not for a grade.

Directions: _____

_____

_____

Performer name: _____   Observer and recorder name: _____

		Write an improvement goal here.

Performer name: _____   Observer and recorder name: _____

		Write an improvement goal here.

We designed the table in the figure using Microsoft Word's Table function. We suggest that you sketch a design on paper first to determine the number of columns and rows. In this example, we began with a table consisting of three columns and three rows. We adjusted the middle column's width to make room for a check mark. To leave room for an improvement goal, we simply merged the three rows in the right column. By now, you should be ready to try your hand at designing a checklist from scratch. You can do it!

Logs

Logs are self-assessment tools that help students record and track their progress over several class periods. They are usually product assessments. Some teachers use logs as instant assessment tasks at the beginning of class. For example, individual logs could be used during a volleyball unit. When students enter the gym from the locker room, they pick up a clipboard, a log, and a pencil. Volleyball tasks might include the serve, wall sets, and self-bumps. Students take a prescribed number of practice trials and then record their personal best for that day. The log is used in this example to help students strive to increase the number of successful serves, sets, and bumps, thus improving their competence. When using

this type of log, we suggest that you set a criterion level to give students a specific goal.

Logs can also be used during station work or during independent practice after skills have been taught. As students go through the stations, they carry a log and a pencil, and record their results at each station. This type of log works well in weight training when students record the amount of weight lifted and repetitions done each day. Even though the record of achievement is not used for grading, students are likely to be more motivated to work harder if they see their progress each day. Their motivation increases if students know the same tasks will be part of a summative assessment at the end of the unit. When students see that they are improving, they have solid evidence of their own learning, which often proves to be highly motivating.

Logs could be used to assist students with keeping track of their steps each day using pedometers. Students can graph results, which helps them apply skills learned in other classes (thus integrating learning from physical education with classroom knowledge). Nutrition logs are often kept to help students track their calories and nutrients each day by recording and analyzing their food intake. As you can see, logs can be used in a variety of ways. Figures 8.6 and 8.7 are two examples of logs that we've used.

**YOUR TURN 8.5**

Perhaps you've used a log of some kind in your own sport or fitness experience. Our examples refer to personal fitness and badminton; can you think of at least three other performances that a log would help assess?

Designing a log is very similar to the strategy used for designing checklists. The first step is to identify a purpose for the log and define what would be helpful to record on a daily or regular basis. You might want to sketch it out on paper before creating it in an electronic format.

**YOUR TURN 8.6**

What kind of log could your students keep during the unit you are designing? Would it work best as an instant activity or would you incorporate a log into stations?

**YOUR TURN 8.7**

Design a log for your unit. In class, share your log with a peer and give each other feedback.

Personal Fitness Log

Name _____ Class period_____

Directions

As soon as you enter the gym, pick up your log and a pencil. Go through as many stations as possible until time is called. Follow the directions for each station and record your personal best at each station. Use your records to set new personal best goals each week. Be sure to set a new goal for each station.

Station	Date Goal/Best	Date Goal/Best	Date Goal/Best	Date Goal/Best	Date Goal/Best	Date Goal/Best
Curl-up: Record the number completed in 1 min.						
Push-ups (regular or modified): Record number completed with no stop.						
Sit and reach: Record R & L distance in inches.						
Jump rope: Record the number of consecutive jumps with no miss.						

Figure 8.6 Sample fitness log for high school students.

Badminton Skills Daily Practice Log

Name _____ Class period _____

Directions

Complete this log during the first 8 minutes of each class period. Your team will earn extra points for each person who completes the daily log. If you are absent, please schedule a make-up session with your teacher. Record your **personal best** number of consecutive hits each day after completing the trials indicated for each skill. **Try to improve your score during each trial.**

Skills/dates	Date	Date	Date	Date	Date	Date	Date
Forehand ups 3 trials							
Backhand ups 3 trials							
Wall volleys 3 trials							
Partner rally tally 3 trials							

Figure 8.7 Sample badminton unit log for high school students.

Statistics Sheets

Anyone who has ever played on an athletic team knows about stats. Put simply, *statistics* are product data about motor performances. Coaches must believe that keeping stats helps players improve performance because they use statistics extensively. We suggest that simplified stats can also be used in physical education *for* learning. Furthermore, we believe that keeping stats can be a great form of peer assessment in secondary physical education. If you are using a sport education model, each team will probably have a head statistician who is in charge of teaching and assigning statisticians. We have included four examples of **statistics sheets.**

High school students can use figure 8.8 to chart where shots land on the court in a singles badminton game or scrimmage. When the player looks at the stat sheet at the end of the game, it is easy to see if the majority of shots are aimed at the middle of the court or whether the player is hitting both back court and front court to move the opponent up and back. During any activity in which there is a need to have some students sitting out (e.g., there is not enough space for all to be active safely), using peer assessment is

a very beneficial way to ensure that all students are learning.

Figure 8.9 is similar, but the focus of the observer's coding is the serve. The resulting stat sheet will let the player know if long and short serves are used appropriately, and the success rate will help players know if they need to practice more on the serves. Players should be attempting to have at least an 80 percent success rate in serving, meaning that the serves go over the net and into the correct court; in addition, short serves should be low and aimed near the short serve line, while long serves should be high and aimed near the baseline. When players know their success rate and have some information about where their shots are going, they can assume more responsibility for their own improvement. This is essential for high school students.

Figure 8.10 illustrates a way for a peer assessor to code shot selection in badminton. Students should be using the clear, smash, and drop shot,

YOUR TURN 8.8

What could you do to simplify the recording form in figure 8.10 for middle school students?

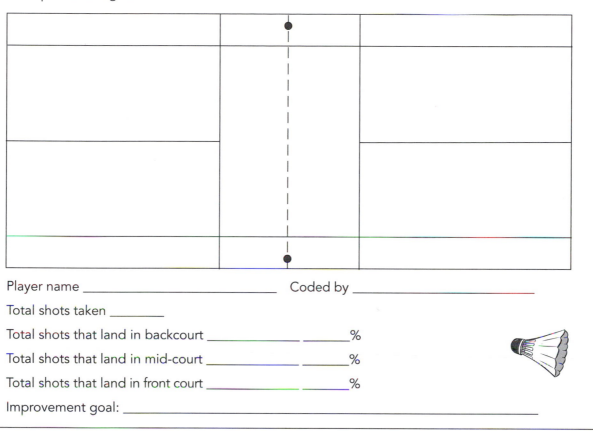

Singles Statistics

Directions

During a singles game, you will code the shots of **one player**. Start by writing a *P* on the side of the court where your player serves. After the serve, mark with an *X* where each hit would have landed or where it actually hit the floor on the opponent's side of the court. **Do not code serves.** At the end of the game, sit down and help your player analyze the shots taken and set an improvement goal.

Player name _____   Coded by _____

Total shots taken _____

Total shots that land in backcourt _____ _____%

Total shots that land in mid-court _____ _____%

Total shots that land in front court _____ _____%

Improvement goal: _____

Figure 8.8 Sample statistics sheet for high school students: badminton shot chart.

so this assessment will give them feedback about whether or not they used a variety of shots during a practice game.

The last example in figure 8.11 focuses students on the return of serve. In badminton, the receiver has two choices when returning serve: high and to the back court, or low and away from the server. This form was designed for use during a sport education badminton season, so there is a space for the signature of the head statistician.

YOUR TURN 8.9

Now it's your turn to design a statistics sheet for your unit. Be sure to include a line for the student's name, date, and class. Write clear and simple directions that include the number of trials. Include some clip art (for now, just draw a little picture) and a title. Think carefully about how and where the stats can be recorded. Then give some thought to the data summary and provide a line for the improvement goal. Bring your stat sheet to class and be prepared to share it with a colleague.

Assessment of Serve Selection and Success

Directions

In today's games, when a person is playing singles, a teammate should be coding serve selection. Each time your teammate serves, you should tally the serve in either the successful or unsuccessful column. Tally marks should look like this: ////

Use the space to the right of the table to jot down any notes to help you give feedback to your teammate. When the game is over, please share your data with the server and help set a specific improvement goal. Remember that the long serve should be used about 80% of the time in singles.

Name of performer _____ Coded by _____

Performer's team name _____

Badminton shots	Successful execution	Unsuccessful execution	Notes
Short serve: Successful execution requires the serve to be close to the net and to the short serve line.			
Long serve: Successful execution requires the serve to be high and near the baseline.			

Short serves: Successful _____ ÷ total attempted _____ = _____%

Long serves: Successful _____ ÷ total attempted _____ = _____%

Improvement goal for the next game: _____

Figure 8.9 Sample statistics sheet for high school students: badminton serve assessment.

Shot Execution Analysis

Name of player _____ Coded by _____

Directions

In today's games, when a person is playing singles, teammates will code shot execution. Work in groups of three. Each time your teammate hits the shuttle after the serve, one person will call to the recorder if the shot was successfully executed and the recorder will place a tally mark in the correct column. Tally marks should look like: ////

Use the space to the right of the table to jot down any notes to help you give feedback to your teammate. When the game is over, please share the data with your teammate and help set an improvement goal.

Badminton shots	Successful execution	Unsuccessful execution	Notes
Overhead clear: Successful execution requires that the shuttle be hit high and in the back third of the court. A shuttle hit to mid-court should be coded as unsuccessful.			
Smash: Successful execution requires that the shuttle be hit at an angle toward the floor. If the shuttle flight is flat or high, it should be coded as an unsuccessful attempt.			
Drop: Successful execution requires that the shuttle drop close to the net in front of the short serve line.			
Other: Code a shot as *other* if it does not meet the criteria for one of the shots above. Code it as successful if it goes over the net.			
Totals/percentages	Total hits = % =	Total hits = % =	

Improvement goal: _____

Figure 8.10 Sample statistics sheet for high school students: badminton shot execution analysis.

Assessment of Badminton Short Serve Return

The purpose of this task is to work together as a team to assess your ability to return an opponent's short serve into the most strategically advantageous place. Remember that the two possible target areas are as follows:

- Low and close to the net, aiming for the area in front of the short serve line
  or
- High and to the back of the court, over the outstretched arm of the server

Directions

Record the names of all team members. Each player returns 10 serves, attempting to hit the first 5 returns to the front and the other 5 trials to the back of the court. To use time efficiently, the server should be the best on your team. Award 1 point for each return of serve that lands in the target area, and mark a 0 for the trial if the shuttle lands in the middle of the court. If the bird fails to clear the net for any reason, record an *X*. Do not rally during this task.

Names	Returns to the front					Returns to the back				

_____   _____   Total points _____

Signature of head statistician   Team name

The signature of the head statistician attests to the accuracy of this record.

Team's improvement goal: _____

Figure 8.11   Sample statistics sheet for high school students: badminton short serve return assessment.

Rating Scales

A **rating scale** for the psychomotor domain contains a list of important elements. The assessor rates each element. The rating scale in figure 8.12 focuses on badminton tactics, and it can be used as formative peer assessment.

Rating scales are used most often as teacher-directed summative assessments. They allow you to give students credit for beginning to understand the concepts listed in the assessment while recognizing that more work and learning are needed. When using rating scales, you must remember that the purpose is to determine levels of student competence. Your evaluation of the component is done to help students learn. In other words, be honest with your students when completing these rating scales. Inflating their level of performance doesn't help your students achieve mastery of the component being assessed.

 YOUR TURN 8.10

Sometimes, when recording scores for others, observers (student teachers, peers, teachers) tend to inflate the scores they give to the people they are watching. This is not always intentional, but we have seen it happen. Why do you think observers might inflate assessment results when observing others? How could you prevent this from happening?

Assessment of Badminton Play

Player _____ Assessor _____

Carefully observe your assigned player and assess the listed components of game play. The purpose of this assessment is to provide honest feedback about the player's strengths and weaknesses. This is not for a grade. Use the 1–3 scale for your assessment:

1 = weakness
2 = neither weakness nor strength
3 = strength

Circle your rating for each question. Does the player do the following?

Hit to the open space (where there is no opponent)	1	2	3
Vary strokes by hitting long and short to move the opponent	1	2	3
Hit left and right to move the opponent	1	2	3
Move back to home position after each stroke	1	2	3
Vary serves so that the opponent does not know what to expect	1	2	3
Keep short serves very low	1	2	3

What was the player's greatest weakness? _____

What was the player's greatest strength? _____

Player's improvement goal _____

Figure 8.12   Sample rating scale for high school students: assessment of badminton play.

Skill Tests

During the '60s and '70s, a lot of masters degree students wrote a thesis to complete their degree. The topic of many of these theses were skill tests for variety of sports. The subjects used to establish the norms for these tests were usually college students. When middle or high school students are given the assessments, they frequently do poorly because they lack the strength to generate the necessary force to complete the assessment and receive a reasonably good score (French et al., 1991). For this and a variety of other reasons, many teachers like to create their own skill tests. We think that skill tests are excellent ways to get students to practice a game skill in a relatively closed environment and to assess their ability to perform the skill away from game play. Just be sure to provide 10 or more trials for a product skill test to guarantee that the results don't happen by chance.

Chapter 7 discusses several ideas for establishing the criteria for skill assessments. Establish the criteria for a skill assessment at a level that gives students a reasonable expectation for success in a game (a mastery criteria approach). In other words, if students do well on the skill test, they should be able to use the skill with confidence in a game. Figures 8.13 and 8.14 are two examples of skill assessments that we have used with students. We have provided the criteria that we used when giving the assessment, but we strongly suggest that you establish your own criteria using the methods outlined in chapter 7.

Typically, teachers want to develop assessments that use the skill in a gamelike manner with an environment that is closed. For serves or skills that initiate game play, this task is fairly easy; for skills used in a game, this is a little more challenging. If possible, avoid using more than one person for the skill assessment. The reason for this is that with two people, the skill of both will affect the results of the assessment. If the person assisting in the setup for the skill being tested is fairly skilled (e.g., a teacher or a very skilled player in class) the influence is lessened;

Serving Test

The server stands behind the end line in the proper service court. Using any legal serve, the student serves volleyballs over the net, attempting to have them land in the zones worth the most points. Ten trials are allowed. Balls that hit the court but do not go over the net count as a trial with no points awarded for the attempt. Balls that fail to cross the net count as a trial with no points awarded for the attempt.

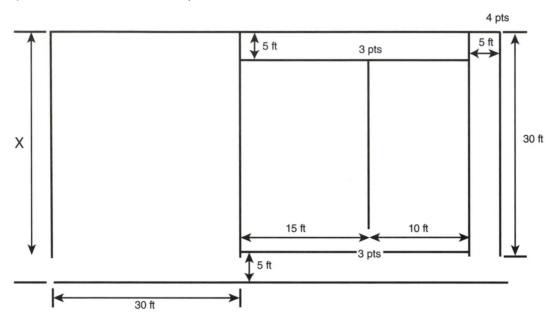

Criteria

A = 30 points and above

B = 24–29 points

C = 20–23 points

D = 16–19 points

F = 15 points or below

Names	1	2	3	4	5	6	7	8	9	10	Total points

This test is adapted from of the AAHPERD volleyball service test (1969).

Figure 8.13 Sample skill test for volleyball serve.

Adapted from *AAHPERD volleyball service test* 1969.

Volley Test

The student waits with the volleyball in hand facing the wall. On the *go* signal, the student tosses a ball into the target area, which is a 2-foot (60 cm) square box located 10 feet (3 m) above the floor. As the ball rebounds, the student volleys it using a set into the target area. The test continues for 1 minute. Only legal volleys are counted. If a student catches or misses a ball, it is put back into play with a toss. Tosses do not count as volleys. Allow student to repeat the test three times and count the best trial.

Criteria

A = 25 and above

B = 20–24

C = 16–19

D = 12–15

F = Below 12

Names	Trial 1	Trial 2	Trial 3	Best score

Figure 8.14   Sample skill test for volleyball volley.

testing two novice players at once can easily spell disaster. To avoid this, teachers sometimes use walls to rebound the ball or implement being used on the test. For example, if running a soccer passing test, instead of having two players move down the field and pass the ball to one another (e.g., they need to make five passes each in 50 yards), you could have the player pass the ball to a wall and then play it off the rebound to set up the next pass. In this latter example, the student would need to complete a certain number of passes within the distance marked. As another example, you might toss a volleyball to a player who then returns the ball with a forearm pass instead of having two students forearm pass the ball back and forth with one another. To find skill tests that will help your students become better players, we suggest that you look up some of the validated skill tests for ideas (Lacy & Hastad,

2006; Strand & Wilson, 1993) and then modify them to fit the needs of your students (e.g., testing setup and criteria for mastery). The solution is not perfect, but it will encourage your students to improve their skills, which is the outcome that you wish to achieve.

Score Sheets

Most sports have scoring systems, so you will need a **score sheet** if you plan to let students serve as scorekeepers. In large physical education classes, it is often not possible to have all students on the floor playing at one time. This means there are opportunities for students to serve as referees, scorekeepers, and statisticians. Who knows, students might even discover a talent or interest that they can pursue later in life. In our teaching experiences, we found that many students enjoyed fulfilling official roles in addition to playing the games.

A score sheet is a type of self-assessment that reflects product accuracy. For example, bowling and archery require score sheets that show how many pins are knocked down and how many times and where in relation to the center the arrows hit the target. Keeping score as a self-assessment allows students to set improvement goals. For example, I bowled a 102 last time, so today I want to score at least 110. Scorekeeping in team sports or net/wall games is usually associated with sport education and tournament play. Keeping score is a way to monitor wins and losses, and a team can use the score to set improvement goals. The key to designing good score sheets for physical education is to *keep them simple!* The following examples of score sheets for badminton and bowling have been used in secondary physical education classes.

In figure 8.15, the badminton score sheet is for a sport education season, which is why there is a space for the team name. Notice that an ethical element is included because the scorekeeper signs the sheet to verify accurate results. In this

teacher's badminton season, fair play is taught, emphasized, and rewarded with points during tournament play. Notice also that the scorekeeper records why the fair-play points are awarded, so the teacher can see if they are awarded correctly. Scorekeepers circle a fair-play point when an instance of fair play occurs. They are not allowed to simply award 3 points at the end of the game.

Figure 8.16 is a simple bowling score sheet that students can use during practice games in the gym. By having students record the number of pins knocked down on every roll, you can see if students really understand scoring; misunder-

YOUR TURN 8.11

It's time for you to try your hand at designing a score sheet for middle school or senior high physical education. We suggest you choose either basketball or softball for this exercise. See if you can come up with a combination stat sheet and score sheet. You're limited only by your imagination. Bring your score sheet to class to share with others.

Badminton Score Sheet

Names of players _____

Team name _____

Points (circle the points as they are made)

   1   2   3   4   5   6   7   8   9   10   11   12

13   14   15   16   17   18   19   20   21   22   23   24

Fair-play bonus points 1 2 3 Given for _____

Names of players _____

Team name _____

Points (circle the points as they are made)

   1   2   3   4   5   6   7   8   9   10   11   12

13   14   15   16   17   18   19   20   21   22   23   24

Fair-play bonus points 1 2 3 Given for _____

Scorekeeper name (print) _____ Team _____

By signing this score sheet, I verify that the results are accurate and complete.

Signature of scorekeeper _____

Figure 8.15 Sample score sheet for badminton.

Bowling Score Sheet

Name _____ Date _____ Class period _____

Directions

As you bowl each frame, record the number of pins you knock down on each roll. Keep a running score at the bottom of each frame box. If all pins fall on the first roll of a frame, score 10 plus the fallen pins from the next two rolls. If all pins fall in a frame, score 10 plus the number of pins that fall on the next roll.

Frame 1	Frame 2	Frame 3	Frame 4	Frame 5

Frame 6	Frame 7	Frame 8	Frame 9	Frame 10

Improvement goal _____

Figure 8.16   Sample score sheet for bowling.

standings are caught right away. When a score sheet is used as formative self-assessment, students should write an improvement goal for the next game. Collect and review the score sheets after each class to see if something needs to be explained or retaught.

Summary

If you successfully completed all of the Your Turn activities in this chapter, you are well on your way to becoming an expert assessor. Once you get started, it isn't nearly as hard as you think it would be. The key to designing good checklists, logs, statistics sheets, rating scales, and score sheets is to first decide on an important purpose. Is your **recording sheet** for the purpose of formative assessment or summative assessment? How will you and your students use the information gained from the assessment?

Now that you know something about designing psychomotor assessment tools, the next step is to consider the types of tools you will need for cognitive and affective assessments (chapters 9 and 10). From there, we will move to the implementation phase of assessment in chapter 11. Take a deep breath, keep going, and remember that any new skill takes practice and time to learn.

Answers to the Your Turn Activities

►YOUR TURN 8.2 AND 8.3

What are the differences between figures 8.2 and 8.3?

1. In example 2, peer observers are looking for critical elements in three trials in a row. In example 1, students mark a response for each of three trials.
2. Example 2 uses a check mark and example 1 asks students to circle yes or no.
3. Example 2 is jump rope.
4. Example 1 is a self-assessment from a video; example 2 is a peer assessment.

What are the differences between figures 8.4 and 8.5?

1. The high school checklist is for a group of three because one person sets up the clear; the middle school checklist is for a pair.
2. In example 3, students check each element for 5 trials; in example 4, students check off each element if it's observed in 3 of the 5 trials.
3. In example 4, there is a product assessment (serve travels low over the net).
4. In example 4, students are told the assessment is not for a grade and honest feedback is stressed.
5. Example 4 shows a court instead of clip art.

NINE

Creating Assessments for the Cognitive Domain

Teachers should supply students with assessment-based descriptive feedback. Descriptive feedback indicates what students can currently do and what they need to do in order to achieve a target curricular aim or master an en-route building block related to that aim.

Popham, 2008, p. 114

LOOK FOR THESE KEY CONCEPTS

- Bloom's taxonomy
- constructed response
- performance-based assessment
- portfolio
- project
- selected response
- table of specifications

The primary goal of physical education is to teach students skills and knowledge so they can successfully participate in at least one activity that they will enjoy for a lifetime. Although this goal is centered in the psychomotor domain, cognitive knowledge is needed as well. Just as chapter 8 presents several different types of assessments for the psychomotor domain, this chapter teaches you how to develop assessments for cognitive learning. When physical educators think of assessing cognitive learning, they typically think of **written tests.** In this chapter, we plan to convince you that students need to learn a lot of cognitive concepts to master the content that you are presenting, as well as show you some of the many ways to assess this learning.

Accountability for Learning

If we go back to the premise that you want your students to have the requisite knowledge to play a game or participate in an activity effectively, then cognitive assessments are needed for *holding students accountable for learning*. Cognitive knowledge includes not only basic facts, but also the ability to apply that information. If you are verifying the application of knowledge, the best way to assess cognitive ability is to observe students while they perform the activity or play the game. However, some students understand concepts, but lack the physical skill to demonstrate their knowledge. This makes it difficult for you to verify whether students actually know the content or if they are relying on others to guide them. The solution to these latter two dilemmas is to have some type of written cognitive assessment, such as a written test or project, to document learning.

Sometimes, you must hold students accountable for knowledge before participation. In situations involving safety (e.g., archery, swimming, golf, outdoor activities), you need ways to verify student understanding of content and safety rules before they participate in the activity. In the case of game play, teachers must ensure that students know various rules before letting them play.

As part of the backward design process, you need to identify the knowledge that supports the skills that you want students to master as you start planning the unit. Let's go back to Mr. Thomas' badminton unit. What knowledge will students need to be successful while playing the game of badminton? Students need to know the rules, but more importantly, they need to know how to apply them while participating in game situations. Since the game of badminton was selected as a way to teach net/wall games, knowledge about net/wall game **tactics** is part of the content that students will be held accountable for knowing. Along with the various shots needed for playing badminton, students will also need to know when to use these skills during game play. If advanced players learn to use the smash, they need to understand how to hit the shuttle so it travels in a downward trajectory.

When determining the cognitive knowledge that you will hold students accountable for during a unit, think about the concepts that are important to success in the game or activity. While you can assess factual knowledge using traditional test questions, it is difficult to assess the application of knowledge using them. Too often, physical education written tests cover only basic facts because it is relatively easy to write questions for this type of information. Unfortunately, students often forget the facts that they memorized for the test, and they fail to learn information needed for successful participation. At this point, we make a confession and a plea: Every time we set up badminton courts for badminton units, we have to look up the court dimensions. Please don't hold students accountable for that type of information; instead, focus on meaningful concepts that you will want students to know 20 years from now.

Part of holding students accountable for learning is to challenge them to grow and improve their skills and knowledge. One way that you can challenge advanced learners is to require students to use the basic facts (e.g., terminology, rules) and apply them to solve problems associated with the activity. **Higher-level thinking** requires students to do more complex thinking, represented by levels 3 through 6 on Bloom's taxonomy (see figure 9.1).

Using **Bloom's taxonomy**, the knowledge needed for responding to these challenges requires students to go beyond memorizing the information, instead using higher level thinking skills (analysis, synthesis, or evaluation) for their responses. Figure 9.1 contains a summary of Bloom's taxonomy of learning, along with verbs that can be used to write cognitive learning outcomes.

Nontraditional Cognitive Assessment Examples

The next section presents five nontraditional assessments that we have used to assess cognitive knowledge. Read the directions for each of the assessments. Then record the type of student knowledge (see Your Turns 9.2-9.6) that it could be used to assess and the level of Bloom's taxonomy that it addresses. Remember that you are analyzing each assessment to decide what type of learning is involved and what level of Bloom's taxonomy is required. Answers for this task can be found at the end of the chapter.

Level	Examples of verbs used to write questions at this level
Knowledge: "awareness of specific facts, universals, and information; it requires remembering and the ability to recall" (Tritschler, 2000, p. 553)	Recognize, recall, identify, define
Comprehension: "the ability to interpret knowledge and to determine its implications, consequences, and effects" (Tritschler, 2000, p. 553)	Interpret, summarize, illustrate, rephrase
Application: "the ability to use knowledge and understanding in a particular concrete situation" (Tritschler, 2000, p. 553)	Apply, use, generalize, transfer, relate
Analysis: "the ability to identify the elements or parts of the whole, to see their relationships, and to structure them into some systematic arrangement or organization" (Tritschler, 2000, p. 554)	Classify, distinguish, discriminate, categorize, compare, analyze
Synthesis: "the ability to structure a whole from understanding of the relationships among specific elements or parts" (Tritschler, 2000, p. 554)	Design, formulate, plan, produce, synthesize, develop
Evaluation: "the ability to form judgments with respect to the value of information" (Tritschler, 2000, p. 555)	Judge, assess, argue, appraise

Figure 9.1   Summary of Bloom's taxonomy of cognitive learning.

YOUR TURN 9.1

Study the six levels and their definitions in Bloom's taxonomy of cognitive learning (see figure 9.1). Then see if you can identify the correct level of Bloom's taxonomy for each of the questions in the following table. If you need to reread Cinderella's story, please look it up on the Internet or in a book.

Question	Level of Bloom's taxonomy
Who helped Cinderella prepare to attend the ball?	
How did the prince know that he had found Cinderella?	
Why did Cinderella's wicked stepmother make her work so hard?	
Why did the prince want to dance with Cinderella?	
Why didn't Cinderella's stepsisters want to help her?	
Do you think that Cinderella lost her shoe on purpose?	
If Cinderella hadn't lost her shoe, how could the prince have found her?	
If you were Cinderella's stepsister, how would you have helped her?	

YOUR TURN 9.2

Scouting the Competition in Badminton

Assessment Task

Today you are going to analyze the people whom you will play next. Watch their game. Ask yourself a series of questions that will help you play smarter when you face off against them. Here are some questions you might want to start with, but feel free to create and answer your own.

- What are their strengths?
- What type of shots might they be vulnerable to?
- What type of serve should you use for each person?
- What will be your strategy for defeating them (up and back, side by side, switching)?

Remember, badminton is not always won by the most skilled players; it is often won by those who play the smartest.

Types of knowledge that the assessment addresses	Level of Bloom's taxonomy

YOUR TURN 9.3

Announcing the Game

Assessment Task

You are seeking employment as a basketball game announcer. To demonstrate your knowledge of the rules and game tactics, your future employer has asked you to create a script for 8 minutes of basketball play. Be sure to include comments on several rules such as the 10-second rule, lane violations, and double dribble. Additionally you should describe the plays that you are watching during the game and the offense or defense used to counteract them. Go ahead and have some fun with this assignment, but remember that the person with the best knowledge of the game will get the job.

Types of knowledge that the assessment addresses	Level of Bloom's taxonomy

YOUR TURN 9.4

Magazine Assignment

Assessment Task

You and a group of friends have a great idea for a new magazine about sport or fitness. The acquisitions editor is requesting a sample of your magazine to see what it will look like in print. For the mock copy of the magazine, your group of six will need to do the following:

- Create a title for the magazine.
- Write a mission statement to clarify what the magazine will feature.
- Identify your editors:
  - Managing editor (someone who oversees the operation; the teacher's contact with your group; this person organizes meetings, sets deadlines, keeps production rolling, and so on)
  - Layout editor (makes sure it is printed in correct format)
  - Copy editor (someone who proofreads copy for grammatical errors, form accuracy, and accurate information)
  - Advertising editor (person who writes and creates ads for your mock issue)
  - Artistic editor (person who adds artwork, such as drawings, clip art, and pictures, to make the publication interesting to read)
  - Miscellaneous editor (your choice on this one—could be in charge of humor, special events, meaningful dates for the readers, and so on)
- Create at least six advertisements (each person in the group writes an ad). The product should be compatible with and support the mission of the magazine. Be sure to indicate which person in the group wrote each ad.
- Each person in your group writes an article for the magazine. The articles should all be on the same theme or topic (e.g., badminton, swimming, golf, fitness). Articles must cite research (at least five sources from publications, not the web). Information from the class is a key part of the article. Be

(continued)

(continued)

sure to include some of the information that you learned in class. Each article will be five or six pages typed and double spaced, using 12-point font and 1-inch (2.5 cm) margins.

- Create the magazine, complete with interesting or enticing covers, artwork, ads, articles, a letter from the editor, and other characteristics of a good magazine. Develop an attractive cover with the title of your magazine on it.

Note: This assessment could be shared with an English teacher who will grade it for writing and grammar, while the physical education teacher assesses it for content.

Types of knowledge that the assessment addresses	Level of Bloom's taxonomy

YOUR TURN 9.5

Task Card Assignment

Assessment Task

Create a task card that illustrates the critical elements of a volleyball overhand serve.

1. Identify the critical elements (limit these to no more than six) important to the serve.
2. Use a photo to illustrate each critical element being performed correctly.
3. Label the photos and critical elements.

Types of knowledge that the assessment addresses	Level of Bloom's taxonomy

YOUR TURN 9.6

Dance Assessment

Assessment Task

Create a personal warm-up based on safe practices for a specific dance genre (e.g., ballet, modern, cultural or folk dance, hip hop). Compare this warm-up to one that you would use for an invasion game (e.g., soccer, basketball, lacrosse, net ball) and explain why the warm-ups for the two activities would differ.

Types of knowledge that the assessment addresses	Level of Bloom's taxonomy

It is important to think about the information that an assessment will provide. Too often, teachers pick up assessments at a conference or online and then use them, giving little thought to what they need to assess or the information that the assessment can provide. Before we go further, we want you to identify the cognitive information that students must know in an activity. You can use our badminton unit or one of your own choosing. As you go through the cognitive assessments in this chapter, look for types of assessment that you could use to assess whether your students have learned the important concepts that you intended them to learn.

YOUR TURN 9.7

List some of the things that Mr. Thomas would want his students to know when he taught the badminton unit. If you are unfamiliar with badminton, choose another sport or activity and write down the important content that you want to assess.

Performance-Based Assessments

Remember that if written tests are used to assess knowledge about a sport or activity, they are actually only an indirect measure of applied learning. Whereas written tests provide a way to assess content knowledge (e.g., naming the rules, history of the game, name of the shot or skill), the written test is not the best measure of whether students can apply this knowledge in a game or activity. As you can see by the examples presented in the previous section, you can use a variety of assessments to hold students accountable for cognitive learning. A **performance-based assessment** can directly measure applied knowledge if it is well conceived and if the rubric targets the appropriate behaviors. According to Lund and Kirk (2010), the characteristics of performance-based assessments are as follows:

- Require the presentation of worthwhile or meaningful tasks that are representative of performance in the field.
- Emphasize higher-level thinking and more complex learning.
- Articulate criteria in advance so that students know how they will be assessed.

- Embed assessments so firmly in the lesson and the curriculum that they are practically indistinguishable from instruction.
- Expect students to present their work publicly when possible.
- Involve the examination of process as well as the products of learning.

We discuss three types of performance-based assessments: projects, portfolios, and performances. In the next section let's begin by exploring these assessment options for cognitive learning.

Projects

Student **projects** are excellent ways to assess application of knowledge; thus, they require students to use higher levels of thinking. They are typically complex and require more skills than just writing. For example, the magazine project shown in the previous section requires students to write a paper about a topic (synthesis) and assess other student papers using a rubric (evaluation). Projects typically take several days to complete. Students will need to complete a portion of the assessment out of class as homework. Another project might require students to create a brochure that informs people about a topic (synthesis). For example, one teacher required students to take notes in class on various facts presented during a heart obstacle course activity and then to develop a brochure for parents to demonstrate their understanding about the functions of the heart. To demonstrate knowledge about cancer causes, early warning signs, and prevention and treatment, another teacher had students in a health class develop a brochure about cancer in their community. They then handed their brochures out during a cancer awareness exhibit at the local mall. Students might show their knowledge of dance choreography by writing a critique of a dance performance after viewing a video or watching a group perform in class (evaluation). Another assessment that we have used required students to scout the competition to demonstrate their knowledge of game-play tactics (see example in a previous section), assess their own skills, and then develop a strategy for defeating that team when playing them in the class tournament (synthesis). You might also have students keep score for a sporting event on television and write a summary or critique using content knowledge from a physical education class to assess the performance (analysis).

Table 9.1 shows some ideas for projects to use as cognitive assessments. Please feel free to add others as you develop new assessments for the cognitive domain.

Portfolios

A **portfolio** is a collection of selected artifacts that shows student growth over time. During the course of the unit, students complete a variety of documents and assessments (artifacts) as they develop competence in the sport or activity. If the goal of the unit was to document learning over time (e.g., I started out here and look what I can do now), then portfolios are useful. With portfolios, specify a few (2 or 3) artifacts that students must include. Students are then allowed to select a few more artifacts (3 or 4) that will demonstrate how they have met the learning outcomes for the unit or class. Teachers should

Table 9.1   Projects for Cognitive Assessment

Type of project	Use to assess
PowerPoint presentation	Rules, history of the activity, knowledge of basic facts and information
Script for announcer or emcee	Knowledge of the activity, history, and rules
Script for a gymnastics meet announcer	Interesting details about the history of the gymnastics, how to score, critical elements of events
Analysis of video performance	Knowledge of correct form; how to improve performance (e.g., relay hand-off, diving, or gymnastics skills)
Critique of a dance performance	Knowledge of dance choreography elements
Brochure	Knowledge about fitness or activity
Dialogue about a concept (e.g. two people discussing or talking; could use avatars)	Understanding of a concept, best way to condition or prepare for an activity
Magazine assignment	Knowledge of fitness; knowledge of various activities; types of dance, history of activity
Create a video	Knowledge of correct form; knowledge of combinations of skills; knowledge about dance choreography
Task cards (use still photos or cells from a video)	Knowledge of critical elements of skills
Teaching others (live or video, could also use avatars)	Knowledge of rules, how to perform skills (critical elements), activity
Wikipedia submission	History of the activity; discussion of rules
Teach younger students how to play a game	Critical elements, correct technique, rules of the game

 YOUR TURN 9.8

Identify three projects that you could use to assess *cognitive learning* for the unit you are developing.

Project idea	What it will assess

require a sufficient number of artifacts so that students will be able to demonstrate their learning, but not so many that grading the portfolios becomes a burden. For each artifact included in the portfolio, students are required to write a reflection explaining what the artifact represents and, in the case of the student-selected artifact, why this particular document was selected over others. Students must learn to be selective and submit the artifacts that best demonstrate their growth or knowledge. For additional information about portfolio development, see Lund and Kirk (2010). Table 9.2 shows possible artifacts for a physical education portfolio.

Performances

Not all measures of cognitive learning require students to write a response to something. You could use a rubric to guide the assessment of game-play tactics or rules knowledge during game play (see figure 4.2). You could also create a rubric to assess student officials' knowledge of game play. Table 9.3 provides a summary of various types of tools that could be used to assess knowledge of or application of skills, tactics, or rules for game play.

When teaching game play, the **game performance assessment instrument (GPAI)** lets you record students' ability to make correct decisions about using the correct skill, note whether students are using the appropriate tactic, or indicate that students are using correct form when executing the various skills during game play. Figure 9.2 is a generic example of a GPAI recording sheet.

The GPAI is excellent for providing feedback to students about how well they are doing relative to the skill or tactic being observed. When using it

Table 9.2   Possible Artifacts for a Physical Education Portfolio

Artifact	Knowledge it will demonstrate
PowerPoint presentation of rules	Understanding of rules; comprehension of rules
Formative and summative assessments of rules or learning	Understanding of rules and basic facts about the game
Study guides created to explain tactics	Knowledge of tactics and analysis of how to utilize them in game play
Plays developed for a coach's playbook	Knowledge of game-play tactics and ways to defend or play against them
Personal fitness prescription	Understanding of fitness elements and how to improve
Diagram of a gymnastics routine choreographed for class	Knowledge about the elements of good choreography
Goals for learning indicating which ones had been achieved	Analysis of own abilities and evaluation of whether they had been met
Stretching routine developed for work at home and log showing days that it was used	Knowledge of flexibility

YOUR TURN 9.9

In the unit you are developing, what other types of artifacts for portfolios could your students use to demonstrate learning in the *cognitive domain*? Think about the types of written assignments you might use for your unit.

Description of the artifact	Cognitive knowledge that the artifact demonstrates

Table 9.3   Tools Used to Assess Knowledge of or Application of Skills, Tactics, or Rules for Game Play

Knowledge of rules	Application of rules
Written essay test	Game play (rubric)
PowerPoint presentation	Analysis of video
Exit slips	Officiating
Dialogue with avatars	Announcing a game
Wikipedia submission	Teaching others or coaching
Knowledge of tactics	**Application of tactics**
Write a coach's playbook	Game play (rubric)
Written test	Game performance assessment instrument (GPAI)
PowerPoint presentation	Announcing a game
Exit slip	Teaching others or coaching
Dialogue using avatars	
Knowledge of skills and correct form	**Application of skills**
Written test	Game-play rubric
Exit slip	GPAI
Announcing a game	Announcing a game
Instructional video	

to observe members of a team, you would observe one person until possession of the ball changes. For example, the observer records whether the player has made correct decisions about when to use game-play skills. When change of possession occurs, the observer selects one player from the other team and makes observations about the correct use of skill. At the change of possession, a different player from the first team is observed until possession changes. The observer systematically rotates through the players on the teams until each player has been observed one time. The observation rotation begins again with the first player observed, and players are all assessed a second or even a third time. At the conclusion of the game or observation session, members of the team are given their scores; thus, they receive feedback so that they can see whether they have made correct decisions during the game. The GPAI is an excellent way to provide formative feedback to teams or individual players about their performances. If the GPAI is used as a graded or summative assessment, a means to calculate a score must be added. Several of these systems are quite complex. The authors suggest the *Teaching Sport Concepts and Skills, 3rd edition* (Mitchell, Oslin, & Griffin, 2013) for in-depth information about using the GPAI and for information on how to use it as a summative assessment.

Written Tests

Written tests are probably the most common assessment tool that teachers use for assessing cognitive domain knowledge. Although good written tests take some time to develop, they are easy to score and are a good way to assess basic facts and content knowledge. Written tests in physical education typically consist of questions about history, game tactics, rules of a game and scoring, player positions and responsibilities, etiquette and safety, and knowledge of critical elements. When developing test questions, teachers must first determine the body of knowledge that they wish to assess.

Two categories of questions are found on most written tests in physical education: selected response and constructed response. **Selected response** questions require students to *select the right answer* from a list of options. Some examples of selected response questions are multiple choice, true–false, and matching. In addition, *classification questions* are a good way to see if students understand the differences between similar elements. *Rearrangement questions* ask students to put elements in order, such as the steps used in the bowling delivery. In **constructed response** questions, students *create the answers*. Common types of constructed response questions are essay,

Game Performance Assessment Instrument (GPAI)

Class: _First period_   Evaluator: _Ms. Smith_

Team: _Gray foxes_   Game: _Soccer_

Observation date: _10/10/11_

Components and Criteria

1. Decision making
   a. Student attempts to pass to an open teammate.
   b. Student attempts to shoot when appropriate.
2. Skill execution
   a. Reception: Student is able to control the pass.
   b. Pass: Ball reaches the intended target.
   c. Dribble: Student controls ball and adjusts and moves position.
3. Support
   a. Students attempt to move into position to receive a pass from teammates (i.e., forward toward goal).

GPAI Score Sheet

Name	Decision making		Skill execution		Support	
	Appropriate	Inappropriate	Efficient	Inefficient	Appropriate	Inappropriate
LaTonya	XXX	XX	XX	XXX	XXXXX	XX
Steven	X	XXXX	XX	XXX	X	XXX
Rashaad	XXXXX		XXX	XX	XXXXX	X
Sophia	XX	XXX	XX	XXX	X	XXX
Yoshie	XXXX	XX	XX	XX	XXXX	X
Nicholas	XXXXXX		XXX	X	XXXXXX	X
Jeffrey	X	XXXX	XXX	X	XXX	XX
Shameka	XXX	X	XX	XX	XXXX	X

Figure 9.2   GPAI template.

Adapted from Mitchell, Oslin, and Griffin 2006.

short answer, listing, and fill in the blank. Another type is called a **Venn diagram**, which can be used when you want students to compare two activities and look for common elements that those activities share. Examples are provided in the next sections.

Multiple-Choice Questions

The two parts to a multiple-choice question are the preliminary statement, called the *stem,* and the possible responses, which will include the correct answer and the incorrect answers, called **distracters.** Questions should be written so they let you know if students have mastered the content; if they have not, the questions should help you diagnose errors or student misunderstandings. As a variation of traditional multiple choice questions, some teachers use best-answer questions in which one choice is preferable, but other questions have a degree of correctness; strategy and skill questions work well for this variation. Table 9.4 demonstrates some important dos and don'ts to guide you when writing multiple-choice questions.

Table 9.4 Dos and Don'ts for Writing Multiple-Choice Questions

Do	Do not
• Use age-appropriate words.	• Do not use negatives in both the stem and distracters.
• Keep the style consistent (same length, verb tense).	• Avoid absolute terms (always, never, only, all, none).
• Bold, underline, or use all CAPS to highlight critical words or draw student attention to some words.	• Avoid using "all of the above" and "none of the above" responses.
• The stem should consist of a positive statement.	• Avoid distracters that are not feasible; use the distracters to diagnose possible student misunderstandings.
• Keep the distracters and answers short.	• Limit the use of "which is not" type questions.
• Keep the stem as short as possible; it should be longer than the distracters.	• Don't ask for the students' opinion or what they think. Every distracter could be correct.
• Distribute correct answers (equal number of A, B, C, D, E responses).	• Correct answers should have no pattern of selection (e.g., 1 = A; 2 = B, 3 = C, 4 = D, 5 = E. 6 = A, and so on).
• There should be four or more answer choices.	• Avoid distracters that have little difference between them.
• Provide one and only one correct answer.	• The stem should not give a clue to the answer to some other test question; each item should be independent.

 YOUR TURN 9.10

Look at the following multiple-choice questions and indicate which questions are well written and which ones violate one of the guidelines in table 9.4. Place a check mark (√) beside the well-written questions.

1. Portfolio assessments are designed to do the following:
   a. Show growth over time
   b. Allow students to demonstrate creativity
   c. Give parents the opportunity to help their child complete an assignment
   d. Give students homework and thus extend the time allocated for physical education

2. Multiple-choice questions are an example of the following:
   a. Performance-based assessments
   b. Selected-response assessments
   c. Projects
   d. Constructed-response assessments

3. Performance-based assessments:
   a. Always require students to use higher-order thinking skills to complete
   b. Require students to use skills frequently utilized by professionals in a real-world setting
   c. Are a superior form of assessment to written tests
   d. Are much easier to develop and score

4. Bloom's taxonomy does not include which of the following types of thinking?
   a. Analysis
   b. Synthesis
   c. Comprehension
   d. Critical thinking

YOUR TURN 9.11

Develop three multiple-choice questions based on information in this chapter for the activity selected for your project. In class, trade with a partner and place a check mark (√) beside each well-written question. If your instructor allows time, put a well-written question on the board for others in the class to review and discuss.

True–False Questions

True–false questions can be constructed and graded relatively quickly; therefore, they are popular with teachers. The problem with true–false questions is that students can guess the correct answer about half the time. Therefore, when using this type of question, we suggest requiring students to correct the false statement so that you can determine if they know why the statement is false (called *correctable true–false questions*). When using this type of true–false question, the correction must actually change a word. It is not acceptable to simply add the word *not* to the phrase. Another way that you can discourage students from guessing is by subtracting the number of incorrect responses from the number of correct responses. When scoring the test, score items left blank by the student as wrong, but do not subtract them from the number correct.

Let's consider some sample questions in figure 9.3. Question 1 is true. Question 2 is false, and it can be corrected by crossing out "constructed" and adding the word *selected*. Question 3 is false. Making the correction will force students to think, since it is insufficient to simply change "unlimited" to *limited*. One way to change question 3 is to cross out "submit unlimited" and write in *select 2 or 3*. Question 4 is true.

Follow these guidelines for writing true–false questions:

- Include roughly the same number of true and false statements.
- Don't create a pattern with the answers.
- Require students to correct false statements.

Matching Questions

Matching questions are useful for assessing knowledge of definitions and rules. When writing matching questions, place the statement in the left-hand column and the list of possible answers in the right-hand column. Number the statements in the left-hand column and leave a blank in front of the number so that students have a place to record the answer. Make sure that there are more possible answers than question statements so that students won't be able to eliminate responses and then guess at the last few questions that they don't know. Be sure that there are multiple possible answers for each statement on the left (e.g., at least two different dates if asking that type of question); you want to test students' knowledge, not their ability to take a test.

Directions

If the statement is true, circle the *T*. If the statement is false, circle the *F* and make a correction. Cross out a word or phrase and add a word or phrase to make it true. Simply adding *not* is unacceptable. False statements that are not corrected will be marked wrong.

T	F	1. A written test is an excellent way to preassess students about safety rules.
T	F	2. True–false questions are an example of constructed-response questions.
T	F	3. Teachers should allow students to submit unlimited artifacts when using portfolios.
T	F	4. If a rubric is not aligned with the intent of an assessment, teachers will be unable to make valid inferences about student learning.

Figure 9.3 Sample true–false questions.

Use the following guidelines in writing matching questions:

- The content in a set of matching questions should be homogeneous.
- All questions in the matching section should be together on one page.
- Include more responses than items to be matched.
- The longer part of the question should be in the left-hand column.
- The response (shorter part) should be in the right-hand column.
- Use capital letters for the distracters so that students won't make a *b* that looks like a *d* and vice versa; sometimes the letter *c* can look like an *e*.
- Alphabetize the answers (right-hand column) to make them easier to find.

Figure 9.4 shows an example of good matching questions.

Classification Questions

Classification questions are a type of matching question with fewer choices. Each choice is used more than once. This type of item lends itself to assessing the ability to organize information and understand the relationship of small items to larger concepts. The list of classifications is usually given at the top. Consider the example in figure 9.5.

Rearrangement Questions

This type of selected-response question emphasizes the order of things. The steps provided should be well scrambled. An error in the sequence means a missed question. This type of analysis question requires that students understand a movement process, so it can be valuable in activities that occur in a step-by-step sequence. Here are some hints for rearrangement questions:

- Make sure that the directions for completion are clear.
- Use capital letters.
- Scramble the responses in a random order.

Figure 9.6 shows an example of a rearrangement question.

Constructed Response Questions

Fill-in-the-blank questions are used to assess students' ability to recall specific terms or rules. They are also useful for assessing student comprehension of a topic. In Bloom's taxonomy, fill-in-the-blank questions are lower-level questions, so use them deliberately only when it is important that students be able to recall specific information as opposed to recognizing a term or definition.

Directions

For each of the items in the left-hand column, select a response from the right-hand column that is the best match. Write the letter of the response in the blank to the left of the number.

_____ 1. True–false questions	A.	Artifact
_____ 2. The criteria used for assessing the quality of a response	B.	Cognitive domain
	C.	Constructed response
_____ 3. An item chosen for inclusion in a portfolio	D.	GPAI
_____ 4. A type of assessment used to assess decision making during games	E.	Psychomotor domain
	F.	Rubric
_____ 5. Short-answer questions	G.	Selected response
	H.	Tactic

Figure 9.4 Example of matching questions.

Directions

Classify the activities below as primarily either *(a)* aerobic or *(b)* anaerobic.

_____ 1. Swimming
_____ 2. Gymnastics
_____ 3. Tennis
_____ 4. Jogging
_____ 5. Softball
_____ 6. Cycling
_____ 7. Soccer

Figure 9.5 Example of a classification item.

Directions

Arrange the following steps in the bowling delivery by writing the letters in the following space in the correct order. What happens first should be 1 and what happens last should be 5.

_____ 1.   A.   Pendulum swing
_____ 2.   B.   Follow-through
_____ 3.   C.   Preparation stance
_____ 4.   D.   Slide and release
_____ 5.   E.   Push away

Figure 9.6 Example of a rearrangement item.

Suggestions for writing fill-in-the-blank questions include the following:

- When writing your questions, make sure that the omitted words or phrase don't make the question impossible for students to answer.
- Grading the responses is easier if you leave a blank on the side of the number for writing the answer.
- Leave adequate space for writing the answer.

- Be sure that the stem has enough words to point students toward the content that you are trying to assess.

Figure 9.7 shows an example of a fill-in-the-blank question.

Listing questions also require that students recall specific information, such as rules, player positions, or courtesy behaviors. Because students are required to write out answers, listing questions are time consuming to administer. Because of the time it takes to write answers, listing questions are not used as often as other formats. The

Directions

For each of the following questions, write in the answer that best completes the statement to make it a true statement. Some of the blanks will require a single word, while others will require multiple words.

_____ 1. A _____ is used to assess growth over time.
_____ 2. Using a rubric to assess game play is an example of a _____.
_____ 3. The _____ domain is associated with student knowledge and thinking.
_____ 4. In Bloom's taxonomy, _____ is the ability to interpret knowledge and determine its implications, consequences, and efforts.

Answers

Note that a teacher would not include the answers on a student test.

1. Portfolio
2. Performance-based assessment
3. Cognitive
4. Comprehension

Figure 9.7 Examples of fill-in-the-blank questions.

same information assessed in listing questions can be tested in a much more efficient manner.

Short-answer questions are the most common types of constructed-response questions used in physical education. Short answer format allows you to ask questions that require students to use higher-level thinking skills, such as evaluation and synthesis, in responses. Short answer questions that require higher-level thinking often reveal misconceptions and errors about a topic. It is fairly easy to assess the lower level of Bloom's taxonomy using selected-response questions, so we suggest that you use constructed-response questions to assess higher levels of student thinking. One important consideration with short answer questions is that they can be written in a short amount of time, but they are extremely time intensive to grade. Figure 9.8 shows an example of short answer questions.

In addition to fill-in-the-blank and essay questions, physical education teachers might want to use some constructed-response questions with a special format. Venn diagrams allow students to demonstrate their ability to compare and contrast information or identify similarities and differences between two concepts. For example, identify the ways that net sports such as volleyball and tennis are different and similar. What is unique about each one? (See figure 9.9.)

Sometimes you may want to make sure that students know certain terminology, such as the names of the lines on the court or field or the names of the parts of various types of equipment. Figure 9.10 is an example of another special

---

Directions

For each of the questions, write a paragraph or more to respond to the prompt.

1. Explain why teachers should use formative assessments.
2. Discuss one advantage and one disadvantage of using short answer questions on an assessment.
3. Identify whether you would use short answer questions and provide a rationale for your response.

Figure 9.8 Examples of short answer questions.

Directions

In the middle circle, list three similarities between tennis and volleyball skills. On the outside lines, list three unique skills for each sport that are not found in the other.

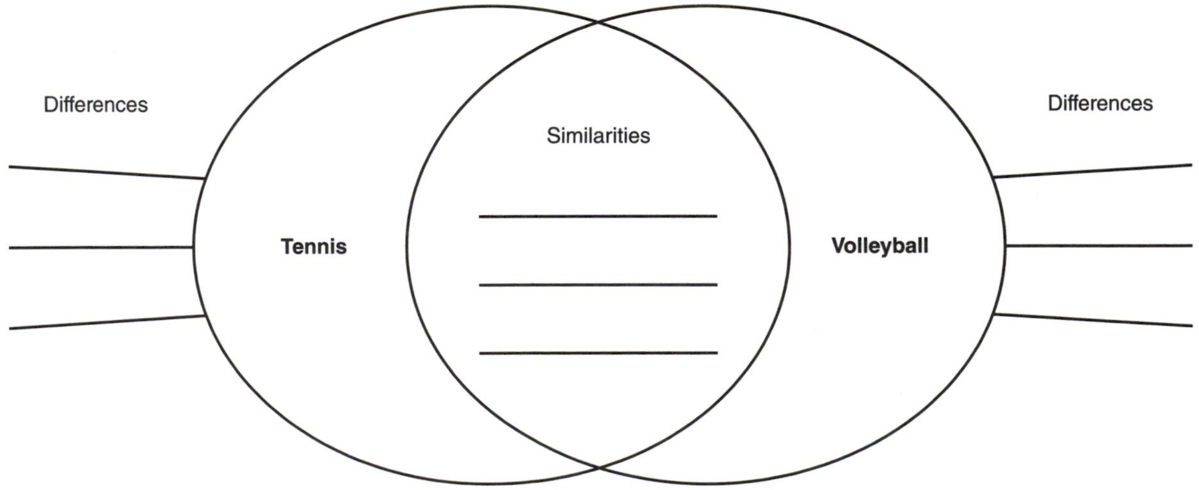

Differences   Differences

Similarities

Tennis   Volleyball

Figure 9.9 Special format question: Venn diagram.

Directions

Label the lines on the badminton court diagram.

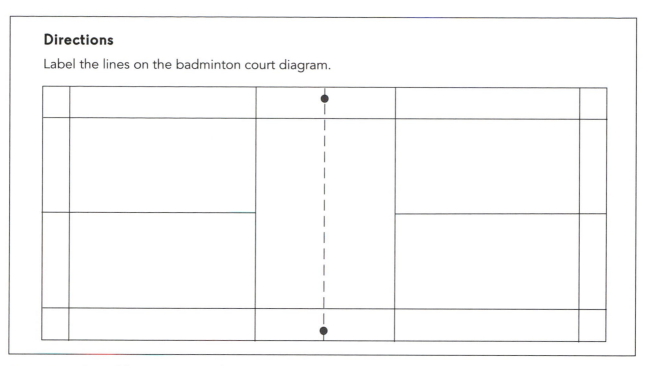

Figure 9.10   Special format question: diagram.

format question that could be used to assess that information.

General Guidelines for Creating Written Tests

When composing written tests, balance the type of content and the number of questions for each area. The areas of information should be assigned proportional weights to parallel the amount of instructional time spent on each area. A **table of specifications** is used to plan a good written test. The percentage of questions in each area depends on how much of the unit was spent on each content area. For example: You want to design a beginning-level knowledge test of 30 questions, so you have to decide how many questions of each content area should be written. If 25 percent of the questions are on rules, multiply

$30 \times .25 = 8$ questions. A teacher used this logic to create the table of specifications shown in table 9.5. Remember the following points about composing a written test:

- Questions need to be **developmentally appropriate** for the age of the students.
- Balance the number of questions with the time spent on each content area.
- If the content area is assessed with other types of assessments, decrease the emphasis of that area on the written test.
- Teachers with advanced test writing skills will use Bloom's taxonomy to analyze the level of cognitive function required by each test question.
- Tests developed for beginner level students usually include items predominately at the

Table 9.5   Table of Specifications for a High School Written Test

Content area	Percent of time	Number of items = 30
Rules and terms	25%	8
Skills and techniques	40%	12
Safety	10%	3
Tactics and strategy	15%	5
History	10%	2

lower levels of knowledge, comprehension, and application.

- Tests for students with advanced knowledge usually have fewer items at lower levels and more items at the higher levels of analysis, synthesis, and evaluation.

- The higher the item is on the taxonomy scale, the more difficult it is to construct.

- Longer tests tend to give more stable results than short ones.

- On average, multiple-choice items require about 30 to 45 seconds to complete; a 50-item multiple-choice test takes about 35 to 40 minutes to complete, on average.

- Other alternative selected-response items take about 30 seconds to complete.

- Include the directions for answering the questions at the top of the set of questions.

- Group items by format and content (e.g., all multiple-choice questions together).

- At the top of the test, include a place for students to record their names, the date of the test, and class period.

- If you staple the test on the right-hand corner, you won't cut off words, which sometimes happens with tests that are stapled on the left-hand corner.

Stay green. When using multiple-choice questions, remember that it take lots of paper to print copies of the test. To save paper, we suggest that you duplicate enough copies of the test for your largest class and then number the tests with a permanent marker and reuse them in each class. Give students a copy of the test and an answer sheet and tell them not to write on the test. On the answer sheet, they write identifying information (name, class period, date, and the number of the test used) and the answers to the test. Be sure to check through the tests and erase any marks that students made before reusing it.

With selected response questions, scantron sheets can be used for faster grading. Put the scantron sheets through a machine to grade them. You will receive a report of the frequency that the various questions were answered incorrectly. You can go back and analyze questions to see if any were poorly written. You don't need to use the scantron sheets; you can create your own answer sheets. This practice will save a lot of paper over the years, which your administrators will appreciate. Using a single-page answer sheet also saves you time when grading exams because you don't have to flip through multiple pages for each student's test.

Many teachers think that written questions are superior to other types of assessment because they are objective. Although selected-response questions are objective (meaning that two teachers could grade the test exactly the same way), they do have an element of subjectivity that isn't always recognized. The selection of content for the test and the wording of the questions is very subjective. The teacher decides which information is important and which information to hold students accountable for. Since in writing the test, teachers determine the content that will be assessed, this part of the process is subjective. Secondly, the teacher decides question format: multiple choice, true–false, matching, essay. Some types of questions are easier to study for than others. All assessments have some degree of subjectivity; they simply will differ as to where this subjectivity occurs.

Written tests provide a fast, easy way to assess basic knowledge; they are useful when assessing large classes. Selected-response questions require more time to write, but they are easier to grade. Good questions require a lot of time and thinking to develop, especially if you use the questions to diagnose student errors or misunderstandings. Constructed-response questions allow you to assess higher levels of thinking, but they will also take you more time to grade.

Errors to Avoid When Assessing Cognitive Learning

Avoid these common pitfalls in creating cognitive assessments:

- Cognitive domain assessments frequently consist solely of written tests composed of selected-response questions (e.g., multiple choice, matching, true–false) and maybe one or two essay questions. While there is nothing wrong with those types of assessments, the problem is with the content of the questions. If the test focuses only on facts about the history of the game (e.g., What year was volleyball invented? Who created basketball?), terminology (e.g., What is this part of the tennis racket called [diagram included]? The strong downward stroke used in badminton is called a smash [T/F].), court dimensions (e.g., How wide is a tennis doubles court?), process elements of a skill (e.g., What are the critical elements of the badminton serve?) or basic rules (e.g., A penalty kick in soccer is worth one point [T/F]. A shot made from behind the 3-point line is always worth 3 points [T/F]), then much relevant and important content is not assessed. These questions all focus on factual information, which is important, but should not be the only goal of cognitive learning in physical education. Too often, teachers ask questions about information that is of minor importance.

• Another common error occurs when teachers prepare a one- or two-page handout for students and then hold them accountable for memorizing the contents of the handout for the test. While basic rules are important to the game, this latter practice fails to hold students accountable for all the knowledge presented during the unit.

• When teachers give only summative assessments, they miss the opportunity both to provide feedback to students and to check for student understanding during the activity. After the completion of instruction, teachers cannot go back and correct errors in student learning. We understand that giving written tests detracts from activity time. However, formative assessments give teachers valuable information needed to reteach unlearned content and thus enhance student learning.

• Aligning assessments with what you intend to assess seems to be a no-brainer. However, we frequently see teachers misusing assessments by using an assessment for something other than the content they are trying to hold students accountable for learning. If you are unsure about the alignment of an assessment to the content presented in class, ask a colleague or another teacher in the district for an opinion. If an assessment is to be useful to you to determine how much your students really did learn, it must align with the intended content and learning outcomes.

• Often, standards specify the level of student learning. Think of Bloom's taxonomy, discussed earlier in this chapter. Using the wrong verb on the assessment may create a mismatch with the intent of the standard. For example, if the standard requires you to assess student ability to analyze knowledge, but you ask only factual questions, you are not meeting the intent of the standard that your content addresses. We encourage you to look at not only the content covered in an assessment, but also the type of learning indicated in the standard. Remember, the standard represents a minimal level of learning. It is okay to go above the level specified; it is not okay to go below that level.

Frequency of Cognitive Assessments

Ideally, you will assess cognitive domain knowledge every day. Realistically, that probably won't happen. A strategy that some teachers use is to provide cognitive knowledge each day (after all, that is your job!), but then hold students accountable for this knowledge every three to five days with a quiz or some type of assignment. If you use projects, portfolios, or some other type of long-term assessment (e.g., requires students several days to complete and work outside of normal class time), hold students accountable with another type of written assessment (e.g., exit slip or short quiz) every few days as a way to check for understanding to ensure that students are not acquiring any incomplete or incorrect knowledge. Teachers should state the cognitive learning outcome on the lesson plan and then indicate that the knowledge will be assessed at a later date with a specific type of assessment (e.g., the student will demonstrate knowledge of the basic rules of pickleball by scoring at least 70 percent on a written test given in lesson 4).

Setting the Level of Competence

The question of how high to set the bar is a little difficult to answer. Many school districts use 70 percent and above as the cut score, below which is failing. However, if the questions are very simple (e.g., Who invented basketball?), the required percentage should be much higher. On the other end of the spectrum, some teachers like to see how difficult they can make tests and how many questions students can get wrong. With our mastery approach to learning, both of these approaches to cognitive knowledge assessments are fraught with problems. Our goal is to have students master the information that they need to play the game, do the dance, or perform the activity with competence. A certain body of knowledge is needed, not just terminology and knowledge of basic rules, but also information important to executing game play tactics and improving the quality of performance. We should strive to help students learn everything that they need to go out and participate with confidence. Set the level of achievement so that you ensure this level of competence for your students.

Summary

This chapter presents a variety of ways to assess cognitive domain learning. As with learning a skill, practicing your cognitive assessment abilities will make you better at doing this type of assessment. We encourage you to be adventurous and try some of the alternative assessment formats suggested in this chapter. However, remember that written tests can be fast and efficient ways to assess the factual knowledge that is the springboard for higher levels of learning.

YOUR TURN 9.12

Here are the cognitive learning outcomes from chapter 7. Create an assessment for each listing the *who* (administers the test), *what* (type of assessment given), and *when* (to give the assessment).

Learning outcome	Who	What	When
Students will demonstrate their knowledge of badminton rules by scoring 70% or better on a multiple-choice test.			
Students will demonstrate knowledge about the tactics of hitting to an open space by identifying that maneuver on a video clip of class play.			
Students will demonstrate knowledge of badminton rules by creating a PowerPoint presentation written in the student's own words (not copied from a rule book).			
Students will demonstrate knowledge of an offensive tactic by correctly explaining it on a YouTube video.			
Students will demonstrate knowledge of the rules of a game by receiving a 2 or better on the game-play rubric.			
The student will demonstrate knowledge of defensive tactics by writing on an exit slip a correct way to cover the court.			

Answers to the Your Turn Activities

⟳ YOUR TURN 9.2

Type of knowledge that the assessment addresses	Level of Bloom's taxonomy
Knowledge of the types of shots	Knowledge
Self-evaluation of own strengths and areas needing more work	Evaluation
Analysis of game-play needs	Analysis
Ability to evaluate others	Evaluation
Game-play tactics (application knowledge)	Application
Ability to design a strategy	Synthesis

⟳ YOUR TURN 9.3

Knowledge assessed	Level of Bloom's taxonomy
Knowledge of rules	Knowledge
Knowledge of tactics	Knowledge
Interpretation of rules	Comprehension
Interpretation of tactics	Comprehension

⟳ YOUR TURN 9.4

Knowledge assessed	Level of Bloom's taxonomy
History of a sport or activity	Knowledge
Understanding about a sport or activity	Comprehension
Understanding about how to participate in a sport or activity	Comprehension

⟳ YOUR TURN 9.5

Knowledge assessed	Level of Bloom's taxonomy
Critical elements of a skill	Knowledge
Understanding of what the critical elements should look like	Comprehension

⟳ YOUR TURN 9.6

Knowledge assessed	Level of Bloom's taxonomy
Principles of a good warm-up	Knowledge
Difference between demands of dance and a sport or activity	Analysis
Knowledge of different muscles used in dance and a sport or activity	Knowledge

TEN

Creating Assessments for the Affective Domain

Because a student's affective dispositions can have an enormous impact on that student's life, educators who fail to promote an appropriate affect for their students are falling down on a significant educational responsibility.

Popham, 2010, p. 2

As we stated earlier in this book, if you assess something, students will perceive it as important. We believe this to be just as true for the affective domain as it is for the psychomotor and cognitive domains. The **affective domain** encompasses the feelings, attitudes, and **dispositions** that students have toward something; in this book, that "something" involves participating in physical education while demonstrating responsible personal and social behavior (NASPE standard 5) and understanding that physical activity provides opportunities for enjoyment, challenge, self-expression, and social interaction (NASPE standard 6). As chapter 1 shows, many physical education teachers also see the affective domain as an important part of NASPE standard 3, which states that students should demonstrate a physically active lifestyle. If students learn approach tendencies to subject matter and find enjoyment in participating in a variety of sports and activities, they will be more likely to actively participate for a lifetime (Siedentop, Mand, & Taggart, 1986). All of this sounds very good. The tricky part is to find ways to assess whether students are actually accomplishing your learning outcomes for the affective domain. This chapter explains how to assess the affective domain and provides several different examples of how you can assess your students. Our goal for this chapter is to give you some strategies for assessing affective domain behaviors. We recognize at the onset that ours is not a perfect system, but what we are going to tell you will give you a good start to finding ways to assess the affective domain.

The Difficulty of Assessing the Affective Domain

Several reasons exist for assessing the affective domain. First, it lets students know that you consider those behaviors important; there are few other places in the school curriculum where the affective domain is assessed. When working with others, it is often affective domain behaviors that spell success. Students need to be aware of their actions and how these actions influence their relationships with others. Holding students accountable for these behaviors in physical education emphasizes the importance of these actions. The second reason for holding students accountable for affective domain dispositions is that if students care about others and act in ways that show this, the class will function more efficiently and effectively. Think of the chaos that would result if students were disrespectful of others and didn't listen to your directions. If affective dispositions are assessed, you can guide students toward becoming more responsible adults while improving the emotional climate of their classes.

As important and beneficial as it is to assess in this domain, why do teachers hesitate to do so?

We are going to guess that some, if not most, of you included at least one of the following three traits or dispositions in your combined top five because they are relatively common traits that physical education teachers like their students to demonstrate. These concepts are **effort,** willingness to cooperate (e.g., teamwork), and **fair play** (formerly referred to as sportsmanship). Now comes the hard part. These words are all pretty abstract; in other words, they will represent different ideas to different people. Let's start by discussing effort: What is effort? Write a definition of effort and identify three behaviors that you would expect from your students that demonstrate effort in your class.

Next, compare what you have written with the results from a person sitting close to you. How are the descriptions similar? Write down which characteristics you have in common. How are they different? The Venn diagram in figure 10.1 shows an example for how your results could be documented: One person would write the answers on the right-hand side of the unshared part of the circle and the other person would write the differences on the left-side of the unshared part of the circle. Write any shared responses in the space where the two circles overlap.

YOUR TURN 10.1

In the middle column, assess the behaviors listed using the **rating scale** that follows. Next, rank the behaviors listed in the right-hand column in order of importance to you from 1 to 17, with 1 as the most important and 17 as the least important.

Rating Scale

> 0 = Not important to assess
>
> 1 = Low importance to assess
>
> 2 = Somewhat Important to assess
>
> 3 = Essential to assess

Affective domain behavior	Rate 0 to 3	Rank 1 to 17
Enjoying the activity		
Making an effort		
Demonstrating a positive sports behavior (e.g., fair play or sportsmanship)		
Demonstrating willingness to participate		
Demonstrating willingness to cooperate		
Demonstrating willingness to follow the rules		
Demonstrating respect for others		
Being supportive of others; teamwork		
Being attentive when teacher is talking		
Consistently demonstrating support for teammates or others		
Demonstrating leadership		
Coming to class prepared for activity		
Staying involved in the game or activity even when not actively participating		
Demonstrating a positive attitude		
Participating safely		
Being enthusiastic		
Being on time every day		

Compare your top five behaviors to those listed by another person in the class. Discuss your ideas and together decide on the five most important behaviors and write them down.

As you can see by the variety of responses, effort means different things to different people. We bring this point up here because teachers often include effort as a factor in determining a student's grade.

Teachers typically want students to display 100 percent effort. What does this concept look like? Many of us say that we will know effort when we see it, but we actually have a very difficult time defining it. This lack of agreement is the crux of the problem with assessing the affective domain.

If there isn't a universal definition of effort and if teachers fail to define it and identify behaviors that will represent the demonstration of effort, how can they expect their students to know what is expected?

When we taught in secondary schools, we wanted our students to put forth their best effort. Sometimes they weren't able to do what we wanted them to do on their first attempt, but *effort* meant not giving up and trying again and again until the skill or concept was mastered.

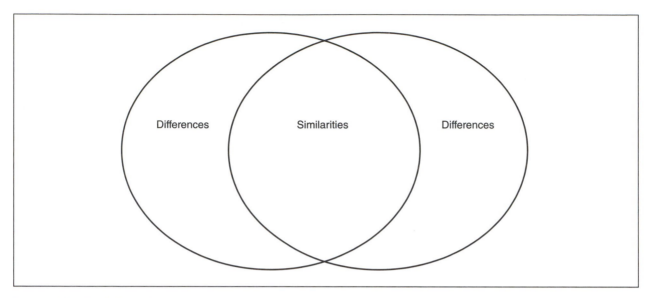

Figure 10.1 Blank Venn diagram.

We didn't want students to goof off (i.e., teacher educators refer to this as students being off task) and we didn't want students to interrupt others who were trying to learn. So, if we were to identify the behaviors that we expected our students to demonstrate, the list would be as follows:

- Persists in practicing a skill or task, even though it may be difficult, until competence is achieved or until the student is as close to competence as possible

- Stays on task at all times; does what the teacher asks even when the teacher is not looking

- Willingly accepts new challenges and tries to meet them

These three items exemplify the behaviors that we looked for when students display good effort. How did our behaviors compare with the ones you identified?

It is difficult to look at students and determine how much effort they are putting forth. We remember watching with frustration as a young man walked a mile (1.6 km) fitness test. When we downloaded his heart rate monitor at the end of the test, we found that he had been in his target zone for each of the 18 laps that we observed. Short of putting heart rate monitors on students, what can you do?

We like the idea of using learning as a proxy for effort; if students learn to do the activity or show they can play the game at the end of a unit, we believe that they have demonstrated effort. Assuming that we are good teachers and

that adequate time for learning is allocated, then students should be able to achieve competence. We know that some students are less skilled than others; this is where the good teaching comes in. If skills are tested in a stable environment and if the skill assessments are reasonable, we believe that when students have accomplished these skills, they have demonstrated effort.

Strategies for Assessing the Affective Domain

When assessing the affective domain, the first step is to define the behavior. Next, identify the actions from students that are acceptable indicators of students meeting your expectations for the trait being assessed. We have put our answers at the end of the chapter so that you can compare your ideas with ours. Remember that many of the definitions and expected behaviors represent what you want from students. Just because your responses are different from ours does not mean that yours are wrong.

If the affective domain is included in the students' grades, then a systematic way to assess each student must be in place. (Remember that the peer and self-assessments suggested in this chapter are formative assessments and should not contribute to student grades. Only teachers should administer assessments that contribute to a grade. See chapter 13 for more information.)

When assessing affective domain behaviors, it is nearly impossible to monitor all students at

YOUR TURN 10.2

The objective of this exercise is for you to begin to define your expectations for the affective domain so that you will be able to communicate your expectations to your students. Write definitions for each of these elements. Feel free to add any other items for which you want to hold students accountable. After you have defined the elements, think of behaviors that will represent meeting those behaviors and some that would demonstrate the absence of the behavior. We provide our answers at the end of the chapter.

Affective domain element	Definition of what the element means	Behaviors that would indicate the presence of the element	Behaviors that would indicate the absence of the element
Effort			
Teamwork			
Fair play (sportsmanship)			
Responsibility for equipment			
Caring for others			
Self-control			
Accepting the decisions of others			
Treating others with respect			

all times, especially when you are teaching large classes (25 students or more, and we know that many of you have class sizes larger than that). It is difficult not only to monitor this many students, but also to record behaviors for a group this size. When assessing large classes, one strategy is to designate a certain number of students that you will observe and assess every day. For example, if you have 50 students, then you should select 10 students each day for assessment. We suggest not doing this alphabetically or by squads, teams, or other grouping patterns that students might figure out. Students know that you are assessing the affective domain traits for some students (probably with some sort of rubric or rating scale), but they do not know which students are being observed that day. You will pay close attention to these students for the day and make a written record of the assessment. The next time that the class meets, choose a different set of 10 students for observation. This continues until the entire class has been assessed using

the criteria established for the affective domain. At the end of the rotation, provide assessment results to the students and have students come up with ways to improve their performance. You also can give specific changes that you want to see from your students and then begin a new observation rotation. This method of observation does not mean that the nontargeted students have a pass for the day. If a nontargeted student does something inappropriate or positive, by all means, make a notation. Sampling students in the manner described is simply a way to ensure that all students are systematically observed on a regular basis.

Tools for Assessing the Affective Domain

The following section provides examples of ways to assess affective domain. The assessment tools include checklists, rating scales, rubrics, journals, event recording, exit slips, anecdotal records, and written tests.

Checklists and Rating Scales

A **checklist** is simply a list of items that you want to see displayed. The assessor checks off the behaviors that are observed. The checklist for the affective domain is similar to the checklists that you developed for looking at correct form of skills in chapter 8. Figure 10.2 is a checklist created using the work of Don Hellison (2011). You can use checklists formatively in self- and peer assessments or for both formative and summative assessments, which you administer.

A rating scale contains a list of behaviors that you want students to demonstrate. Does that sound like a checklist? The difference between a checklist and a rating scale is that with a rating scale, the user (peer, self, teacher) is asked to assign a level of quality for the trait instead of merely checking for the presence of an item. Figure 10.3 is an example of a rating scale. With a rating scale, it is important to give a verbal description for each of the levels. These descriptions, although brief, allow the user to know what the different levels represent. Good descriptions of the levels help ensure consistency, meaning that everyone using the rating scale should arrive at the same score. For example, if you are watching an afternoon class, you will score them in the same way that you did for your morning class. Figure 10.3 was used to assess during a badminton class. To save on paper, we put two copies of the rating scale on the same sheet of paper and let a team assess their opponents.

Levels of Responsibility Checklist

Name_____ Date_____ Class period _____

Directions

Check each of the behaviors you used in today's class.

My respect:

_____ I did not make fun of others.

_____ I did not hog the equipment.

_____ I did not interfere with others.

_____ I did not interrupt when someone was talking.

My participation:

_____ I followed all directions.

_____ I tried my best.

_____ I avoided people who were trying to cause trouble.

_____ I let others participate.

My self-direction

_____ I encouraged others.

_____ My teacher did not need to remind me to keep practicing.

_____ Even though I saw someone doing something wrong, I chose to mind my own business.

My caring:

_____I tried to help others.

_____I helped my teacher.

_____I gave someone a compliment.

My improvement goal: _____

Figure 10.2   Self-assessment checklist using Hellison's levels of responsibility.

Badminton Peer Assessment

Your name_____ Opponent's name_____

Use this form is to assess the etiquette of your opponents. Circle 1 if the statement is not at all true, 2 if it is true some of the time, or 3 if it is true most of the time. Please answer each question fairly and accurately. This assessment is not part of the grade.

	Never true	Sometimes true	True most of the time
Encourages others (says things like "nice shot," "good hustle," and so on)	1	2	3
Wins or loses gracefully (doesn't throw temper tantrums)	1	2	3
Both partners on the other team played equally (the person being rated did not hog the court and try to dominate play).	1	2	3
Correct calls were made; they didn't try to cheat.	1	2	3
Courteous to others (We really enjoyed playing the other team because they were so nice.)	1	2	3

Figure 10.3   Example of a rating scale.

Rubrics

Affective domain behaviors can be embedded in other rubrics for participation in sports or activities. Figure 4.2 (chapter 4) is an example of a game-play rubric for a culminating activity that has affective domain traits embedded in it (fair play and etiquette). You might also develop behavior rubrics for your students. Figure 10.4 is a rubric that we have developed just for affective domain traits.

Journals

Journals provide students a way to record affective domain elements. They are useful as formative assessments because they can let you know when the class is not meeting the needs of the student or whether students are enjoying certain aspects of the class. Ask students to respond to a prompt that will focus their comments on a relevant topic. By requiring students to write a response to a prompt, you can gain insight into the feelings that they might have regarding an activity. If students want to add other information beyond the response to the prompt, this should be allowed. Do not grade the response for the content; just require students to complete the assessment. If you grade on the correct answer, the journal entries will be less effective because students will write what they think you want to hear instead of how they really feel about the class. Here are some prompts that you might use for journal entries.

1. Did all members of your team have a chance to be successful? Explain your

YOUR TURN 10.3

After studying figure 10.4, create your own four-level rubric for one affective domain trait using the following table. Choose a trait that you personally value and plan to promote with your students.

Affective domain trait	Unacceptable	Passing	Target	Exemplary

Behavior	Unacceptable	Passing	Target	Exemplary
Safety	Is unaware of or ignores potentially dangerous situations; participates recklessly with little concern for others	Is cautious while participating; when learning something new, waits for assistance (e.g., spotting) when appropriate; avoids getting hurt or using behaviors that could harm others	Uses equipment in a safe and conscientious manner; stops participating if there is potential danger and tells others so that the situation can be corrected	Alerts others to potential safety hazards; is constantly on the lookout for potential safety problems and seeks to correct those with easy fixes
On task behavior	Constantly modifies a task and does not practice as the teacher instructs; talks with friends instead of participating; moves to the end of the line to avoid taking a turn	Stays on task usually without a reminder or prompt from the teacher or another person	Practices tasks that the teacher specifies; continues to practice even when having limited success	When encountering a task that is too easy or hard, requests a modification from the teacher; encourages others to stay on task
Effort	Completes task with little personal exertion or enthusiasm	Completes tasks in a satisfactory manner; does activities expected by teacher	Is engaged in all activities mentally and physically; others can count on this student's performance; gives one's best performance; shows persistence when task is difficult	Looks forward to new challenges posed by the teacher; eager to learn new skills or cognitive information
Teamwork	Hogs the ball; fails to support others; seeks to dominate play	Works with others to achieve success for the team; communicates with others to ensure group success	Encourages good play by others; allows others to experience success	Demonstrates leadership and the strong desire for all students to work together to accomplish a task; willing to experience personal sacrifice for the good of the team

Figure 10.4   Rubric for affective domain traits.

role in making that happen. If it did not happen, what could you have done to change things?

2. How did you help or encourage someone else today?

3. What skills do you feel confident about and which ones do you struggle doing?

4. How could someone help you participate at a more competent level?

5. If you had someone on your team who wasn't very skilled, how could you make this person feel welcome?

6. What was your favorite part of the dance unit?

7. What would you do if you knew that someone had cheated to win?

YOUR TURN 10.4

Create three journal prompts that you could use to assess the affective domain. Be sure that they will require students to write a response and that they cannot be answered with a simple yes or no.

Figure 10.5 is an example of a response die. You can create one by putting questions in each of the boxes on the form. The cube is then cut out and taped together to make a cube. Students roll the cube and then respond to the question that appears in the square of the cube facing the ceiling. The question can be used as a journal prompt. Students can also go around in a small group (4 or 5 students) and respond to one another regarding the question.

Event Recording

Event recording is a simple way to tally student behavior. Compose a list of behaviors that you want students to demonstrate and then record a tally mark or check mark each time the behavior is observed. Table 10.1 is an example of a simple behavior recording sheet. To save time, you can run off multiple copies of class lists with blank columns. When it is time to assess certain behaviors, write them in at the top of the columns. You can also create an Excel document for the class and record behaviors using a handheld device or a tablet computer.

Another type of event recording is a T chart, which is often used in adventure education to record incidences of students giving a compliment. Table 10.2 is an example of a T-chart template for recording behaviors. As you can see, the key is to keep a written record of the desired behaviors. The written record can be used as formative assessment to give feedback to students.

Exit slips are used to require students to respond to a question at the end of class, kind

Table 10.1   Simple Behavior Recording Sheet

Names	Unsafe behavior	Helped others	Complimented others
Sue	XXX	XX	XXXX
Darius	XXXX	XX	X
Jamillah	X	XXXXXX	XXX
Maria	XXXXX	X	
Yuan	XX	XXX	XXX
Dwayne	XXXXXX	X	X

Table 10.2   T-Chart Template for Recording Behaviors

Name of student	Compliments seen	Compliments heard

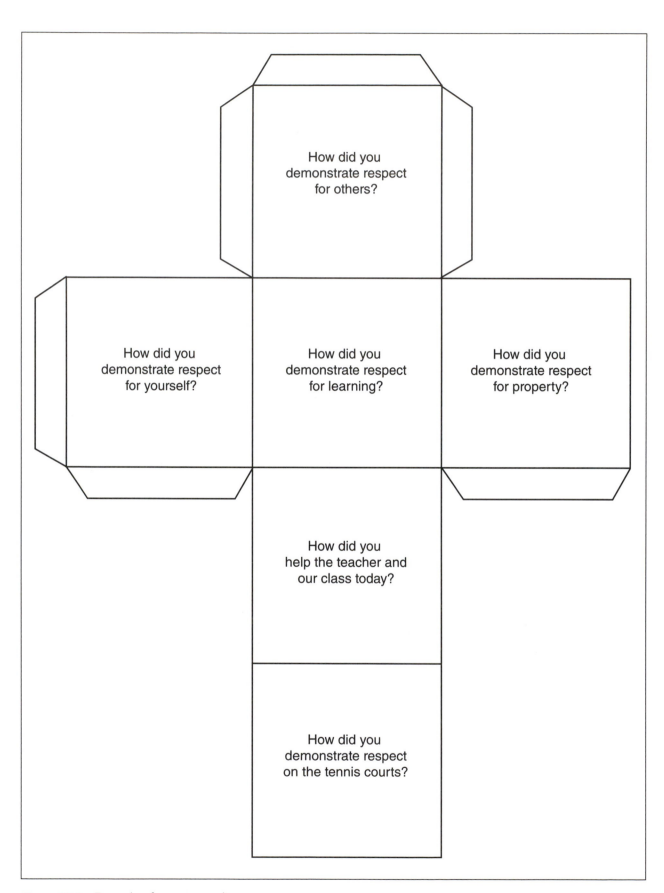

Figure 10.5   Example of a response die.

Using this template, create your own response die for the affective domain.

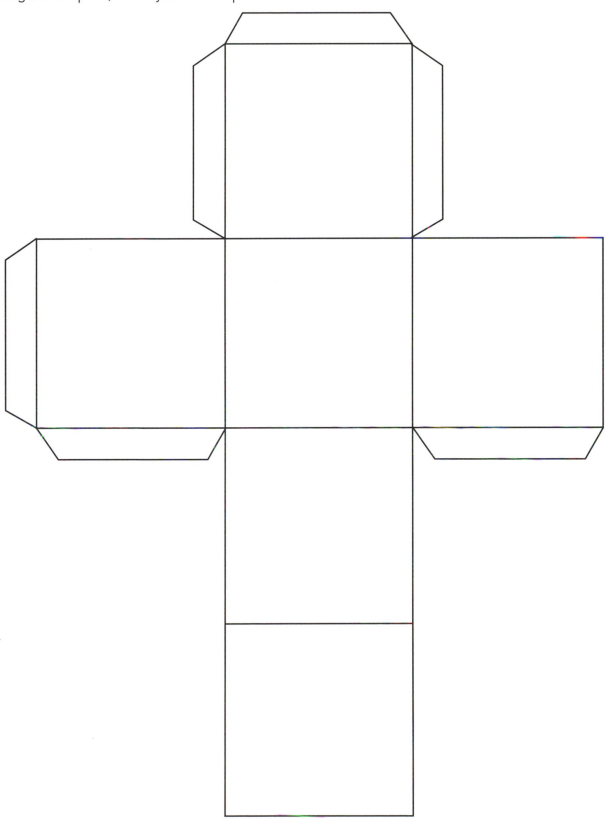

of a ticket out the door; students must complete the exit slip before leaving class. As with journal entries, you are encouraged to give definite prompts when requiring students to complete exit slips, such as "What three words describe the way your team worked together today?" If you want to save paper, you may elect to use the back of scrap paper as exit slips. They do not need to be preprinted. The most important part of the exit slip is the student response to the prompt.

Anecdotal Records

Anecdotal records are a way to capture the affective domain behaviors of students throughout the semester or grading period. Use file cards (3 by 5 inches or 5 by 8 inches); when an event occurs in class, take a few minutes to jot down some notes outlining the incident. You can also create files on computers or use handheld devices to record these comments. Figure 10.6 is shows a card with some sample comments.

Written Tests

Some would argue that knowing different affective behaviors is an important first step in participating responsibly. For this reason, you might give written tests on the class behavior rules or appropriate behaviors. If students miss any of the questions, you will know what you should cover in subsequent lessons to ensure that students understand your expectations concerning behavior and participation in class. NASPE's *PE Metrics: Assessing National Standards 1–6 in Secondary School* (2011) contains several examples of questions for standards 3, 5, and 6, which all contain elements of the affective domain. Following are some examples of questions for the affective domain.

1. You are practicing hitting with a 5-iron with your physical education class. You have hit your allotment of balls. The best thing to do is:
   a. Help your neighbor hit any remaining balls.
   b. Move around the class and give feedback to others.
   c. Remain at your designated spot and wait for others to finish.
   d. Go to the bulletin board to check the elements of correct form for your swing and do some practice swings.

2. You are still practicing with your 5-iron. Following one of your swings, it slips out of your hands, landing on the hitting range. You should:
   a. Yell to others to stop hitting and run out to retrieve your club.
   b. Run out and quickly retrieve the club.
   c. Move around the class and give feedback to others.
   d. Wait until everyone has completed hitting their balls before retrieving the club.

3. According to golf etiquette, when on the putting green, the player who putts first is:
   a. The player whose ball is furthest from the hole
   b. The player who is the oldest
   c. The first person to have his or her ball hit the green
   d. The player whose ball is closest to the hole

Name of student ___Julie Snow___

Class period __2nd__ Semester/marking period ___3rd quarter 2012___

Comments

3-11 Julie assisted a special needs student in class today; after her help, others in the class started helping as well; demonstrated good leadership.

3-15 Today Julie refused to participate; she was placed on a team with students that she did not like and opted to sit out; I tried to encourage her, but she refused to participate.

Figure 10.6 Example of an anecdotal record card.

Compose three questions of your own that would assess student knowledge about the affective domain in a physical education class. You may use any type of selected response question.

How Do I Hold Advanced Students Accountable for Affective Domain Behaviors?

If you want to challenge students to demonstrate advanced levels of affective domain behaviors, consider giving those students leadership opportunities. For example, students with advanced skills in a sport might become a coach for a class team during a sport education unit, helping others improve their skills. They also could be given plays to teach members of their teams and then coach their classmates during games instead of actually participating in the game itself. Table 10.3 shows expectations in the affective domain for advanced learners.

Table 10.4 summarizes the affective domain assessments we've discussed here.

Assessing Participation Outside of Class

NASPE content standard 3 indicates that students will participate in physical activity. The intent of this standard is that students would learn a variety of skills and activities in a physical education class and then use this information to be active during times beyond the class. NASPE advises that students should be active for about one hour per day; most physical education programs are not of sufficient length to allow for this amount of activity. Additionally, strive to prepare students for life beyond graduation and beyond the regular physical education class. You should help students develop habits that involve being physically active on a regular basis.

Ideally, schools have programs that will allow students to be active beyond the school day: intramural programs, club sports, dance teams, and athletics. If students participate in programs organized with a school, documentation of participation outside of the school day is fairly easy. If your school does not have a program or if students choose to participate beyond the school program, you could hold students accountable with **activity logs** or **activity tickets.** Figures 10.7 and 10.8 are examples of recording forms that you could use for tracking student participation outside of physical education classes. Notice that the form in figure 10.8 asks students to record the type of health-related fitness that the activity promotes. These could be optional or extra credit activities if you are reluctant to hold students accountable for activity outside the school day.

Why Isn't Dressing for Class an Indicator of Affective Behavior?

In some physical education programs, students pass or fail a class depending on whether they dress out for class. This topic is further addressed in chapter 13 when we talk about grading. For

Table 10.3   Expectations in the Affective Domain for Advanced Learners

Affective domain element	Definition of what the element means	Behaviors that indicate the presence of the element	Behaviors that indicate the absence of the element
Willingness to accept leadership responsibilities	Volunteers for various management roles or offers to help others while learning	Offers to help the teacher; agrees to serve as a coach or as an official; when given leadership responsibilities, tends to follow through	Leads efforts to disrupt the class; nonparticipation in class
Leadership: willing to sacrifice self-glory for the team	Supports the efforts of others to help them be successful	Passes to teammates so that they can experience success; agrees to take a supportive role in a dance production or game instead of the lead	Takes a shot at the goal even when out of position; constantly calls for the ball and then refuses to pass it back to others on the team

Table 10.4　Summary of Affective Domain Assessments

Type of assessment	Some things it will assess
Checklists (teacher)	Ability to follow rules; cooperation with teammates during practice; safety; responsibility
Rating scales	Student attitudes toward an activity or participation
Rubrics	Safety and personal responsibility as a stand-alone rubric or embedded in a game play or activity rubric
Journals	Student feelings toward participation Things that went well What students would like to learn
Activity tickets	Participation in activity beyond the physical education class
Activity logs	Participation in activity beyond the physical education class
Event recording	Frequency of behaviors: good and disruptive
Checklists and rating scales: peer and self	Often used for self- or peer evaluation of behaviors; excellent formative assessment
Game-play rubrics	Accepting calls by the official, being nice to teammates and opponents during games, honesty
Exit slips	A way to record short responses to a teacher prompt about some type of affective domain behavior
Anecdotal records	Notes to teacher: Use symbols to represent certain types of commonly viewed behaviors (desirable and undesirable).
Written test	Used to assess student knowledge of rules or appropriate behaviors for the class

Activity Ticket

This certifies that I have participated for 30 minutes or more in the following activity during this week.

_____Walking

_____Jogging

_____Dancing

_____Cycling

_____Skating

_____Swimming

_____Jumping rope

_____Playing soccer

_____Playing basketball

_____Other

Student's name _____

Parent or guardian's signature _____

Date _____

Figure 10.7　Recording form for outside activity.

My Activity Record

Name_____ Date submitted_____ Class period _____

Directions

Use this form to keep a record of your physical activity outside of school. Remember that the goal is to be physically active at least five days each week.

Date	Activity	Type of health-related fitness promoted	Number of minutes

Figure 10.8 Recording form for physical activities.

now, we will simply state that dressing for class is a managerial concern. If the grade is to represent the degree to which a student has learned something, then dressing for class is not something for which we should have an instructional goal. Dressing for class is simply a prerequisite for participation. It can be compared to bringing a textbook to a history class. It would not be acceptable to grade a student on bringing a book to class: If a student forgets the book, you can simply provide one. In the same way, you can have extra clean clothing on hand for physical education students to borrow if they forget their own clothing or uniform. Ensuring that all students are dressed appropriately for class is the first step toward promoting a positive learning environment in physical education.

Instructional Models

Two instructional models (IMs), as described by Metzler (2011), allow you to emphasize the affective domain. The first one is called the Teaching Personal and Social Responsibility (TPSR) instructional model, originally developed by Don Hellison. Although it was developed when he was working with underserved youth (e.g.,

juvenile delinquents, very-low-income children in an inner city), it has a place in today's schools. Hellison has spent much of his career working with the affective domain and has identified four different levels of affective domain behaviors, summarized in figure 10.9.

The TPSR instructional model does not focus on any one type of activity or sport, but it can be used by all teachers who want their students to develop responsibility for their actions. If you wish to know more about the levels of responsibility, try reading Hellison (2011).

The second IM is Sport Education, which offers you many opportunities to assess affective domain behaviors. When teachers use the Sport Education IM they set up a physical education class and the teacher assumes the role of general manager for a league. Students are given leadership roles in class ranging from managing the team, coaching, leading exercises, writing publicity articles, handling equipment, officiating, and keeping statistics. During a Sport Education unit, teachers have an opportunity to require students to complete several different documents and assessments that are linked to the affective domain. Here are a few common ways to hold students accountable for affective

Level 0	Represents irresponsible attitudes and behaviors
Level 1	Respect for the rights of others: Student has personal control of emotions and does not interfere with the actions of others but does not engage in the activity for the lesson.
Level 2	Participation: Student accepts challenges and participates under supervision.
Level 3	Self-direction: Student shows respect for others and participates without direct supervision.
Level 4	Caring: In addition to showing respect for others and participating, student has a sense of responsibility beyond self and gives support and help to others.

Figure 10.9 Levels of responsibility.
Based on Hellison 2011.

domain behaviors when using a Sport Education IM:

- Completion of tasks given by the coach
- Participation points (team)
- Points for completing tasks
- Spirit (cheers)
- Wearing team colors
- Completing team roles
- Completing duty team roles

The notebook that a team keeps contains much information about affective domain behaviors. Unfortunately, we have seen too many people miss these indicators of good affective domain behaviors. If you use this instructional model, we encourage you to use the documents generated as indicators of affective domain achievement. For more information about the Sport Education IM, refer to the book by Siedentop, Hastie, and Van der Mars (2004).

Setting the Level of Competence

Typically, for affective domain behaviors, there is an implicit recommendation for when the behaviors should occur (at all times). The rubrics that you write for affective domain behaviors will help students realize where you are setting the bar. We encourage you to set the bar at a level that will encourage students to be good citizens of your class and to treat others (yourself included) with respect.

One of the key parts of making this happen is to communicate to students what you expect them to do and then hold them accountable for doing it.

We also feel that when students demonstrate higher levels of achievement, they will demonstrate these behaviors without direct teacher supervision. Perhaps your strongest students will not only model good behavior, but also encourage their classmates to behave appropriately.

Affective domain assessments should outline the various behaviors and expectations; it is up to you to hold students accountable and ensure that these levels are met. Giving students credit for something that they don't deserve or earn does little to help them grow. We have seen student teachers give students credit on affective domain assessments when, in fact, the students did nothing to earn this. Keep the bar high, and your students will rise to meet your expectations.

Summary

We have presented several different ways to hold students accountable for affective domain behaviors. If you first explain your expectations to students in clear and explicit terms and then hold students accountable for demonstrating them, you will provide students with an education that will benefit them for a lifetime. We know that it is not easy to assess the affective domain. We've provided several suggestions and examples in this chapter that should help get you started assessing these very important life skills.

YOUR TURN 10.7

Here are the affective objectives from chapter 7. Create an assessment for each, listing the *who* (administers the assessment), *what* (type of assessment given), and *when* (to give the assessment).

Learning outcome	Who	What	When
The students will demonstrate responsible behavior toward others by not dropping them when serving as a spotter during gymnastics.			
The student will demonstrate willingness to help others by volunteering to help others during free skate time.			
During practice, the student will demonstrate support for teammates by giving encouraging comments to each person on the team.			
Students will demonstrate personal responsibility by picking up equipment without being asked by the teacher.			
Students will demonstrate cooperation with a partner by equally sharing opportunities to return the ball.			
Students will demonstrate fair play by accepting the decisions of an official without arguments.			
Students will demonstrate a desire to participate by being on time and dressing out every day.			

Answers to Your Turn Exercises

YOUR TURN 10.2

Affective domain element	Definition of what the element means	Behaviors that indicate the presence of the element	Behaviors that indicate the absence of the element
Effort	Full participation to the extent possible; keeps working on assigned tasks even if others stop	Does one's best; tries hard; engaged at all times; willing to work hard to improve one's own skills	Plays at half speed; walks instead of trying to keep up with the play of the game; doesn't try to learn new skills; refuses to participate
Teamwork	Works cooperatively with others to accomplish a common goal	Helps others succeed; listens to and respects ideas from teammates; encourages others on the team	Rejects the suggestions of others; plays for self instead of team; argues with others on team
Fair play (sometimes referred to as sportsmanship)	Plays within the rules and shows respect toward others	Shows courtesy to others; shows dignity whether winning or losing; compliments others; accepts decisions of the official	Calls a play incorrectly to gain advantage; gloats when the winner; complains if the loser; argues with officials

(continued)

(continued)

Affective domain element	Definition of what the element means	Behaviors that indicate the presence of the element	Behaviors that indicate the absence of the element
Responsibility for equipment	Handles equipment carefully and returns it to specified location when asked; makes sure that equipment is accounted for and not lost	Reports broken equipment to the teacher; uses equipment for its intended purposes; volunteers to help with equipment	Throws equipment; tries to break equipment; leaves equipment where it was used instead of putting it away
Caring for others	Helps others; is nice; is polite to others	Invites people to join one's group; helps someone when they are acquiring new skills; allows all to participate in activities	Socially isolates others; intentionally tries to hurt someone when committing fouls; doesn't apologize for negative actions
Self-control	Controls emotions and actions without being told by others	Remains calm even in stressful situations; keeps hands to self	Plays with aggression to the point of being destructive; talks while others are talking
Accepting the decisions of others	Supports the judgments of those in authority	Accepts a call by the official; follows the wishes of the team captain; when appropriate, compromises to come to common agreement	Is rude to others to get own way; refuses to participate when isn't getting own way; complains incessantly
Treating others with respect	Demonstrates good manners and polite behavior	Listens when the teacher is talking; appreciates the efforts of others; waits for one's turn; listens to others	Calls others out for unintentional errors; makes fun of others; bullies others

PART III

Developing Assessment Skills

ELEVEN

Using Assessment Data

Assessment [is] the process of gathering evidence about a student's level of achievement . . . and of making inferences based on that evidence.

NASPE, 1995, p. vii

Throughout this book, we stress that assessment always results in a written record of student performance. The written record is made up of **assessment data,** consisting of numbers, check marks, tally marks, or words. These are all examples of **raw data** used to describe students' performance. But raw data means little to the students or the teacher. Making sense of the raw data is a process called **data analysis.** To analyze the raw data from student performances, you must become comfortable with several mathematical processes, such as calculating an average, sum, or **percentage.** Fortunately, data analysis is a fairly simple process when you use a computer program like Excel. This chapter shows you what to do, step by step. In the first part of the chapter, we explain how to use formative student-directed assessment data to make decisions and set goals. Later in the chapter, we address using teacher-directed assessment data to make decisions about teaching and learning, both at the individual and class level. Chapter 13 addresses the use of summative data, so this chapter primarily focuses on formative data analysis.

Descriptive Statistics

In every case when assessment data are collected, you need a procedure for summarizing and analyzing the data. Data summaries can consist of tally counts for various categories or **descriptive statistics,** which are used to describe a set of scores. Descriptive statistics most commonly used by teachers are the average, the range, and the sum. The **average** (also called *mean*) is a numerical score calculated by dividing the sum by the total number of scores; it is a measure of central tendency. The average is often used in statistics sheets to report the batting average or average percentage of basketball free throws made by a team. The **range** represents the difference between the lowest and the highest score; it is obtained by subtracting. Use it when you want to visually examine data to see patterns and make

decisions about how individual students and the group are progressing toward competence or toward meeting a lesson's learning outcome. The *sum* is the total of a group of scores, such as the number of bowling pins knocked down in each frame, when added together.

Descriptive statistics can be helpful for the following reasons:

1. You can organize and analyze the data (result of assessment) collected about student learning.

2. Progress toward competence can be calculated for individual students and a class.

3. Both you and the students can understand the results of **assessment.**

In standards-based assessment, your most important step is reflecting about the meaning of the assessment data and then making decisions based on the data. The examples that follow will take you through different types of assessment data, the analysis of the data, reflections about the meaning of the data, and the steps to take after analysis and reflection.

To find the sum of the scores using a calculator, carefully enter each score, followed by the plus symbol. An easier way to analyze data is to enter the raw data into a computer program called Excel, which comes with Microsoft Office. An advantage of using Excel is that you can check that each score was entered correctly. After you complete the process of data entry, a couple of mouse clicks will yield the sum, the average, and several other statistical processes. Here are some basic steps describing how to use Excel.

1. Enter your data for a class into column A.

2. Check the data to be sure you have entered each score accurately.

3. Place your cursor in an empty cell at the bottom of the column.

4. Click on the Function (*fx*) symbol, click on the function you want to compute, and click on OK.

5. A box appears called Function arguments, where you will see the column and numbers. For example, if you have 45 scores in column A, you should see the following: A1:A45.

6. If the formula is correct, click OK; if it is not correct, you can change it by typing the correct number and column.

7. The answer will appear in the cell you preselected.

8. Next to the answer, type a label so you can remember what the number represents.

9. Repeat the process for other desired functions.

The following Your Turn exercise gives you an opportunity to use the Excel program.

YOUR TURN 11.1

Analyze the data below from a written test using Excel to find the sum and the average. Bring your Excel sheet to class showing the raw data, the sum, and the average. Answers are at the end of the chapter. Be sure to label each result.

75, 80, 82, 78, 90, 43, 88, 96, 61, 80, 89, 92, 71, 70, 67, 39, 54, 92, 91, 83, 84, 76, 68, 67, 59, 95, 88, 74, 73, 72, 65, 83, 87, 85, 97, 56, 62, 76, 77, 84, 83, 90, 56, 76, 73, 72, 80, 80, 90, 93, 68, 70, 83, 93, 64, 65, 70, 81, 85, 90, 73, 74, 78, 82, 79, 65, 70, 77, 92, 65, 85, 86

Frequency Distribution

When using formative assessment, look at the class data to see where students are in relation to the criterion level. For example, if more than half of the students are well below the criterion level, you will need to reteach, change practice tasks, or simply allow more practice time. One rule of thumb is when about 80 percent of the class has reached the criterion level, it's time to move on to a new skill, a combination of skills, or game play.

Sometimes, descriptive statistics alone don't answer your questions about the assessment data. A way to view scores for a group in an organized way is to make a **frequency distribution.** When the range is small, use a simple frequency distribution (see figure 11.1), in which you list every possible score and tally the number of students who had each score. In figure 11.1, the

Frequency refers to how often a score occurs. List the scores in order from high to low in a column as shown. Then tally how many times each score occurs. Each tally mark represents a score (e.g., three students had a score of 9).

Scores	Tallies
10	/
9	///
8	///
7	//////
6	///////////
5	////
4	/////
3	//
2	//
1	/

Figure 11.1 Simple frequency distribution.

assessment scores range from 10 to 1. Notice that even with a small range of 9, the students' scores are quite spread out. In this example, if the criterion level is 8, there are 31 students below that score, and only 7 students are at or above the criterion level. Clearly, this teacher needs to address the fact that the majority of students are below the criterion level.

When the range is large, it would be cumbersome to list every score, so a grouped frequency distribution is used (see figure 11.2), meaning that several scores are grouped together into **intervals** and then tallies are made for each interval. *If the range for a group of scores is more than 35, you will probably choose a grouped frequency distribution.* It's best to have between 10 and 20 intervals, but 15 intervals are ideal. The interval size should be a whole odd number. In physical education, interval size is usually either 3 or 5.

To compute the interval size, do the following:

- Determine the range by subtracting the low score from the highest score.
- Divide the range by 15.
- Compose the 10 to 20 intervals that best represent the data.

Curl-Up Data (N = 100)

High score = 58
Low score = 9
Range = 49
49 ÷ 15 = 3.2 (interval size is 3)

Intervals	Tallies	Frequencies
56–58	///	3
53–55	//	2
50–52	/////	5
47–49	/////////	9
44–46	///// //	7
41–43	////	4
38–40	/////	5
35–37	/////////	9
32–34	///// ///// //	12
29–31	///// ///// ///	13
26–28	///// ////	9
23–25	///// ///// /	11
20–22	///	3
17–19	//	2
14–16	////	4
11–13	/	1
8–10	/	1

Figure 11.2   Grouped frequency distribution.

Notice in figure 11.2, when the interval size is 3, it means that three scores are grouped together (e.g., 56, 57, and 58). If you study the intervals, you will see that every score is represented. To see trends in the data, we will create a grouped frequency distribution using an interval size of 3, which yields 17 intervals. If we had used an interval size of 5, there would have been 11 intervals. Remember that to best see the data, 15 is the ideal number of intervals. Normally, intervals start with the highest score, and they are listed down to the lowest possible score. Sometimes, with written tests that have a possible 100 points, you would start the intervals with the highest possible score, but a better picture of the data usually appears by using the range to build the intervals. After creating the intervals, you're ready to tally

the scores. Each score is tallied into an interval. To check your work, add up the numbers in the Frequencies column. If you have 100 scores, the numbers indicated in the Frequencies column should add up to 100.

When you finish tallying scores, look at the class results to see if the scores tended to group in the middle or if they were skewed toward the top or the bottom. When the majority of scores are grouped at the top, it means the majority of students have reached the intended criterion level. It might also mean that the assessment was too simple. If the scores are grouped at the bottom, the assessment is probably too hard or is not developmentally appropriate. Scores that are bottom heavy may also indicate that students need more practice. Of course, you will need to identify the

YOUR TURN 11.2

For the test data set for tennis serves that follows, do these tasks (answers are at the end of the chapter):

1. Find the range (subtract the lowest score from the highest score).
2. Determine the size and number of intervals.
3. Start the intervals with the highest score at the top.
4. Compose the remaining intervals by the determined size (either 3 or 5).
5. Tally each score by placing a tally mark to the right of the appropriate interval.
6. Sum the frequencies in the next column (see figure 11.2).
7. Compute the average using a calculator or Excel.
8. Write a brief analysis of what you have learned about the tennis serve test.

You administered a tennis serve test to three 10th grade physical education classes (N = 75) and grouped the scores into a frequency distribution for analysis purposes. The scores were as follows:

83, 75, 81, 56, 82, 86, 62, 87, 79, 93, 58, 61,
61, 75, 73, 94, 48, 79, 72, 81, 85, 52, 73, 62, 80
73, 84, 63, 61, 67, 63, 75, 73, 67, 72, 73, 72, 77
73, 85, 82, 70, 57, 58, 54, 79, 68, 54, 70, 77, 81,
68, 83, 65, 77, 90, 52, 75 ,62, 84, 69, 56, 68, 69,
63, 70, 91, 70, 80, 65, 70, 88, 72 ,63, 88

students whose scores are well below the criterion level so you can give them individual help.

A large range is an indication that the class is very heterogeneous. Here, you may need to differentiate instruction by skill level. You might allow an extra day or two of practice on isolated skills or skills in combination to help students develop competence before using them in game play. On the other hand, a small range means that teaching can be aimed toward the middle performance and that it will be appropriate for most students in the class.

Using Data From Student-Directed Assessments

When students use self- or peer assessment to improve their learning, the most important way to use the data is through **goal setting.** Ask students to set improvement goals. When they set goals and monitor their learning along the way, they assume more responsibility for their own learning. They also gain a strong sense of competence when they see improvements, so their motivation goes up. Sometimes the improvement goal moves students closer to the expected criterion level. If you are using Fitnessgram, the goal should move students closer to the healthy fitness zone.

A suggested guideline is to ask students to aim for a 5 to 10 percent improvement. You can integrate math into your physical education lessons by teaching students to multiply their current score by 5 or 10 percent (to multiply, convert the percentage to .05 or .10). Then add the result to the current score. For example, Amanda performed 20 curl-ups. Compute the new goal by multiplying 20 by 5 percent (20 × .05 = 1 + 20 = 21) or 10 percent (20 × .10 = 2 + 20 = 22). Amanda's new goal is 21 or 22. Keep in mind that improvement comes gradually with practice, so you may need to implement weekly goals or even longer-term goals. If the starting score is a small number, the 5 percent added will also be a small number, but if the starting score is larger, the value of 5 percent will be much larger than before. Be careful to help students set reasonable and attainable improvement goals.

YOUR TURN 11.3

Phil's pedometer showed he averaged 2,200 steps this week during physical education classes. What is his new goal for next week if he wants a 5 percent improvement? The answer is at the end of the chapter.

At times, students will need to analyze data in order to track their progress toward a goal or outcome. Figure 11.3 shows a learning outcome and assessment task for basketball shooting, while figure 11.4 shows a sample completed assessment form from two eighth-grade students named Jeremy and Nakesha. In this example, data analysis consists of addition to obtain a total score.

When the assessment task was completed, the forms were submitted to the designated box in the gym and students went on to the next learning task. The teacher listed all the scores by each student's assigned number. A student in the class could not participate actively because of a broken finger. She volunteered to record all of the scores (with her good hand) for the teacher

Basketball Unit

4 WEEKS (20 LESSONS)

Skill

Midrange shooting

Learning Outcome for Lesson 10 (November 6)

Students will make at least 21 out of 30 points (70 percent) shooting the basketball from various marked positions inside the 3-point line.

Assessment Task

Using formative peer assessment, one partner shoots 15 shots while the other partner records success rate, giving 1 point for hitting the rim and 2 points for making the basket

Figure 11.3 Sample eighth-grade coed basketball assessment.

Shooting Assessment

NOVEMBER 6

Directions

In this task, you and your partner will work together to practice shooting at marked spots inside the 3-point line. This task is not graded. While one partner shoots the basketball, the other partner will record; then switch places. Use correct form as we've been practicing. Your goal is to score at least 21 points.

This arc shows the proper trajectory.

82% off all missed shots are short or on too flat of a trajectory

For each trial, record 1 point if the ball hits the rim, 2 points if the ball goes into the basket, and 0 points if the shooter misses. After the 15 shots, help your partner set an improvement goal.

Shooter __Jeremy__   Recorder __Nakesha__

1	2	3	4	5	6	7	8	9	10	11	12	13	14	15	Total points
0	0	1	2	1	1	0	1	2	0	2	2	2	1	1	16

Shooter's Improvement Goal

This time, I only made 5 out of 15 shots. I want to make at least half of my shots next time. Nakesha told me I need to follow through and that I will improve my shots.

Shooter __Nakesha__   Recorder __Jeremy__

1	2	3	4	5	6	7	8	9	10	11	12	13	14	15	Total points
2	2	1	0	0	1	2	2	1	2	0	2	2	2	1	20

Shooter's Improvement Goal

I made 8 shots, but missed the goal completely on 3 shots. Next time I want to at least hit the rim on every shot. I think I can do that. Jeremy says that my form is great! My team is counting on my shooting in tomorrow's game.

Figure 11.4 Completed assessment form.

20	16	6	19
17	8	19	22
16	24	21	15
10	18	23	16
22	15	17	12
23	19	19	21

Figure 11.5 The numbers represent the total points for each of the 24 students in Nakesha and Jeremy's class.

in an Excel spreadsheet using a laptop computer. Keep in mind that a student should not see other students' scores with names, but if scores are recorded by assigned numbers, it is permissible for students to help with data entry.

Figure 11.5 shows the total scores for the 24 students who completed this assessment in Jeremy and Nakesha's class. If the teacher wants to compare the scores of all her classes, she can enter the total points for each student into an Excel program. After data have been entered, the teacher clicks on the Function symbol (*fx*) and a box appears, allowing her to choose from a list of functions like sum, average, and standard deviation. If she were using a calculator, she would simply enter each score, obtain the sum, and divide the sum by the number of scores (N).

Using Data From Teacher-Directed Formative Assessments

Teacher-directed assessment data is generally more accurate than student-directed assessment data, partly because students may feel the need to exaggerate their own scores or the scores of a partner. In addition, students may be distracted by other students or personal problems. For this reason, only teacher-directed assessment data are used for grading. Even though student-directed formative data may be less accurate, you can use them to help make teaching decisions, as demonstrated previously. If you use formative assessment regularly, and students understand that it does not affect their grades, they will be more likely to record accurately.

While teaching an assessment class, I had students assess 4-year-olds using a motor development test. As part of the assignment, teacher candidates had to write a letter to the parents of the child telling them what the child could do that was developmentally appropriate, whether the child was doing things that were more advanced for the age, and suggestions to remediate any skills on which the student was performing below expectations. On the day following the testing, we looked at the data. It appeared that we had a bunch of superstars because the scores were all so high (remember that these were 4-year-olds). Finally, one of the candidates raised his hand and said "I can't write a letter to this child's parents telling them how great he is. He has a hard time even galloping, let alone skipping and leaping." The teacher candidates were reluctant to give the child the rating that was appropriate because they did not want to hurt the child's feelings. Lesson learned: Even big people have trouble giving appropriate scores.

The most important idea here is to collect some data about learning, analyze the data, and reflect on what the data tell you about students' progress toward meeting learning outcomes. This whole process should result in decisions about what to do in the next lesson or series of lessons. If you assess and just set the data aside, you have wasted your time. Figure 11.6 summarizes the

➔YOUR TURN 11.4

Using Excel or a calculator and the data in figure 11.5, compute the mean for the data set from the basketball shooting peer assessment. Then answer the following questions and make your suggestions to the teacher about where to go next with Nakesha and Jeremy's class. Answers are at the end of the chapter.

1. What is the average? _____ Range? _____
2. How many students met the learning outcome for lesson 10? _____
3. How many students did not meet the learning outcome for lesson 10? _____
4. What do you think the teacher should do in the next lesson related to midrange shooting?

- Reteach the same concept or skill.
- Back up to something simpler.
- Move on to the next lesson.
- Slow down your instruction.
- Provide more student practice in a variety of tasks.
- Use a peer assessment to reinforce important cues and improve technique.
- Group students for homogeneous instruction (groups are similar).
- Group students for heterogeneous competition (mixed groups).

Figure 11.6   Types of teaching decisions.

different teaching decisions that you can make based on assessment data.

What follows are five examples of how you might use assessment data to inform your teaching. In each example, the learning outcome is given, along with the type of assessment performed so you can see how the learning outcome and assessment are aligned. A discussion follows of how you might use the data to improve teaching and learning.

Example 1: High School Fitness Unit

Learning Outcome
All students will demonstrate abdominal strength by scoring in the healthy fitness zone on the curl-up test.

Formative Assessment
Administer the curl-up test from Fitnessgram and have students self-record their scores each week using the computerized Fitnessgram program.

Using the Data
The diagnostic fitness assessment reveals that 75 percent of the students were below the target zone, so abdominal strength was selected for special emphasis. Various abdominal exercises are included in every class. Ask students to set a goal of at least 5 percent improvement each week. They administer a weekly curl-up self-test to check their progress. Monitor individual and class progress using the computerized Fitnessgram program.

Example 2: Cardiorespiratory Fitness

Learning Outcome
Students will demonstrate cardiorespiratory fitness by achieving an average heart rate (HR) in the target zone during class time.

Assessment
Use heart rate monitors to check students' level of activity (i.e., average heart rate during the class period). Students record their average HR on a daily log.

Using the Data
If students' heart rate is not in the target zone, change the task to increase or decrease the physical activity level. Ways to change the task include the following:

1. Increase the amount of equipment in use.
2. Decrease the number of players on a team.
3. Modify game rules.

Monitor regularly with HR monitors.

Example 3: Seventh-Grade Volleyball Unit

Learning Outcome
Students will demonstrate successful serving by using correct form and serving the ball underhanded over the net and in bounds at a 75 percent success rate or better.

Assessment
In lesson 8, the teacher administers formative assessment at one small-sided (3v3) 10-minute game to sample serving success rate (see table 11.1). Modified rules = 1 serve, rally, rotate so each player serves five times during the game.

Using the Data
Jerry may be ready to learn the overhand serve. Since the overall success rate is only 40 percent, this group of students is not yet serving successfully. Reteach the mechanics of the serve to this group and then use a checklist with peer assessment. Then, to increase their success, try the following changes:

- Move students closer to the net.
- Allow two serves per student, if needed.
- Allow a teammate to help serve over.

Example 4: Sixth-Grade Overhand Throw to a Target

Learning Outcome
Students will demonstrate the ability to throw a softball overhanded from second base to first base with a success rate of 70 percent or better. A successful throw must be catchable by the player on first base.

Assessment
After the overhand throw has been taught and practiced, assess students during a practice activity. Select a higher- and a lower-skilled student, and code their 15 practice trials and success rate (see example in table 11.2). If success rate is less than 75 percent, adjust the task. Then code the same two students again. Code several other pairs if you need more information about the class.

Using the Data
These data clearly show that Judy is consistently able to throw the ball accurately from second to first base with good form. Sylvia however, needs to improve her form by taking a long contra-lateral step. This will also help her increase rotation and force so that the ball reaches the intended target. Pairing Judy and Sylvia for a peer-assessment practice should help.

Example 5: Ninth-Grade Pickleball

Learning Outcome
Students will demonstrate the ability to hit the ball from a good toss down the line to a target area near the baseline using a forehand drive with a success rate of 70 percent.

Assessment
Students work in groups of four to record the number that hit within a large hula hoop located near the baseline. The hitter stands in the center of the service area; the tosser stands about 5 feet (1.5 m) from the net and tosses the ball to a target in front of the hitter; the recorder counts and records the number out of 10 that are hit down the line into the hula hoop. The fourth student retrieves balls to keep the assessment task moving quickly.

Results (All scores are out of 10 trials.)
2, 4, 5, 3, 2, 1, 7, 3, 4, 0
1, 1, 0, 5, 4, 3, 0, 2, 1, 3

Table 11.1   Assessment of Volleyball Underhand Serve

Names	Successful serves	Unsuccessful serves	Notes
Joe	///	//	
Sarah	/	////	Sarah needs to take a step to apply more force.
Jerry	/////		
Cindy	/	////	Cindy tosses the ball and often hits off center.
Sherika	//	///	
Jacob		/////	Jacob is serving with his fist so the ball goes out of bounds.
Totals	12	18	
Overall success rate	12/30 = 40%		

Table 11.2   Assessment of Softball Overhand Throw

Names	Successful trials	Unsuccessful trials	Success rate	Notes
Sylvia (lower skilled)	////	///// ///// /	4/15 = 27%	Needs a longer step to increase force
Judy (higher skilled)	///// ///// ///	//	13/15 = 87%	Consistent good form

YOUR TURN 11.5

Let's see if you can use our examples to create your own learning outcome, assessment, and reflection for your unit. Choose one of the psychomotor learning outcomes that you wrote in chapter 7 and complete the following exercise.

Activity unit:

Learning outcome:

Formative assessment:

Using the data:

Using the Data

Note that only 1 student out of 20 met the criteria for this outcome. Clearly, either students need more practice in order to meet the learning outcome or the task was too difficult. You may need to reteach the lesson on hitting down the line with a greater emphasis on why it is important to hit the ball to the back of the court. Correct mechanics may also need to be emphasized. If you decide that the problem is the difficulty level, you may decide to use a larger target to improve students' success rate. Finally, using the targets during practice task may also serve as reminders of the target area for drives.

Summary

This chapter shows you how raw assessment data can be analyzed to help you make decisions to improve instruction and learning. In rare cases, you can accurately analyze how well students are learning without data. We strongly recommend that, *most of the time,* you base your instructional decisions on assessment data about student learning. This means that assessment should routinely be intertwined with learning.

A good rule of thumb to follow when using formative data is if the class success rate is about 75 percent or better, it's time to move on to the next step in the teaching progression. There may be one group that is ready to move on before others, and that's okay. When the individual or class success rate is below 75 percent, students probably need more practice. The activity may also need to be adjusted for students' level of ability. Making teaching decisions based on students' success rate will help you ensure that students' time in physical education is more enjoyable. A high success rate is also a good predictor of future interest in physical activities.

We are very aware that some physical education teachers do not enjoy math, and may even try to avoid using it. This chapter explains how to do some simple calculations that help you understand assessment data. By all means, we encourage you to use a calculator or a computer program like Excel to analyze your data. However, a computer can't do the thinking that is required for understanding the meaning of your assessment data. You will have to do that with your brain and, hopefully, with a fellow teacher. With practice, you will become proficient at data analysis and reflection.

Answers to Your Turn Activities

YOUR TURN 11.1

Analyze the following data from a written test. Bring to class your Excel sheet showing the data, sum, and average.

75, 80, 82, 78, 90, 43, 88, 96, 61, 80, 89, 92, 71, 70, 67, 39, 54, 92, 91, 83, 84, 76, 68, 67, 59, 95, 88, 74, 73, 72, 65, 83, 87, 85, 97, 56, 62, 76, 77, 84, 83, 90, 56, 76, 73, 72, 80, 80, 90, 93, 68, 70, 83, 93, 64, 65, 70, 81, 85, 90, 73, 74, 78, 82, 79, 65, 70, 77, 92, 65, 85, 86

Sum = 5537
Average = 76.9

YOUR TURN 11.2

Formative Tennis Serve Test

1. Range: 94 – 48 = **46**
2. Intervals: 46 ÷ 15 = **3** (This size interval will give you 16 intervals.)
3. Determine the top interval: 92 – 94 (because 94 was the highest score)
4. Construct a table and tally scores (see following table)
5. Average = 72
6. Write a brief reflection on what you learned about the tennis serve test.

Intervals	Tallies	Frequencies
92–94	//	2
89–91	//	2
86–88	////	4
83–85	//////	6
80–82	///////	7
77–79	//////	6
74–76	////	4
71–73	//////////	10
68–70	//////////	10
65–67	////	4
62–64	///////	7
59–61	///	3
56–58	/////	5
53–55	//	2
50–52	//	2
47–49	/	1

Reflection

The first thing that stands out is that the scores appear to be distributed normally, with 31 scores above the average, 10 scores at or near the average, and 34 scores below the average. This tells me that the test was neither too hard nor too easy. The wide range of scores on the tennis serve test matches my observation that some students are still struggling on the serve. Enough students are well above average that it might be worthwhile to pair the top half with the bottom half of students for some peer teaching. We will repeat this test several more times, and I'll ask students to set an improvement goal of 10 percent over the next week.

YOUR TURN 11.3

Phil's pedometer record showed that he averaged 2,200 steps this week during physical education classes. What is his new goal for next week?

2,200 × .05 = 110

2,200 + 110 = 2310 steps

YOUR TURN 11.4

Using Excel or a calculator and the data in figure 11.5, compute the mean for the data set from the basketball shooting peer assessment. Then, answer the following questions and make your suggestions to the teacher about where to go next with this class.

1. What is the average? _17.4_ Range _18_
2. How many students met the learning outcome for lesson 10? _7_
3. How many students did not meet the learning outcome for lesson 10? _17_
4. What do you think the teacher should do in the next lesson related to midrange shooting? Answers might include the following:
   - Reteach the correct form for midrange shooting.
   - Use a peer assessment emphasizing correct form; pair weaker shooters with strong shooters.
   - Move students a little closer to the basket and provide more shooting practice time.

BASKETBALL SHOOTING ASSESSMENT TASK

Excel worksheet showing data from the basketball shooting assessment task. At the bottom are the sum and average.

20	
17	
16	
10	
22	
23	
16	
8	
24	
18	
15	
19	
6	
19	
21	
23	
17	
19	
19	
22	
15	
16	
12	
21	
418	Sum
17.41667	Average

TWELVE

Managing Assessment

We realize that teaching does not cause learning; rather, learning occurs when the learner, with high-quality and appropriate feed-back, attempts to use knowledge to achieve some meaningful goal.

Lambert, 2007, p. 11

Although never is not a good word to use, we never—or maybe very rarely— have seen real teachers have enough time to do everything that they want to accomplish. Note, we are talking about real teachers, not teachers who don't really teach. As a teacher, it is quite typical that you don't have quite enough time to really put the finishing touches on a lesson that you want to perfect or to accomplish everything that you want to do with your students in class. Time is a constant, and you must work hard to use every available minute in class to improve student learning. In this chapter, we talk about managing assessment and not wasting time while administering assessments. We approach time from two perspectives: first, finding ways to teach your classes most effectively so that you have time to do assessments, and second, maximizing the use of your time when you are preparing to teach your class.

Importance of Organization and Efficiency

Becoming an assessor means learning to be organized. If you tend to be a disorganized person who procrastinates on important tasks, this chapter may represent a difficulty for you. We have seen teacher candidates who have a hard time keeping track of papers when all they needed was a hole puncher and a notebook. It only takes a little extra time to keep papers organized, but the payoff is huge as the semester draws to a close. The same is true in teaching. Putting in a little extra time at the beginning of the semester means that your job will be easier at the end of a unit when grades are due. Your organization tasks begin in your office. The old saying "A place for everything, and everything in its place" is a great guideline for organizing your office. Later in the chapter, we provide a list of equipment and **assessment supplies** you'll need. All of those things must be stored in your office. Preparing multiple copies of forms at the

beginning of the unit is great, but you'll need a place to store them so you have easy access. One teacher we know uses a storage system that has numerous thin shelves to hold papers. Your office desk can easily be equipped with small baskets to hold supplies like rubber bands, paper clips, and pens so you can find things quickly.

When you think about time for assessment, you need to remember that not all assessments contribute to the grade. Going back to what you learned in chapter 5, a big role of assessment is to help you know what to teach; in other words, assessment is formative. Here's an example: Let's say that your car engine often stalls. Because you are trying to save money, you keep doing little things to fix it: changing where you buy gas, changing the type of gas that you use, putting a fuel additive in your gas, and so forth. After about a month of frustration, you go to a mechanic, who does a diagnostic test of the car and discovers that the spark plugs don't have the appropriate gap (you had tried to save a little money and did that yourself). This is the root of the stalling problem. If you would have had the diagnostic test run a month ago, you would have saved yourself a lot of aggravation and would have been able to do other things with your time. Just like the mechanic, as a teacher, you can use assessments to help pinpoint a problem or lack of student learning that in fact allows you to move on to bigger or more complex (and fun) learning. To save time while maximizing instruction, we have learned ways to weave assessments with instruction. The rule of thumb on assessment is that 10 percent of your class time should be spent doing assessments. If you have a 50-minute class, you should allocate 5 minutes for assessment. If you don't assess on one day, the next day, you can spend 10 minutes assessing. You also can do individual rather than whole-class assessments so that only a few students are missing their activity time as they are assessed. Although 10 percent sounds like a lot of time, if you become a more efficient and effective teacher, you will easily have that 5 minutes a day to devote to assessment.

YOUR TURN 12.1

To see how you spend your time when you teach, have a friend or colleague observe your classes. With a stopwatch, the observer will note how much time you spend taking attendance, doing exercises, getting equipment out, talking and giving instruction, transitioning students from one activity to the next (either from lecture to activity or from task A to task B), engaging students in activity, and so on. After reviewing the data from the observation, look for noninstructional times that could be decreased or see whether you can present your lesson with less teacher talk. Can you find 5 minutes? Write down what you will do to increase your teaching efficiency. Be honest when looking at the results. You are administering your own self-assessment, and the goal is to make your teaching more efficient.

Note: If you do not have a colleague who can observe you, get a video camera, record your lesson, and do a self-analysis of your teaching.

Management	Fitness	Teacher instructions	Transitions	Motor active
Total:	Total:	Total:	Total:	Total:
Reflections on use of time:				

Management Routines

We have found that the teachers who use assessment most effectively are also very organized. They know that they are going to assess their students, they preplan the assessments before starting a unit, and they teach their students **management routines** so that students can complete the assessments as quickly as possible. Management routines are automatic: When you have a management routine, you do not need to explain to students what they should be doing. Routines must be taught and practiced, just as you would teach a skill. If you assess often, students will learn these routines, and you will be able to assess them efficiently. Most of the management routines that teachers use require students to learn to be responsible about handling equipment and supplies. You will usually have several students in a class who love to help hand out materials, but all students should be expected to act responsibly. In fact, students like to be asked to help. The only way they will learn responsibility is if you give them responsibilities and teach them how to behave.

Here are some management routines for assessment that you should teach your students:

- If using pencils, have a way to distribute them quickly.
  - Ask a student to hand them out.
  - Post a sign students will see as they enter the locker room telling them that they will need a pencil for the day.
  - Give students an attendance number (located on the outside perimeter of the gym), so they can go to that spot to pick up the assessment and pencil from a box.
  - Attach a pencil to a clipboard and have a squad leader pick up the materials needed for the assessment.
  - Establish an assessment station that students rotate to, and provide pencils there.
- If you provide pencils, make sure you have more than you will need for the class. This way, if someone breaks a pencil, it does not cause problems.
- Put the pencils in a box or container that is large enough to make it easy to distribute, and then collect pencils. The box should have a lid so pencils can be put away without spilling.
- Have a student assistant sharpen pencils every once in a while, or do it when you are unwinding at the end of the day. Don't try to do it while you are on your way to a class—we guarantee that this will cause problems (Murphy's law).
- If using written materials, devise a way to distribute them quickly.

○ See ideas listed previously for distributing pencils since they apply to both types of materials.

○ Use a file box of folders to keep recording sheets organized for each class.

Here are a couple of other suggestions for assessment management routines:

- At the beginning of the semester, create a multipurpose recording form for every class with the names of students in the class, and then make multiple copies of each class list. If you do this, you will not need to write in the names each time you use the form. You can create a good form using Excel—just be sure to put lines around all the cells (See table 12.1 for an example).

- Use colored paper to code parts of the test or different areas if you are doing several assessment stations with students self-recording. Different colors make it easier to sort and organize the results.

- For each class, assign each student an attendance number. Whenever the student completes an assignment, assessment, or a written test, students will put their number on the paper. When recording scores, it is easier to put items in numerical order than to alphabetize the set of papers. When recording scores, you can quickly enter them into your grade book or computer if they are in alphabetical order. We suggest that you wait a week or so before assigning these numbers. Our counselors used to shift students around during the first couple of weeks of the school year. Wait until students have stopped changing their schedules before assigning numbers to your students.

Managing Skill Assessments

Never test a single student in view of the rest of the class. We have seen teachers do this during fitness tests, and it is wrong. First, it is embarrassing for the student being tested. Second, students being tested are under a lot of extra stress and will probably not perform to the best of their ability. Third, you are wasting the time of those students who are watching. Fourth, these inactive students are prime candidates for causing problems because they are probably bored.

To maximize activity during assessment, we have seen teachers use the following ideas:

Table 12.1   Sample Multipurpose Recording Form

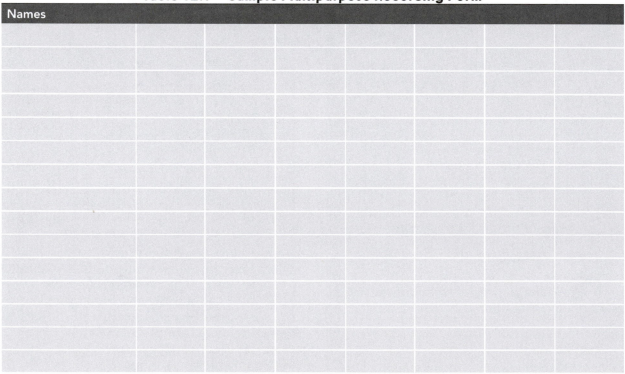

Names						

- Use a testing station: When students rotate to that station, they do the assessment.

- During game play, the game will keep students engaged with relatively little teacher attention (you also could use student referees). This is a good time to administer psychomotor tests to students whose teams are not playing.

- During game play that involves all students, pull one person from each competing team and do the skill assessment for those two students. When the testing is completing, allow those students to re-enter the game and pull two more students out for testing. Be sure to pull students of like ability from the games so that you don't accidently give one team an advantage during the assessments. Continue pulling students out until all students in both teams have completed the assessment.

- Administer game play assessments while students are engaged in game play.

When giving psychomotor skill assessments, there is typically a protocol, or set of directions, that students must follow so that their scores can be compared to the criteria established for mastery. Following the stated protocol is essential if you want to make valid inferences about the data. Many teachers set aside a skill assessment day to administer the test. If students haven't ever seen the assessment, you must teach the protocol for the assessment before administering it. When time is used to explain the assessment, it often is difficult to assess an entire class on a single day; you will save much time if you teach students the protocols and give them a chance to practice during instruction.

We have found that skill assessments can increase student response rates on the days preceding the actual assessment if they are presented to students in advance and if students are informed about the criteria that they will need to achieve for mastery (i.e., they need to get that score before moving to the next task) or for a certain grade (Lund, 1992; Lund & Shanklin, 2011). You can use the assessment as a learning task during instruction, which provides students with the opportunity to practice doing the assessment and simultaneously familiarizes them with the test protocol. If students have an opportunity to practice for the skill assessment, the scores tend to be better. Students also might administer the assessment as a peer assessment and report the results so that you can use the information for planning lessons. We strongly suggest that you let students see the skill assessments before the actual day that they will be administered.

When it is time for you to administer the skill assessment for a grade, a variety of equipment must be gathered. You should always be the person conducting the assessments that will lead to a grade. However, if you have a reliable student assistant (one who has already completed the class and who is assigned as a teacher aide, someone who is older than the students taking the class) or a paraprofessional teacher, you may allow that person to administer skill assessments that do not include an assessment of correct form (i.e., counting the number of serves that land in the proper court, timing a dribbling test, or measuring a long jump).

Following are some general guidelines about preparing for and managing skill assessments efficiently.

- *Managing students.* If you are calling students up to be assessed, maximize testing efficiency by having three students waiting to be assessed: one who is actually completing the assessment, one who is on deck (waiting to be assessed next), and one in the hole (will be assessed third). The students who are waiting will observe the assessment protocol, and you will be able to complete the assessment quickly. As soon as the student completes the assessment, have that student send the next student over to the testing station, so that three students are always ready for the assessment.

If the assessment is being completed in a random order (i.e., students come up when they are ready to be assessed), be sure to have the names already filled in on your score sheet. The precompleted recording form will save time when you transfer the data to the record book because it lists the students in alphabetical order. Don't allow more than four students to stand in line to wait. Having more than four students watching puts extra pressure on the student being assessed and wastes student time. Students can also cause problems if they become bored. Create some type of a numbering system where students receive their number in the assessment order instead of standing in line waiting for a turn.

If doing a group assessment (e.g., several students are being tested simultaneously during a formative assessment), arrange students in lines so that, if using a manipulated object (ball or racket), all the implements will go the same direction. It is easier to see when someone is making an error, and it is also much safer because balls are not flying randomly in the gym. Also, try to use lines that are already painted on the gym floor or on the field so that you don't need to put down a taped line. Always use floor tape when putting a line down on the gym floor—it is much easier to remove than masking tape.

When possible, arrange the students so that a wall or a fence will stop the ball. For example, if students are completing a pitching assessment, have them throw the pitch to the catcher, who is positioned next to the wall or fence. If the catcher misses the ball, the wall or fence will act as a backstop. Last, when assessing students as a group, always make sure there is enough space between students to make the assessment area safe.

• *Method and materials for recording results.* You will need recording sheets and a writing implement or some type of electronic device to record results. If you are writing the answers by hand, always have a second pencil handy in case the first one breaks or gets dull. If using an electronic scoring format, remember to charge the battery before use. If assessing several classes in a row, it may be necessary to have a second battery charging so that you don't get caught without power. If students need a recording sheet, prepare these in advance.

• *Managing writing materials.* You need to provide directions to students for using writing materials. Students need to know what to do when they finish the assessment. If they are doing a written assessment before moving to an activity, what should they do with their pencil and papers that they used? With peer assessments, students need to know where to put their papers when they are working and what to do with papers and writing utensils when they finish using them. This is especially important if students will be engaging in psychomotor activity either during or after the assessment.

• *Materials for setting up the testing station.* Typically, a teacher sets up several testing stations in a gym or on a field so that multiple tests can be completed on the same day. Be sure to have all the areas for the assessments set up before students enter the activity area. Use floor tape to mark the walls or floor. Be sure to have enough cones on hand for the actual assessment and to mark areas between the assessments so that students stay in their assigned area. In some cases, teachers create several instructional stations and an assessment station. Stand at the assessment station to record data on student performance.

• *Materials to time and measure.* You also will probably need one or two long tape measures to mark the areas. If you need tape measures to record distances for the student trials, make sure

Set up fitness testing stations ahead of time so all the needed materials are on hand.

to have enough of them and make sure that they are long enough. Sometimes it is impractical or unnecessary to exactly measure each attempt. If this is the case, mark your area in zones to save time. For example, if assessing golf drives, mark zones at 20 yards, 30 yards, 40 yards, and 50 yards. Write the criteria for the assessment so that students are given credit for hitting the shot at least 20 yards or at least 30 yards, instead of requiring the exact distance to be recorded. Some assessments require stopwatches or a timing device. If the class is doing an activity that doesn't require individual stopwatches, consider using the clock that is used for games as a start and stop signal.

• *Saving paper.* Some teachers have limited amounts of paper or copies to use during the school year. Chapter 9 explains how to save paper when administering written tests by copying tests and then requiring students to put their answers on an answer sheet or a scantron form. You can also save paper by recycling paper from the copy center at school that was used on one side. We have used this recycled paper for exit slips and recording sheets for formative skill tests. On a white board, draw a template of the score sheet needed for the assessment, and have students create one on the recycled paper.

You can also make your own white boards by buying a 4-by-10 sheet of white board (it is used to finish bathrooms) from the lumber store and having students cut the sheet up into recording tablets. One sheet of the material will yield 40 boards that students can use to record assessment results. Students will use erasable dry markers (the kind that are used with white boards) to record their answers. At the conclusion of class, you can record the assessment results in a grade book and wipe the boards clean for the next class. White boards are also useful for making tally marks when keeping statistics for a game. You can also print copies of the recording sheet and then laminate them. These too can be wiped clean after assessment results are recorded. If your school does not have a laminating machine, clear contact paper will also work, but it is much more difficult to prepare the forms for use.

• *Managing time.* Be sure to set up the stations so that students flow from one area to the next. Use cones of different colors at the stations to make it easy to distinguish between stations. Number the stations by writing on the cone and be sure to have students rotate through the stations in numerical order (e.g., from station 1 to 2, 2 to 3, and so on) even if they begin at station 5. If using stations, arrange students so that each station will take about the same time to complete. If one station is slowing down the rotation, you may need to include a double set of assessment equipment to avoid a rotation delay or slowdown.

Technological devices can be an asset in compiling and recording data about your students.

Managing Electronic Devices

Many teachers like to record data on a tablet, laptop computer, or a personal digital assistant (PDA). If you are planning on using any of these electronic devices for recording data, you will need software to record the results. Commercial products are available, but they tend to be expensive. However, once purchased, they can be used for many years. If buying a product, be sure to buy something that will allow you to download data and dump them into a program in which you can manipulate the data following the assessments. If you have a basic working knowledge of Excel, you can easily develop recording sheets for your data. You can develop the data sheets on a desktop computer and then sync the computer with a mobile device, such as a PDA.

We confess to being old fashioned: We really like using clipboards and paper to record results, since we never have to worry about power failures and lost files. For us, the PDA screens are small and difficult to read. A tablet has a larger screen, but you will need to download results into a computer if you want to do any calculations. You should use the recording device or format that you feel most comfortable with. If your school has a grading program, it probably has software that will allow you to download data into it. If you don't have a grading program, you can use Excel software for grade storage and calculation. It is easy to write simple formulae to automatically do the calculations for grades.

When allowing students to use electronic devices such as heart rate monitors, pedometers, or clicker response systems, assign each student a number that corresponds with the device that the student is using (or just use the student's assessment number). Be sure to include some type of accountability for the item so that students benefit from taking their assigned device. We have seen teachers give students credit for using the clicker to respond to questions asked during class. There also is a way to track correct answers at the end of class so that you can see which students were successful and likely understood the content and which students were still struggling. Similarly, we encourage you to download the heart rate monitors that you use with your students to maximize their effect on student learning. Don't bother using equipment if you are not going to use the data that they can yield.

Make sure that you have a way to transport your electronics. Students should be able to

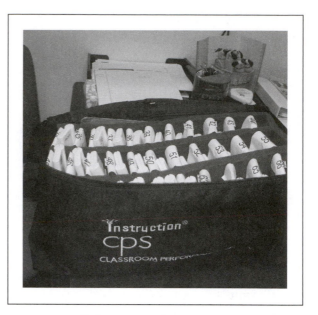

Figure 12.1   Clicker-carrying bag.

quickly remove the device from the case used for transport and return it to the proper place, ready for transport, when the class is finished. Be sure to number both the electronic device and the spot in the case to make it easy for you to ensure that the device was returned. Figure 12.1 shows one example of a useful carrying device—a bag to organize and transport clickers.

Managing Peer Assessments

When doing peer assessments, be sure to have enough clipboards, answer sheets, and pencils ready for students. It is best to have everything in one place (i.e., load the clipboard with a pencil attached with a string and place the answer sheets on top of it). Establish your groups first and then have one person from each group retrieve the clipboard.

Make sure that your groups are large enough to do all the tasks needed. As a minimum, you probably cannot have fewer than three people per group if you have some type of setup for the skill (i.e., a person tossing a ball that is hit with a racket). If this is the case, you will have the person being tested, the person providing the setup and the person recording the data. Some assessments require a person to retrieve the ball. If that is the case, be sure to provide enough equipment for each group so that the test isn't slowed down, and then designate a person or two to retrieve the balls. You'll also want to provide some type of container for the equipment (e.g., a hula hoop keeps balls from rolling into other areas).

If you use peer assessments to gather data during game play, you might want to have one student observing the game and a second student recording results. If recording statistics for a game, have two students work together, with one student looking at the game at all times and the other student looking at the recording sheet or handheld device and putting the data in the correct spot. If you use this procedure, the data are much more likely to be accurate.

Managing Written Work

- When setting up a written test, be sure to group all the matching, true–false, and multiple-choice questions together.

- Number the questions consecutively throughout the test (i.e., multiple-choice are 1–20, true–false are 21–26, fill in the diagram are 27–35, and so on). Consecutive numbering makes it easier for students if you are using a separate sheet to record answers; it also is easier for you to answer student questions after the tests are graded and returned.

- If allowing students to write on their tests, leave an answer blank to the left of the question's number so that you don't need to hunt for the answer. Tests with this format are much faster to score.

- Staple the test in the upper right-hand corner; you won't chop off any words or answer blanks.

- Write out the answers to the essay questions and decide ahead of time what answers you will accept and reward with points.

- When grading an actual test, go through and grade page 1 first for all the tests in the class, turning the test so that page 2 is showing. When you grade page 2, you won't need to turn the page. By grading all the page 1 questions, you will learn the answers and it is much faster to score the test. Continue this practice for the entire test. If you have essay questions, it is much easier to grade them consistently if you use this method. An extra benefit of this method is that if your essay questions are at the end of the exam, you won't know whose paper you are reading and you can be completely objective when scoring the answers.

- If giving a long test and using a score sheet, set it up as in table 12.2.

  You can fold the answer sheet on the line and place it next to the student's answer sheet. This way, the test will be adjacent to the answers and will be easy to score.

- If using a score sheet, use a red pencil for your answers to avoid scoring the wrong paper. It is easy to get mixed up and start grading the answer sheet with the student's paper instead of vice versa.

  It is always best to give a written test in a classroom where students can sit at desks. Some librarians might allow you to use the tables in the library for a test. The cafeteria is another option for using chairs and tables.

  However, if you don't have the luxury of having desks or tables for testing, you will need to give the test in the gym. Here are some suggestions:

  ○ Lay the tests face down on the floor. Spread the tests out so that students have space to wiggle a little and so that they cannot look at a neighbor's answers. While you are spreading out the tests, the students wait on the edge of the gym. On a signal, allow the students to move to a test. When everyone has a test, instruct students to turn the test over and begin to complete it.

  ○ Have all students face the same direction while taking the test; this will keep them from looking at someone else's paper. It

Table 12.2   Sample Score Sheet

1. _____	6. _____	11. _____	16. _____	21. _____
2. _____	7. _____	12. _____	17. _____	22. _____
3. _____	8. _____	13. _____	18. _____	23. _____
4. _____	9. _____	14. _____	19. _____	24. _____
5. _____	10. _____	15. _____	20. _____	25. _____

really doesn't matter whether students lie down or sit; just make sure that they all face the same direction.

- ○ You may provide a pencil (place it on top of the test as you are spreading it on the floor) or ask students to bring their own writing implement.

- ○ If you have an activity planned following the test, make sure to provide a box where students can leave their pencils when they finish.

- ○ Don't allow students to write in red ink if you are using red ink to grade the tests.

You should also have management routines for handling papers in their classes. As students enter class, you might have a basket or cardboard box in which they deposit their homework. We also use this technique when teaching in a classroom—assignments are handed in before the start of class.

You may prefer a different routine from the one described previously. If your students sit in squads for attendance or if you teach in a classroom with desks, you may want to develop a routine to have students pass the paper to the right or left. You will then walk down the row and gather papers up from the person sitting in the last row. Some teachers prefer to have students pass the papers forward. When distributing papers, such as a handout or a test, it is unnecessary to hand a copy of the assessment or assignment to each student. You can give copies to each person at the front of the class and then have them pass the papers back or give papers to students sitting in the first row and have them pass papers across the room. The advantage of distributing papers this latter way is that you can go to the opposite side of the class and collect any of the extra papers.

When handing back homework, we prefer to hand the assignment to the student it belongs to. Fold the paper in half so no other students can see the score on the front of the paper. If students wish to share the results with others, they can; however, if they wish to keep the results private, they also have that option.

We have provided you with several different ideas for distributing and collecting papers. Please select the method that you prefer and then teach your students the routine so that the process becomes efficient and doesn't require much time to complete. When teaching routines, use a stopwatch to see how much time it takes to complete the routine. Then, monitor the time occasionally to see if you are using time efficiently.

If you are using portfolios with only one class, a file box will probably be sufficient to store them. If you are doing portfolios with multiple classes, you might want to invest in a large type of file on wheels so it can be taken into the gymnasium.

Regardless of the storage box or file used, we recommend that you use individual folders or hanging files with a manila folder inside that has the student's name written on it to store student artifacts. If you are using portfolios with several classes, consider color coding the files by grade level (sixth grade is blue, seventh is red, ninth is green) or type of class (advanced physical education is blue, outdoor education is red, and so on). If using folders, allow students to decorate the cover so that they can readily find their own file. Be sure that students write their student number on the folder or manila file so that it is easy to reorder once the files are pulled for use. Teachers who use portfolios often have a routine for use such as the following: one student gets the files for a squad, teachers spread the files along the edge of the room, students retrieve them and then return them to a box after use, students retrieve their file or folder and then turn it in as they exit the class, and so on. Ensure that students take responsibility for keeping up with their own portfolios and papers. See Lund and Kirk (2010) for suggestions on how to use portfolios. One final note: Portfolios can take a long time to grade. Try not to assign portfolios for all of your students that are all due at the same time—stagger the dates for submission. Another suggestion is to score the papers that will become the artifacts before submission with the portfolio.

We always make a point to provide an activity for students who finish their tests early. We have a game set up at the end of the gym. If game play is possible, students who are finished have a fun activity to keep them occupied and students who need a little more time don't need to feel like they are holding up the class. Note that this is one advantage of administering the test in the gymnasium.

Assessment Equipment

Figure 12.2 is a list of assessment equipment that every teacher should have. We have discussed the uses of this equipment throughout this chapter and provided some ideas for using it. We suggest

Clipboards (For a class of 30, you'll want 15 clipboards.)

Lidded box for pencils

Pencils

Extra erasers for pencils

Electric pencil sharpener or a manual one if electricity is a problem

White board, markers, and eraser

Multi-use recording sheets

Stopwatches—enough so students can use them for peer assessments

Paper in at least six different colors

File box with a divider for each class

File box to organize blank and completed forms

Multicolored file folders

Rolling cart that can be used to move assessment materials from your office to the gym

Calculator

Record forms—enough for all classes

Hole puncher

Several large measuring tapes

Floor tape

Masking tape

Containers for equipment in the gym

Figure 12.2 Assessment materials.

that you gather your assessment materials so that they will be ready for use whenever you need them. We have seen teachers load these items onto a cart. When it is time for the assessment, roll out the cart, and you'll be ready to go.

Here are some other helpful tips related to equipment and organization:

- If you don't have an unlimited supply of pencils or if students aren't good about bringing their own writing implement to class, you can check out pencils. The student who needs to borrow a pencil is required to give some type of collateral—a shoe, sock, or other item another item not needed while the pencil is being used. After students finishes with the pencils, they will get their collateral back. Students will get a kick out of the system, and you won't need to keep adding pencils to your depleted collection.
- Always carry a clipboard with you to record data. If you are going outside, cover the pages with clear plastic in case of unexpected rain or sprinkler activity.

- Use index cards for recording assessments when you are outside.
- Peer assessment is also an ideal way to organize a class when there is not enough space or equipment for all students to practice at one time.

YOUR TURN 12.2

This chapter provides several ideas for managing assessment. Write down two things that you read about that will be useful to you for administering psychomotor assessments and two things that will help you with written assessments.

Compare your answers with another person and see if you both selected the same items.

Summary

This chapter provides you with several ideas for managing assessment with your students. Remember that you must establish **assessment routines** and teach them to your students. Also remember that it is important to be organized. Make sure that your assessment equipment is ready to use at all times. Last, find a way to organize the data that you will gather as you assess your students. If you have 200 students, you will drown in paper or lose important documents. A wise teacher once told us that it could take you X number of hours to grade a set of papers. It is your choice to spread that time over several weeks or to discipline yourself and complete it right away so that the papers can be returned to students and provide feedback. If the papers are returned to students, they are not piling up in your office. You will also be less likely to lose them. Please think about this and return all student work in a timely manner.

THIRTEEN

Using Assessment Data to Assign a Fair Grade

In other words, grades are not about what students earn; grades are about what students learn.

Brookhart, 2011, p. 12

If we want to have a heated discussion, we ask, "What elements should physical education teachers use when calculating student grades?" Teachers attending in-service workshops become incensed at the suggestions of others that differ from their own. Our teacher candidates weigh in with very strong opinions on this topic as well. The underlying theme in all these viewpoints is that teachers want grades in physical education to be fair. However, *fair* can mean a lot of different things to different people. For some, fair means that teachers consider how much a student improves, while others feel that students who try hard should be rewarded with good grades. In other words, they feel that the grade should be based on *earning* and not *learning*.

In this chapter, we share our views about grading in physical education and provide some guidelines as you develop a grading plan for your classes. Because this book is geared toward secondary physical education, we assume that you are required to assign letter grades to students, thus we also assume that you are not giving *S* and *U* type grades (i.e., satisfactory and unsatisfactory as the rating elements).

YOUR TURN 13.1

When looking at a concept that represents a personal philosophy or belief system, it is good to know your own philosophy before reading about that of others. So, we want you to begin by pretending that you are going to assign grades for a nine-week grading period. Write down the elements that you would include when calculating grades. Be sure to include the percentage for each of the elements that will contribute to the student grade. To make it a little easier, assume that you taught soccer for five weeks and badminton for four weeks.

We aren't going to discuss your ideas right now; we will use this information for our discussions later in the chapter. We simply want you express your thoughts and record them on paper before we start to talk about grades and grading.

The Purpose of Grading

One of the primary purposes of grades is to communicate to others the degree to which students have achieved the learning outcomes specified for the class. In a standards-based classroom, these outcomes are typically tied to the standards associated with the grade level of the class being taught. However, there are other purposes for grades. In some instances, grades are used by university or college administrators to decide if a student will be admitted to that institution. At some of those institutions, admission is quite selective and competitive. If everyone who applied had identical grades, it would be impossible to sort students and to decide which applicants to admit. In physical education, sorting by grades might be done to determine who is allowed to take an advanced course or a specialty course in physical education. For example, a B average in freshman physical education might be required to participate in an advanced physical education class because the B represents the requisite level of pre-learning needed for success in the advanced class. For some, grades are a way to motivate students for their efforts or to give students documentation that they are learning and achieving. Whatever the purpose, the grade should represent the amount of student learning so that those evaluating the student's grades can make a valid **inference** about learning and achievement.

In a standards-based physical education program, the grade should represent the degree to which the student satisfied learning outcomes. In our opinion, a fair grade means that students were required to exert a reasonable amount of effort and that learning did occur. Students were challenged; their knowledge and skills increased. The teacher coached students to high levels of skill and learning and students fulfilled their responsibility to practice and learn. Because of this hard work, students were able to achieve competence.

In physical education, we have standards for all three domains. Thus, the grade should be representative of learning and achievement in the psychomotor, cognitive, and affective domains. Previous chapters of this book explain several different types of assessments for each of these domains. Your grading system should be based on something from each domain. A fair grading system weights these three domains appropriately so that learning outcomes are represented and the intent of the standard is satisfied.

Last, a fair grade means that the final grade is based on data, not just on your opinion. You must be able to justify your grades for students and provide documentation to support your final decisions. Student grades should be consistent and accurate across students. In other words, one student shouldn't get a B because of **improvement,** while another student gets a B because of trying hard, and a third student gets a B because of a high level of skillfulness coupled with some bad behavior.

In chapter 8, we discuss several different types of assessments used to assess the psychomotor domain. If the grade is supposed to represent the degree to which students meet the standards, and if the purpose of physical education is to teach students how to play sports, dance, and do other types of activities, then assessments that represent student competence in those sports or activities are used for a grade. Skill assessments ensure that students can do the skills independent of the game or activity; we have used game play and culminating activity assessments to ensure that students can combine those skills in a meaningful way and demonstrate that the important elements from the psychomotor domain were met.

Chapter 9 contains several performance-based assessments (projects and performances) that represent cognitive domain learning. It also includes a section that explains how to develop written tests. We have used all of these assessment formats to document whether students met the cognitive intent of the standards; any of the summative assessments found in that chapter could be used when calculating student grades. Since formative assessments are used to enhance learning, they will not be included in the grade.

Chapter 10 covers assessments for the affective domain. The key to affective domain assessments is to define the elements that you want students to learn and demonstrate and then identify behaviors that are representative of that element. The teacher-directed assessments found in chapter 10 can be used to document student achievement and to calculate student grades.

Why Don't Physical Education Teachers Base Their Grades on Data?

We suspect that the answer to this question is very complex. For one thing, physical educators tend to love sports and being active. Many young professionals (and, we suspect, many older ones) feel that if students receive high marks in physical education, they will be more likely to enjoy the class. Siedentop, Mand, and Taggart (1986) write about subject matter approach tendencies. When applied to real-world settings, this means that if people are successful at doing something, they will be more likely to continue to do it. For many teachers, *success* is defined by getting a high grade in physical education; by giving high grades, they feel that students will find the class enjoyable.

In addition, we also realize that some teachers will trade compliance and good behavior for a good grade in physical education. In large classes, if students don't follow teacher directions, chaos will result. Tying the grade to behavior makes your life easier. Last, we believe that tradition stands in the way of using data for grades. For many years, grades in physical education have been based on management components, such as attendance and dressing for class. In today's standards-based climate, grades based only on behavior and managerial issues are simply not acceptable. Programs that cannot document student learning with evidence are vulnerable to budget cuts.

⟳ YOUR TURN 13.2

Read the follow scenario. Did this teacher have a fair grading system? Explain your answer.

> One of our beginning teachers was overheard discussing his first grading cycle. He had one student who was very unfit at the beginning of the six weeks (couldn't do one sit-up) and by the end of the grading period could do five sit-ups. This student received a B for her efforts. A second student was a great athlete but his behavior was terrible. This student also received a B because the teacher didn't want to reward bad behavior with a top grade. The third student had missed a few days during the grading period. He was a good student when he was there, but received a B for poor attendance. All three students received a B for different reasons.

Weighting

In many instances, the **weighting** (i.e., giving more emphasis to a given area) of the grading categories is highly connected with your philosophy toward physical education. We both feel quite strongly that the main purpose of physical education is to develop skillful movers. For this reason, we emphasize the psychomotor domain by weighting that domain higher than the other domains and allocating a higher percentage of the grade to psychomotor learning. When the NASPE standards were first published, the writing team gave a lot of thought to the order of the standards. Student achievement in the psychomotor domain was deemed most important; therefore, it became standard 1. If you think about it, student achievement in the cognitive and affective domains is related to performance in the psychomotor domain, so this order makes a lot of sense.

If you want a starting point for a standards-based grading system, we suggest that you develop your grading system so that 50 percent of the grade comes from the psychomotor domain. The remaining 50 percent will come from the cognitive and affective domains. If you are worried about students who struggle with psychomotor domain learning, this split gives those students a chance to boost their final grade with strong performance in the cognitive and affective domains. This also holds that superstar athlete accountable for learning the information important for high levels of performance; it ensures that the student will need to demonstrate reasonable levels of affective domain achievement to receive a top grade.

How you divide the final 50 percent of the grade between the cognitive and affective domains will depend on your philosophy and the content being taught. If you view the cognitive learning as more important, you might assign 30 to 35 percent of the grade to that domain and 15 to 20 percent to the affective domain. Some teachers might feel that they are equal, and other teachers may feel that with their students, affective domain learning should receive greater emphasis.

Content of the units or the instructional model used will also influence how the domains are weighted for grading purposes. For example, if using the Teaching Personal and Social Responsibility (TPSR) instructional model, the affective domain is very important. This would mean that the affective domain would receive greater emphasis on the weighting system. A similar argument could be made with a cooperative instructional model or with adventure education. On the other hand, the Teaching Games for Understanding (TGfU) instructional model emphasizes cognitive learning; if using that model, you will place greater emphasis on the cognitive domain. Most schools do not have a policy for weighting student grades; ultimately, the teacher usually determines the weighting of the domains. However, if your school has a mandated weighting system, by all means, you must follow that.

How are grades calculated when they are weighted? Teachers often have multiple grades for each domain, so the first step is to establish the percentage allocated for each domain (or standard). If the grades for each domain were weighted exactly the same, it would be a simple matter to just add up the grades and divide by 3 (the number of domains). When grades are weighted, calculating the grade is slightly more complicated, but schools often have computer programs that do the work for you. If not, you would take each grade and multiply it by the percentage it is weighted. Add up the results to calculate the grade. In table 13.1, we will weight the domains as follows: psychomotor = 60 percent; affective = 15 percent; cognitive = 25 percent. Of course, when you use weighted grades, the percentages should add up to 100 percent.

We have done a calculation showing how weighting the grade affects the score (see table 13.2). If we had weighted the domains the same and simply averaged the grades (88 + 70 + 90 = 248 ÷ 3), the student's grade would be 82.6. By assigning different weights, you can to emphasize some areas and de-emphasize others. Although, in this example, there is not a large difference, weighting can make a difference in some instances, especially when a plus or minus system is used.

Grading on Fitness

Did you notice that we didn't mention fitness in the previous discussion on weighting grades? The National Association for Sport and Physical Education (NASPE 2010) recommends that student performance on fitness tests not be used to calculate grades. Many reasons exist for this:

- Fitnessgram was never intended to be used as part of a student's grade (www.fitnessgram.net/faqparents).

Table 13.1   Examples of Weighting Scores by Standard

Standard	Percent of grade	Sport or activity	Percentage allocated by unit
1. Demonstrates competency in motor skills and movement patterns needed to perform a variety of physical activities	60%	Team handball	40%
		Badminton	20%
2. Demonstrates understanding of movement concepts, principles, strategies, and tactics as they apply to the learning and performance of physical activities	25%	Team handball	15%
		Badminton	10%
3. Participates regularly in physical activity	5%		5% from activity logs
4. Achieves and maintains a health-enhancing level of physical fitness		Team handball	For these units, fitness will not be directly measured; participation in outside activities will be the goal (see standard 3).
		Badminton	
5. Exhibits responsible personal and social behavior that respects self and others in physical activity settings	5%	Team handball	3% team handball
		Badminton	2% badminton
6. Values physical activity for health, enjoyment, challenge, self-expression, or social interaction	5%		3% team handball
			2% badminton

Table 13.2   Calculating Weighted Grades

Domain	Grade	Weight	Calculation	Result
Psychomotor	88	60%	$88 \times .60 =$	52.8
Cognitive	70	25%	$70 \times .25 =$	17.5
Affective	90	15%	$90 \times .15 =$	13.5
Grade =				83.8 = B

⟳ YOUR TURN 13.3

Calculate the grade for the student described in the following table.

Domain	Grade	Weight	Calculation	Result
Psychomotor	72	60%		
Cognitive	97	25%		
Affective	95	15%		
Grade =				

⟳ YOUR TURN 13.4

Write down the domain and the percentages that you will use to develop your grading system. Note: After reading the discussion in the previous two sections, your responses might be different than you originally thought, which is perfectly all right. Discuss your answers with a partner. Reach consensus and write down the weighting system that you both agreed on.

- The purpose of the Fitnessgram is to give students feedback about their levels of fitness so that they can determine needs and then address any deficiencies (Quinn, personal communication, November 16, 2011).
- To improve cardiorespiratory fitness, students need to have a minimum of 20 minutes of moderate to vigorous activity five days per week. Most physical education classes are not of sufficient length to devote that much time to fitness.
- It takes a lot of class time to do fitness testing correctly. We would rather that you spend that time engaging students in learning activities instead of testing fitness on multiple occasions for a grade.

Therefore, we don't advocate holding students accountable for the results of fitness testing unless you have a class that is devoted to fitness-type activities. Certainly, a weight training class that makes students stronger would be one of those classes. Students in a gymnastics class that meets several days per week might also be held accountable for various flexibility or strength assessments. We do feel that it is permissible to hold students accountable for *participating* in fitness testing. We have done fitness units where students need to take the initial fitness test to determine the types of activities that they should do to address weaknesses or deficiencies regarding fitness. In these cases, we have given students points or credit for completing the assessment. These completion points fall under the affective domain; the actual results of the fitness test were not used to contribute to the final student grade.

Grading on Management Issues

In physical education, teachers often want to grade on management issues such as attendance, turning in daily work or homework, or being a good citizen in class. Teachers often want to include these items in a grade because they want to reward these behaviors. Because the grade should represent the degree to which students have met the learning outcomes of the class (what students learn, not just earn), we feel that these elements should not be included as part of the student grade. Some school systems report an achievement grade (based on learning) and a behavior grade, which includes attendance and those other managerial items. A behavior grade is often indicated with either an *S* (satisfactory)

or *U* (unsatisfactory) grade symbol. Additionally, web-based grading programs allow parents to view test scores, homework completion, and attendance for their children, thus eliminating the need to develop a reporting system for those items. In a standards-based grading system, the grade should represent the amount of learning demonstrated by the students.

We frequently hear stories about the strategies that teachers use to get students to dress for physical education class. Recently, a teacher related his policy on dressing for class. According to him, it was impossible to fail physical education because he allowed make-ups for not dressing for class. On a make-up day, students are required to come to class in street clothes and meet in the center of the gym. The students then have 90 seconds to run to the locker room and change into participation clothing and then return to the center of the gym. Three successful changes in the allotted time would negate one of the no-dress days accumulated during the grading period. When we were in high school, our physical education teachers allowed shower make-ups: For all the days that girls skipped showering, they were allowed to change out of their street clothes, shower, and redress to make up for those skipped showers.

As you read this, you might think this is really dumb. No doubt, your students would agree. The purpose of dressing for physical education classes is to promote safety and good hygiene. Make-up showers and make-ups for dressing out simply are not valid or useful. We strongly feel that dressing for class is a managerial issue; if dressing for class is important for the activity, it should be handled in other ways. You should not use a grade as a way to get students to dress for participation. Since dressing for class is a managerial concern and not a learning outcome, find ways other than a grade to encourage students to dress appropriately.

Here is something else to consider; most elementary children change their shoes to prepare for class. Additionally, several different physical education activities (e.g., social or square dancing, archery, bowling, golf) taught at the secondary level could be safely performed if students only change their shoes; a full change of clothes is not necessary. Many middle school programs have adopted this policy, having decided that for relatively short classes (40 to 45 minutes), changing clothes is simply not worth the effort. They would rather keep students active for those 10 to 15 minutes than require them to dress out.

We suggest that you use common sense; do not include these items in your grading system. This policy eliminates the need for making up missed showers or changes of clothes.

Grading on Improvement

Grading on student progress or improvement is another practice that we avoid. Again, the grade should represent the degree of student learning with relation to the standards. In a standards-based grading system, it doesn't matter where the students begin. It only matters that they are able to cross the finish line of learning. If you let students know what they are expected to accomplish and then provide the content development and instruction to get students to that goal, then students should be able to achieve competence. If students reach it more quickly than others, then they should be challenged with more advanced material and allowed to maximize their learning potential. If it takes some students longer than others to achieve competence and they are required to practice outside of class, that is okay. With this approach, we know that after the physical education class is completed, students will have the skills and knowledge to participate in various activities; thus taking the first step toward achieving the ultimate goal of physical education—a physically active lifestyle.

Creating a Grading System

Some teachers like to use percentages to calculate grades. We have found that the use of percentages is abstract to students, so we suggest that you translate these percentages to a **point system.** In the following example, we have assigned 60 percent of the points to the psychomotor domain, 25 percent of the points to the cognitive domain, and 15 percent of the points to the affective domain. Table 13.3 shows this breakdown, as well as the assessments that we will use. Note that the points are divided between the two units taught this grading period according to time spent on the unit. Students played badminton for four weeks and team handball for five weeks.

60% psychomotor skill (240 points)

25% knowledge (100 points)

15% affective (60 points)

100% total (400 points)

Table 13.3   Breakdown of Points in Two Physical Education Units

Psychomotor	Cognitive	Affective
Team handball		
150 points	**60 points**	**40 points**
Game play assessments (2 @ 30 points each)	15 points—game play officiating (3 @ 5 points each)	20 points—journal
30 points—team handball practice log	20 points—game play assessment (2 @ 10 points each)	10 points—peer assessment completion (2 @ 5 points each)
20 points—shooting test	25 points—student project choice (write article for newspaper, create a game broadcast, write a script for a broadcast, analysis of a video tape of game play)	10 points—teacher assessment (2 @ 5 points each)
20 points—passing test		
10 points—goalkeeping test		
10 points—dribbling test		
Badminton		
90 points	**40 points**	**20 points**
15 points—serve test	20 points—game play assessment (2 @ 10 points)	Sponge activity self-assessment completion (2 @ 5 points each)
15 points—wall volley test	10 points—scouting the competition strategy analysis (2 @ 5 points)	10 points—exit slips (2 @ 5 points each)
15 points—continuous rally test	10 points—written test	
45 points—game play assessment (3 @ 15 points each)		
Grading scale		
A: 360–400 points, B: 320–359 points, C: 280–319 points, D: 240–279 points, F: 239 and below		

On the preceding grading system, the standards were represented by the three learning domains. Standard 1 is the psychomotor domain, standard 2 is the cognitive domain, and the remaining standards are represented by affective domain assessments. The grading system shown in table 13.4 represents the same units, but assigns points by standards instead of grouping standards 3, 5, and 6 together for the affective domain. Standard 4 is not represented, since the primary fitness benefit for these units is cardiorespiratory fitness, which is captured with standard 1.

You may ask why this example is based on 400 points. The decision to use 400 points was arbitrary. Some teachers like to use 100 points because it makes it easy to do percentages. When you have a low number of total points, teachers will start giving half points for an assignment, which really makes it complicated to calculate grades. It is far easier to use whole numbers when adding final grades. We have found that using 400 points allows us to assign an adequate number of points to certain assignments, and it makes the final calculation fairly simple. If you want to use 500 points, 300 points, or something else, go ahead. Our suggestion is to allocate enough points so that you are using whole numbers, but not so many points that you have to use higher levels of mathematics to do the calculations.

Disadvantages of a Negative Grading System

Some teachers like to start out with the premise that all students have an A in the class and that when they do something bad, their grade is decreased. This is called a **negative grading system.** We simply don't like this way of approaching a grading system because it focuses your attention on what students are doing incorrectly. Using a negative point system means that students could fail the class very early in the grading period, thus giving you no way to hold students accountable for any behavior or

YOUR TURN 13.7

One of our students indicated that he liked the negative grading system. This student was a waiter so we asked him if he liked it when his customers put their tip on the table when he greeted them and then told him that it was his to lose—any incident of poor service would result in less money left for a tip at the end of the meal. He didn't like the system.

How is this method of tipping the waiter similar to the negative grading system? If you had a colleague that used the negative grading system, what would you say to convince this person that it was not an effective way to evaluate student learning?

YOUR TURN 13.5

Go back to Your Turn 13.1 and look at the grading system that you created. How have your ideas changed? Record the major changes in your system. Use this exercise to think carefully about how your ideas about grading might be evolving.

YOUR TURN 13.6

Referring to the template in the following table, create a grading plan for a sport or activity lasting five weeks. Indicate the assessments that you will use for each domain and the number of points or percentage of the total grade that each assessment will represent.

Psychomotor	Knowledge	Affective

Grading scale

A 000–000 points, B 000–000 points, C 000–000 points, D 000–000 points, F 000 and below

Table 13.4   Points Assigned by Standards in Two Physical Education Units

Standard	Percent of grade	Sport or activity	Assessment and points
1. Demonstrates competency in motor skills and movement patterns needed to perform a variety of physical activities	60%	Team handball (150 points)	60 points—game play assessments (2 @ 30 points each) 30 points—team handball practice log 20 points—shooting test 20 points—passing test 10 points—goalkeeping test 10 points—dribbling test
		Badminton (90 points)	45 points—game play assessment (3 @ 15 points each) 15 points—serve test 15 wall—volley test 15 points—continuous rally test
2. Demonstrates understanding of movement concepts, principles, strategies, and tactics as they apply to the learning and performance of physical activities	25%	Team handball (60 points)	15 points—game play officiating (3 @ 5 points each) 20 points—game play assessment (2 @ 10 points each) 25 points—student project choice (write article for newspaper, create a game broadcast, write a script for a broadcast, analysis of a video tape of game play)
		Badminton (40 points)	20 points—game play assessment (2 @ 10 points) 10 points—scouting the competition strategy analysis (2 @ 5 points) 10 points—written test
3. Participates regularly in physical activity	5%	(20 points)	10 activity tickets @ 2 points each
4. Achieves and maintains a health-enhancing level of physical fitness	0%	Team handball	
		Badminton	
5. Exhibits responsible personal and social behavior that respects self and others in physical activity settings	5%	Team handball (10 points)	10 points—peer assessment (2 @ 5 points each)
		Badminton (10 points)	10 points—sponge activity self-assessment (2 @ 5 points each)
6. Values physical activity for health, enjoyment, challenge, self-expression, or social interaction	5%	Team handball (10 points)	Teacher observation during game play 2 @ 5 points each
		Badminton (10 points)	Teacher observation during game play 2 @ 5 points each

learning. Additionally, the system is typically based on managerial items (e.g., misbehavior, not dressing for class, or attendance) instead of basing the grade on the degree to which a student achieves the learning outcomes of the class.

Bonus Points

We are not opposed to giving students a few bonus points here and there, but we have two caveats. First, when giving bonus points, you must be certain that the bonus points represent additional learning. Giving students bonus points for participating in a 10K road race during a cross country running unit is very different from giving points for buying a shirt to support school spirit or bringing in chip dip for a class party.

Second, we have seen teachers who give so many bonus points that the bonus points actually distort the grading system. Remember that the grading system was weighted so that it represented student learning in the various learning domains. Giving an extra 10 points during a quarter in which students have possible 400 points will not disrupt the system. Giving 150 points during this semester will distort the grade. Remember that the grade is a way to communicate to others the degree to which students achieved the learning goals for the class. Do not give out bonus points to the extent that the amount of student learning is not clearly represented.

For example, consider an English teacher who assigns a term paper worth 150 points, then offers 150 potential bonus points during the course of the grading period. In this system, students who did poorly on the term paper could receive the same grade as those students who spent many hours toiling on the project. This extreme example illustrates how bonus points can negate learning.

We all have had negligent students who were absent, didn't participate, or didn't practice during the quarter and suddenly find themselves with a low or failing grade. Imagine that a student comes to you and says, "Is there any way that I can do extra credit and bring my grade up?" Your answer here should be No! When you show that students can appeal to your soft heart in this manner, the lesson taught is that they can do whatever they want—fail to study for tests, participate, or learn the appropriate skills—without being penalized in any way. This may be harsh, but by declining this request, you

are doing students a favor, even if it means that they will not be able to play football, run track, or participate in their upcoming dance recital. Students must learn that there are consequences for their actions. It is better to learn this over a quarter grade than in another scenario with even more dire consequences.

YOUR TURN 13.8

Do you agree or disagree with not allowing students to earn extra credit to pass the class? Write down your answer and then share your response with a partner.

What ideas did you have in common? How were your responses different? If you were colleagues you would need to develop a departmental policy toward bonus points. Write down that policy.

Grading Skill Assessments

Some teachers might argue that a skill assessment is really a formative assessment—it is something that students use on their way to being able to use the skill in a game or activity. We view skill assessments as an intermediate stopping point on the way to incorporating the skill into the culminating activity, so we do include skill assessments when calculating grades. The skill assessment should not be the only way that students are held accountable for psychomotor domain performance; you should always be trying to move students toward competent performance on the culminating activity when skills are used in an applied setting. Skill assessments are an excellent way to observe student attainment of the skill in a closed environment. In this setting, you can ensure that the student will have the opportunity to perform the skill (this doesn't always happen in the game), and that outside factors (reaching to save the ball and demonstrating poor form in order to win the point) don't influence skill performance. Our students got a lot of extra practice on their skills when we held them accountable on skill assessments. Using the skill in a closed environment is an excellent way to teach your body how to perform the skill automatically, without having to think about when or how to do it. When professional athletes want to improve their skills, they practice the skills in a closed environment. Think about all the times you have seen tennis players hit balls against the wall instead of with an opponent, the Pistol Pete ball-handling skills used in basketball, and Forrest Gump practicing his table tennis skills against the other half of the table. We see the value of skill assessments away from the game and advocate including these data when calculating student grades.

The level of performance students need for a certain grade should be determined from the skill level required for participating with competence. To set these levels, we ascertain the performance levels of people who can participate with competence and then set the criteria there. To arrive at grades for skill assessments, we decrease the criterion score by 10 percent for each level. Let's say that a volleyball player who plays with competence can, after some practice, set the ball to a target on the wall 25 times in 30 seconds. Using the 10 percent rule, we establish the following range: 23–25 = A, 20–22 = B, 18–19 = C, D = 15–17, and below 15 is unsatisfactory. If, after administering the assessment, your best students are unable to reach those scores despite lots of practice and fairly good skill competence, then you should make adjustments so that the students are not penalized on their grades; the next time that the assessment is administered, you will use the adjusted range. Similarly, if students who have 15 reps on the skill assessment can play a passable game, then the bottom score of the skill test needs to be adjusted as well. On the other end of the spectrum, let's say that the criteria established are too low, and everyone winds up in the A range with rather minimal effort and low game play competence. In this instance, the ranges need to be adjusted the next time that you use the assessment; however, for this first time, you will allow all students to receive their A. Never change your grading scale after you've announced it if the change will negatively affect your students' grades.

YOUR TURN 13.9

While teaching a racket sports unit, a teacher established some pretty high standards for the forehand volley skill (pickleball). No student made it into the top category, so the teacher adjusted the grading scale down. A badminton unit followed, and all students received an A on the first day of the serving assessment. The teacher did not adjust the test criteria even though some students demonstrated weak performance during a game. Did the teacher do the right thing in both of these cases? Write down your response.

Giving Students Opportunity to Retake Skill Assessments

With the mastery approach used in standards-based learning, think of yourself as a coach trying to help students reach a given level of performance or meet a criterion. For this reason, we give students multiple chances to pass skill assessments. When they reach the criterion score for the assessment, they no longer need to do that assessment. With a lower-skilled student, this approach rewards student effort in a measurable way; with good effort and practice, they will be able to reach a reasonable level of performance. Remember with a standards-based approach to learning, the goal is for all students to become competent performers. Allowing multiple opportunities for students to complete skill assessments takes some of the pressure off the testing situation and provides an opportunity for a student who had limited prior experience with the sport or activity to become more skilled and more successful.

One caveat is offered on the retest philosophy: When allowing students to retake skill assessments, they must not be allowed to constantly retake the assessment, thus wasting your time. When allowing students to retake assessments, you should insist on a practice period or certain number of repetitions before allowing the student to do the retest. If you fail to specify a practice interval, students will take the assessment continuously, since they figure they have nothing to lose. This takes up your teaching time and prevents you from helping others. All students should have the opportunity to retest for a higher goal; this should not be a privilege afforded only to low-performing students. We understand that class time may force you to put a limit on the number of times a student can retake a test; however, we hope you consider adopting this philosophy whenever possible.

Should you give feedback during psychomotor assessments? If you are assessing some type of student learning other than psychomotor skill during the assessment, the answer is no. You cannot assess student knowledge and tell them the answers at the same time! However, as stated earlier, we allow students to do skill assessments multiple times. In these instances, a little hint or encouragement is probably okay. We like using skill assessments for learning tasks in class because students can improve skill levels and learn the protocol used for the upcoming assessment. During these formative practice sessions, it is very appropriate to give feedback and coach the students.

One of the drawbacks of giving feedback during the actual grading experience is that you can negatively influence a student's performance. Let's say that you are assessing the tee shot in a golf unit. You remind the student to do a certain task, and the student remembers that critical element, but forgets all the other good things that he or she has been doing during the tee shot for the past two weeks. The one critical element is done correctly at the expense of all those other things. A person's mind can play games at times. For this reason, if doing a summative assessment, let students get into a good frame of mind, concentrate on the task at hand, and do their best.

Grading on the Curve

Grading on the curve is correctly used in reference to a normal curve, and it is called **norm-referenced grading.** It is a way of comparing the performance of students with other members of the group. Let's say that you have decided to use the normative curve to assign grades. In this system, it is assumed that a class of students will be distributed according to the normal curve (see figure 13.1), so 3 percent of the students receive a grade of A, 15 percent of the students receive a B, 64 percent of the students receive a C, 15 percent of the students receive a D (the same percentage as received a B), and 3 percent of the students receive an F (same number that received an A). With a norm-referenced grading system, you can see how students compare with one another, but you have no idea how well they performed against an external criterion. If you have a group of low-skilled students, they would like this system, since 3 percent of the students will receive As and 15 percent will receive Bs. However, with a highly skilled group of students, they would not like the system, because 15 percent of the students must receive a D, and 3 percent must fail.

Many people incorrectly use the term *grading on the curve* to make adjustments to the grading criteria. When students don't perform on an assessment as well as was expected, the teacher will lower the standard and then create a grading scale based on this lower student performance. Most teachers do not use a true normative curve (the same number must fail as receive an A), but they do make adjustments to the grading scale so that fewer students receive lower scores. This practice is really not grading on the curve.

In standards-based grading, teachers set a level of performance, and all students who reach that level will receive the corresponding grade. This system is referred to as a **criterion-referenced grading** system. If the entire class reaches mastery, the teacher is a genius, and all students receive an A for their performance.

YOUR TURN 13.10

Some published skill tests have different criteria for male and female students (boys tend to have more strength and can often perform better than girls). Respond to the following questions in writing: Is this practice fair? Is it consistent with a criterion-referenced philosophy? When you establish skill assessments, will you require better performance from your male students? Justify your answer.

Averaging Scores for a Final Grade

Consider the grades in table 13.5 for Darius and Demetri:

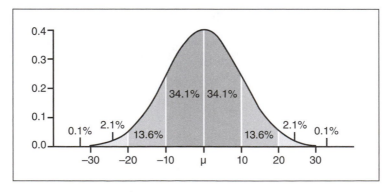

Figure 13.1 A normal curve.

Reprinted from http://commons.wikimedia.org/wiki/File:Standard_deviation_diagram.svg.

Table 13.5   Examples of Student Grades

	Test 1	Test 2	Test 3	Test 4	Average grade
Darius	25%	50%	75%	100%	62.5%
Demetri	100%	75%	50%	25%	62.5%

YOUR TURN 13.11

Given the scores in table 13.5, has either student achieved competence? Explain your answer.

Let's put the test scores into perspective. From the data, Darius began the unit not knowing much about the topic, but by the end, he was able to achieve competence. On the other hand,

Demetri had a good background in the skill, and started quite strong, but failed to practice and improve; by the end of the unit, he didn't demonstrate much learning. Where students begin in terms of skill level and knowledge should not affect the final grade. If you stop to think about it, coaches are not evaluated on the quality of their practice sessions. Players are allowed to make mistakes during practice. What is important is the learning that players demonstrate when

YOUR TURN 13.12

React to the statements in the following table and write a sentence or two to explain your reaction. Indicate whether you agree or disagree with the statement. We suggest you discuss each statement with a colleague.

Our thoughts	Your reaction	Agree or disagree? Why?
If using a group project for a grade, find a way to grade individual students' effort. Never base a student's grade on the work of others.		
Never give students a lower grade than they deserved to motivate them to try harder. Too often, this will backfire and have a negative effect on student motivation.		
Don't use grades as a weapon or to retaliate for bad behavior. The grade should be based on the scale established at the beginning of the grading period.		
If you want to grade behavior, give a separate grade for it. The main grade should be for learning and achievement.		
If your top students aren't getting your highest grades, you need to change your grading system.		
If all students aren't achieving competence and all are getting the same grade, you need to change your grading system.		

they play the game. The same holds true here: Allow students to practice and make mistakes while progressing through the unit. If they are able to achieve competence at the end, you have accomplished your instructional goal. If using a game-play rubric, don't average scores. Instead, use the final evaluation to determine learning.

Zeros and Missed Work

Some people feel that students who fail to turn in assignments or do work should be penalized and should not be allowed to make up the assignment. However, giving a **zero** with a grading system based on 100 percent will make it almost impossible for a student to end up with a passing grade; zero scores can skew the grading system if you are using a 100-point or percentage system. For this reason, we strongly advise using a grading system such as the one given earlier in this chapter. If a student misses an assessment, this does not devastate the grade for the grading period. Remember that students' grades should reflect the degree to which they have accomplished the learning outcomes established for the class. A single missed assignment should not distort that reflection.

Summary

Figure 13.2 is a summary of assessments that we have used to assess learning and subsequently grade our students. Others exist; feel free to add your own.

This chapter provides examples of a standards-based grading system and alerts you to several things to avoid when establishing your system. Ultimately, how you grade your students must be compatible with the system established by your school district. If possible, we strongly encourage you to try our ideas and base your grades on learning instead of earning.

Psychomotor	Cognitive	Affective
Skill tests	Written tests	Completion of sponge activities
Game-play assessments	Projects	
Dance performances	Quizzes	Completion of journal entries
GPAI (Note: must have a way to use data to calculate a grade)	Officiating (Note: need a rubric to determine a score)	Teacher observations using a rubric for the behavior
	Scorekeeping during a game	Completion of exit slips
Fitness test results (when teaching fitness units)	Announcing a game	Fulfilling team duties for sport education units
Video of simulated game (students are required to demonstrate certain shots)	GPAI (Note: must have a way to use data to calculate a grade)	Fulfilling duty team requirements for sport education units
Scores in a target game (e.g., golf, archery, bowling)	Video of simulated game (students are required to demonstrate certain rules or tactics)	Completion of fitness testing
Performance in individual sports (e.g., gymnastics, diving)	Coach's playbook	Completion of peer assessments
Statistics from game play	Portfolio	Heart rate monitor printouts
	Analysis or critique of a game or dance performance	Activity tickets
	Scouting the competition	Participation in activities related to sport and activity units outside of class
	Fitness plan	

Figure 13.2   Summary of assessments useful for calculating student grades.

FOURTEEN

Developing Your Plan to Become an Assessor

You can't go forward with only passionately argued opinions. To succeed in tearing down old traditions, you must have new traditions to take their place.

Guskey, 2011, p. 21

Going back to our opening story, Mr. Thomas completed his badminton unit, and his students had a blast. They learned a new game and became quite skilled. Although some students initially struggled with the skill assessments on the serve and forehand drive, eventually all students were able to reach criterion scores of a C or better. For the clear-shot skill assessment, the majority of the class reached the level of performance to receive a B or better. The best part about using the skill assessments was that students were encouraged to practice and help one another. They even cheered for the people who struggled initially, but were eventually able to succeed. The badminton tournament was very competitive, and the better skilled players learned to place their serves and forehand shots so they were difficult to return. On the final journal entry, students indicated overwhelmingly that they had enjoyed playing and that they were especially proud of their personal efforts that went into learning to play the game. Initially, during the games, some students demonstrated poor behavior that was not readily apparent to Mr. Thomas until students turned in their affective-domain peer evaluations of game play. By having students do game-play affective-domain evaluations on their opponents, he was able to pinpoint the students who were struggling. After watching games played by those students, Mr. Thomas discovered that some of the disputes were caused because students didn't know the rules, which was easily remedied. Because of the game-play rubric, students understood his expectations for game play and played according to that standard. One student's parents questioned their child's grade, but Mr. Thomas was able to provide data that explained the reason for the grade. Even though it was a lot of work initially, Mr. Thomas is now convinced that the assessments helped his students become more competent and that the entire unit ran much more smoothly as a result of the assessment system he implemented. Mr. Thomas will tweak some of the assessments after he finishes grading this unit in preparation for the next time he teaches badminton. By making changes now while the ideas are fresh in his mind, he will not have to rely on his memory when he prepares to teach badminton the next time.

Changing Assessment in a Standards-Based Educational Climate

During our discussions about writing this book and while using it to teach an assessment course to future teachers, we have identified several differences between the way that we were taught to assess our students and the way that we approach assessment today. These differences are summarized in table 14.1.

We think that most of the items on this table have been explained throughout the book. Student learning should be central to the delivery of instruction, and assessments developed before the start of instruction are a key part of student learning. You need to identify a level of competence that allows students to enjoy participation in the activity, and then use diagnostic, formative, and summative assessments to encourage and verify learning. These assessments will allow you to make valid inferences about whether students have learned and to point out areas still in need of instruction. We have three items on this list that we wish to discuss in more detail.

Students Are Informed of Criteria and Expectations at the Beginning of a Unit

To illustrate the power of prior knowledge about grading (Lund & Shanklin, 2011), a teacher taught badminton to two classes that, at the start of the study, were of about the same ability level. Initial ability was determined by an analysis of

Table 14.1   Differences Between Traditional and Standards-Based Approaches to Assessment

Traditional approach to assessment	Standards-based approach to assessment
Teaching is central to the delivery of units.	Student learning is central to the delivery of units.
Emphasis is on delivering the content and then testing students on that content at the completion of instruction.	Emphasis is on helping students reach a level of competency that will allow them to participate in activity at an enjoyable level.
Characterized by pre- and posttesting with an emphasis on improvement	Characterized by diagnostic, formative, and summative assessments with an emphasis on competence
Assessments are developed and administered at the conclusion of instruction.	Assessments are developed before instruction begins and delivered throughout the instructional process.
Good tests are valid and reliable.	Teachers are able to make valid inferences from assessment tools.
Evaluation is primarily summative for the purpose of grading.	Formative assessments are used to determine student progress toward reaching the final goals of instruction and to provide feedback to the teacher for use with planning lessons.
Grade is based on a one-time testing experience.	Grade is based on a longer culminating activity.
Criteria and expectations are not shared with students at the beginning of instruction.	Students are informed of criteria and expectations at the beginning of a unit.
Teachers believe that only athletic students are capable of learning.	Teachers believe that all students can learn.
Teacher assumes a gatekeeper role to see how many students pass the class.	Teacher assumes a coaching role to assist all students in meeting the standards.

the number and quality of responses performed by the students before the unit began. After three days, students in the treatment class were told that they would be held accountable for skill tests on serving, forehand and backhand strokes, and participation in game play. They were given the criterion scores for each of the assessments. Students in both classes improved (better form and more responses), with lower-skilled students in the treatment class showing the greatest gains. Response rates for lower-skilled students went from approximately 30 hits per class during the initial days of the unit to 180 responses by the end of the unit. The low-skilled students in the treatment class became almost as proficient as the higher-skilled students in the control class, while their counterparts in the control class did not even approach those types of improvements. Lest you think that there were other factors, the same teacher taught the same lessons in both classes. The only difference between the two classes was the knowledge that they would be held accountable. These kinds of results make it clear that assessment can be a powerful factor in student learning.

Teachers Believe That All Students Can Learn

We have noticed that several of our teacher candidates feel that if students do not possess inherent athletic ability, then they cannot be taught new skills. According to the achievement goal theory, people have one of two orientations toward learning new skills (Cox, 2012). For people with a **task orientation,** their goal is mastery of a particular skill. They believe that if they work hard, they will be able to learn the task, and if they are better today at the task than they were a week ago, then they have high ability. In other words, self-improvement is a goal. In contrast, people with an **ego orientation** to achievement perceive a difference between ability and effort. Their sense of self-confidence is linked to performing better than others instead of to improvement. People with an ego orientation believe that ability is too great a barrier to overcome and that low-ability students cannot learn to perform a skill or play a game. To make the grade fair, teachers with an ego orientation want to grade on student effort, or the proverbial act of trying hard, because they believe that students are really not capable of achieving mastery of a task.

Some of our teacher candidates have an ego-oriented approach with their students because they feel that if the student is not athletic, then the student cannot learn. Too often, this translates into a gender issue. We see female students sitting out of an activity while the teacher does not try to engage them. Learning becomes a self-fulfilling prophecy because the low-skilled students are left out of practice activities, and they never learn new skills and activities.

We believe that assessments enhance learning and that teachers should use assessments to determine what students have learned as well as gaps in learning, as was demonstrated in the Lund and Shanklin (2011) study. If students know what the goal for the assessment is, and if they have a way to measure this and practice activities that will help them learn, they can take a task-oriented approach and gain competence.

YOUR TURN 14.1

Do you believe that all students can learn or that only those with natural ability can be successful? Provide a rationale to back up your view and record your thoughts. Discuss this topic with a partner and see if you agree or disagree.

Gatekeeper Versus Coach Approach

In the past, we have observed teachers who acted like gatekeepers: They wanted to see how hard they could make the material, and they actually took pride in the number of students who failed their classes. They perceived that if several students failed, the course held rigor. Today, we want teachers to act more like coaches who motivate students to learn and give lots of encouragement and multiple chances so that students have every possible opportunity to learn. Which will you be—the gatekeeper or the facilitator of learning?

Concept Map

In the preface, you were encouraged to complete a concept map. After reading this book and completing the questions in the chapters, we want you to go back to the assignment and complete a new concept map that represents your current

understanding of assessment and assessment practices.

This assignment is one that we use with our teacher candidates. We find that they are amazed at the difference between the two maps and how their understanding of assessment has changed during the course. We hope that you feel much more confident about your ability to assess your students.

YOUR TURN 14.2

Compare your first concept map with the one that you just completed. What differences do you note between the two maps? Has your knowledge of assessment increased?

The Need to Keep Learning

Beginning teachers often struggle with developing assessments for their units. Research tells us that the best teaching occurs when teachers have a strong knowledge base for the content of their unit. Teachers who are skilled in the sport or activity that they are teaching typically provide more tasks for students (Hastie & Vlaisavljevic, 1999). They know what is important for player success and hold their students accountable for learning those items. We think that if teachers know what students need to be held accountable for in familiar units, it will be easier for them to develop assessments. We have taught units in which we have competence and, by far, these are our favorites. However, we also have taught things that we were far less familiar with, but we have been able to develop reasonable levels of skill with our students. So, how did we do it?

First, we realized that what we learned in the activity and sport classes during our undergraduate years was not going to be the last thing that we ever learned. Since graduating from our undergraduate institutions and as certified teachers, we have learned to teach, play, or participate in gymnastics, trampoline, ultimate (disk), pickleball, team handball, and country western dance, to name just a few sports and activities. If you can participate even at a minimal level, this will help you teach. We strongly recommend that you keep learning new activities and sports.

Second, over the years, we have acquired extensive libraries of books with ideas for drills and lead-up games that we have modified and used during our classes. Recently, we have noticed a strong reluctance from our students to purchase these books. Today, many teacher candidates and teachers rely on the web for information. Our caution here is that sometimes novices write and post information on the web that is incorrect. Books tend to be written by experts (the publishing company does a lot of investigation before they invest in publishing a new title), and these writers often have really good ideas arranged in a teaching progression that they have used with success over the years. We see a lot of information published on websites by beginners presented in a random order, with no indication of which steps should come first. We are not saying that you should stay away from web sources, we are merely advising you to check your sources for expertise. We know that several sites are great. Most of the sports and activities taught in physical education have a national association that provides excellent information on the association's website. If you are hooked on getting information online, these websites would be a good place to start. However, please remember that there are other good sources of information that are not on the web.

Third, we have learned over the years that if you focus on the tactics of a game, you will probably have a good start on what you need to assess. This revelation came when we were working with a group of teachers to develop middle school assessments. We had spent two days identifying things that we should assess in a variety of sports: soccer, badminton, basketball, volleyball, and so on. As we looked at the various sports, we saw a pattern emerging. The items we had included for soccer, basketball, team handball, and lacrosse were all pretty similar. The same was true for volleyball, badminton, and pickleball. We found that we could actually use a generalized rubric for all the sports grouped in the same game category. About a year later, while reading articles and books written by authors connected with the Teaching Games for Understanding and the tactical games movement, we realized that we had simply reinvented a wheel that someone else had discovered several years before us. (Well, not really. We were working on the assessment part and it was a little different, even though the principles still applied.) So, when trying to figure out what to assess when you are unfamiliar with a sport, start with the tactics of the game.

Fourth, we do what every great teacher does: We borrow from others and modify things to fit our needs. We attend conferences and talk with colleagues. Many times, the assessment we get from them isn't exactly what we need, but it will work with some modifications. We've also found that game-play assessments with some modifications can work for other sports in that tactical category. Go back to chapter 4 and convert the qualitative badminton rubric to another net/wall game to see if what we say is true.

Becoming a Good Assessor

We are going to encourage you to think big but to start small as you begin to incorporate more assessments into your teaching. The road to becoming a quality assessor is not easy, but it is one that you can start to travel on right now. For example, you might develop assessments for one unit and then ask a colleague for feedback. If both of you develop assessments and agree to work together, you will have assessments for two units. Try the assessments out (pilot) and then reflect on student learning and the effectiveness of the assessments. Make the appropriate revisions for the next time you teach the unit and share these revisions with your assessment buddy.

With regard to instructional skills, administering assessment is a teaching skill, just like giving feedback, presenting tasks, or motivating students. The skill of administering assessments has to be planned and practiced, just as you do other teaching skills. It won't come easily at first, but it does get easier with practice. When working to improve your skills for implementing assessments, start with one class. Select your best class—the students who are most cooperative—and begin administering assessments with them.

Often, the hardest part of being a good assessor (and teacher) is making the commitment to improve the way that you currently do things and then follow through to make the appropriate

▶ YOUR TURN 14.3

Write down three things that you intend to do as a result of reading this book that will make you a better assessor. Indicate the expected date that you plan to complete each item and any preparatory work that you need to do in order to complete it.

Place this list on your desk, refrigerator, and a few other places so that you see it often. This list represents your promise to yourself to continue to improve your teaching skills and to become a better teacher.

changes. Now is the time for you to make a commitment to being a better assessor and teacher.

Summary

We hope that the information provided in this book has helped you become aware of the various ways that you can use assessment to enhance student learning. Just as we began our assessment journeys more than 40 years ago, we encourage you to start yours now. Take that first step, and use the ideas in this book as your roadmap. It is a journey worth starting. We wish you safe travels!

GLOSSARY

accountable (chapter 4)—Occurs when a teacher holds students responsible for learning or completion tasks.

activity logs/tickets (chapter 10)—Types of self-assessment in which students keep track of participation in physical activities outside of the physical education class.

affective domain (chapters 1 and 10)—In physical education, this concerns the feelings, attitudes, and dispositions that students have toward participating in physical activities.

alignment (chapters 2 and 6)—Teachers assess what they teach by ensuring that assessments give information about the learning outcomes and standards.

analytic rubric (chapter 4)—Allows discrete analysis of the various descriptors necessary to the performance or product.

anecdotal records (chapter 10)—Written records, kept by a teacher, to capture the affective domain behaviors of students throughout the semester or grading period.

artifacts (chapter 9)—Documents and assessment records completed and selected by students for inclusion in a portfolio to demonstrate growth over time.

assessable (chapter 7)—When a learning outcome contains a clear criterion, the teacher and students are able to determine if the learning outcome has been met.

assessment (chapter 1, 11)—NASPE's (1995) definition is "the process of gathering evidence about a student's level of achievement. . . and of making inferences based on that evidence" (vii).

assessment data (chapter 11)—The written record of the assessment process.

assessment for learning (chapter 1)—Ongoing assessments used to help students learn by providing feedback that leads to goal setting and improvement; they also help the teacher adjust instruction to meet students' needs.

assessment of learning (chapter 1)—Assessments used for grading; they are final because there is no chance for the teacher to adjust or for learners to improve.

assessment routines (chapter 12)—Management strategies for administering assessments that are taught and used frequently so that students automatically know what to do when the assessment is used.

assessment supplies (chapter 12)—Materials like pencils and clipboards that help assessment tasks run smoothly.

assessment task (chapter 5)—An activity during which students are assessed.

average (chapter 11)—A numerical score calculated by dividing the sum by the total number of scores.

backward design (chapters 2, 3, and 9)—The process used to develop a unit of study.

baseline (chapter 5)—A beginning score that represents what students know or can do before instruction and practice.

block plan (chapter 3)—A way to briefly indicate what you are going to teach every day.

Bloom's taxonomy (chapter 9)—Defines six levels of cognitive learning from factual knowledge to more complex thinking.

checklist (chapters 8 and 10)—Contains a list of critical elements that should be present in competent performance.

closed environment (chapters 2 and 4)—Reasonably stable circumstances while skills are practiced or played.

cognitive domain (chapters 1 and 9)—Knowing and understanding tactics, problem solving, rules, skills, player positions, and key elements of performance.

competence (chapters 2 and 3)—Students are able to perform a skill fairly automatically when in the applied setting.

competent (chapter 7)—Students leave your program with sufficient skills and concepts to enjoy being physically active for a lifetime.

condition (chapter 7)—The part of a learning outcome that specifies exactly how a task is performed (influenced by equipment, space, rules, number of players, or number of skills).

constructed response (chapter 9)—In this type of cognitive assessment, students create the answer.

content standards (chapter 2)—Define what students should know, be like, and be able to do.

covert learning outcomes (chapter 7)—Learning that may not be readily observable (e.g., cognitive domain).

credible (chapter 6)—Believable and trustworthy assessment results.

criteria (chapter 7)—The plural of criterion.

criterion (chapter 7)—Expected level of performance needed to satisfy the learning outcome.

criterion-referenced grading (chapter 13)—Student performance is compared to a standard that represents competence.

critical elements (chapters 3 and 8)—Parts of a movement that are important to correct performance.

culminating activity (chapters 1, 2, 3, and 4)—A final task or set of tasks that requires students to use all the skills and knowledge acquired during the unit.

data analysis (chapter 11)—Making sense of the raw data through mathematical processes such as calculating an average, sum, or percentage.

descriptive statistics (chapter 11)—Mathematical processes used to analyze data.

descriptor (chapter 4)—The name given to the characteristic or trait that is one of the major elements that will be assessed on a rubric.

developmentally appropriate (chapters 6 and 9)—An assessment task is one that most students, as determined by age or prior experience, can accomplish with a reasonable level of success.

diagnostic assessment (chapters 1 and 5)—Occurs before instruction begins to determine the baseline level of performance or ability.

dispositions (chapter 10)—Traits that are encouraged by teachers in the affective domain.

distracters (chapter 9)—The incorrect answers in a multiple choice item.

domains of learning (chapter 1)—Categories of learning that include psychomotor, affective, and cognitive.

effort (chapter 10)—An important disposition often encouraged by teachers that is associated with motivation, hard work, and doing one's best.

ego orientation (chapter 14)—In people with this orientation, self-confidence is linked to performing better than others instead of improvement; counterpart of task orientation.

essential questions (chapters 1 and 3)—The key concepts or outcomes of the unit or lesson phrased in the form of a question.

event recording (chapter 10)—A way to tally student behavior in which the behavior being observed is recorded each time it occurs.

exit slip (chapters 9 and 10)—Used to assess student learning in a lesson; students are required to respond to a question at the end of class.

fairness (chapter 6)—A fair assessment is one that is aligned with the content and that results in an accurate appraisal of students' learning.

fair play (chapter 10)—An affective behavior that is the gender-neutral equivalent for the term *sportsmanship*.

feasible (chapter 6)—An assessment is user friendly and doable.

formative assessment (chapters 5 and 7)—Occurs during instruction and is an assessment *for* learning.

frequency (chapter 11)—How often a behavior or event occurs.

frequency distribution (grouped or simple) (chapter 11)—A method of displaying scores showing the number of scores in each interval.

game performance assessment instrument (GPAI) (chapter 9)—Provides a way to record students' ability to make correct decisions about using the correct skill.

game-play rubric (chapters 1, 2, and 4)—Guides the observation of skills, dispositions, and knowledge that are important for students to learn, but are not readily observed away from game play; allows the observer to look at the application of skills, dispositions, and knowledge important for learning.

goal setting (chapter 11)—A way for students to aim for continual improvement based on their previous performance.

grading on the curve (chapter 13)—Norm-referenced grading based on the normal curve.

graphic organizer (chapter 3)—The diagram that shows the relationships between the various types of knowledge and skills.

higher-level thinking (chapter 9)—Requires students to do complex thinking represented by levels 3–6 on Bloom's taxonomy.

holistic rubric (chapter 4)—Used to give a single score or rating for the overall performance.

improvement (chapter 13)—Gradual gains in performance.

inference (chapters 6 and 13)—Assumption about student learning made by teachers based on an assessment.

instant activity (chapter 5)—Begins when students enter the gymnasium from the locker room.

intervals (chapter 11)—Used in frequency distribution to group scores.

invasion games (chapter 2)—Games that require players to move a ball into an opponent's goal area, such as soccer, flag football, basketball, and floor hockey.

journal (chapter 10)—Students respond to a prompt that will focus their comments on a relevant topic; often used to assess affective traits.

learning (chapter 1)—In the psychomotor domain, this is a permanent change in behavior.

learning outcomes (chapters 1 and 7)—Statements written by teachers that define a performance, condition, and criteria for successful performance; they guide teaching and assessment.

log (chapter 8)—Self-assessment tools that help students record and track their progress over several class periods.

management routines (chapter 12)—Methods for distributing equipment and supplies or forming groups that are taught to students in a way that uses class time efficiently.

meaningful (chapter 6)—An assessment that serves an important purpose for the teacher or students.

multiple performances (chapter 13)—Students have more than one chance to take an assessment.

negative grading system (chapter 13)—Students begin a grading period with an A and lose points when they do something wrong.

net/wall games (chapter 2)—Games that require players to hit an object across a net or against a wall, such as pickleball, volleyball, badminton, tennis, or racketball.

norm-referenced grading (chapter 13)—A way of comparing the performance of students with other members of the group.

objectivity (chapter 6)—The lack of any instructor influence over the results of assessment.

open environment (chapters 2 and 4)—Variables are constantly changing, requiring constant adjustment to the performance.

overt learning outcomes (chapter 7)—Learning is usually readily observable (e.g., psychomotor domain).

pace (chapters 3 and 7)—Instruction is planned so that students learn something new each day.

peer assessment (chapter 5)—Type of formative assessment conducted and recorded by peers.

percentage (chapter 11)—Mathematical procedure used in sports to indicate the ratio of success in terms of a decimal; to calculate free-throw percentage, divide the number of shots made by the number taken.

performance (chapter 7)—In physical education, this occurs when a student displays a motor skill.

performance-based assessment (chapters 1 and 9)—Assessments that are designed to let students demonstrate what they know and can do.

planning (chapters 2 and 3)—The process used by teachers to design curriculum and lessons.

point system (chapter 13)—A grading system in which the value of an assessment is stated in terms of points rather than percentages.

portfolio (chapter 9)—A collection of selected artifacts that show student growth over time.

process criterion (chapter 7)—Expected level of the form or technique of a movement.

product criterion (chapter 7)—Expected level of performance in terms of the outcome of the movement.

project (chapter 9)—A performance assessment that requires students to create something.

psychomotor domain (chapter 1)—Involves movement skills and fitness.

qualitative rubric (chapter 4)—Provides written descriptions of the levels of performance used for complex performances that involve multiple skills or supporting actions.

quantitative rubric (chapter 4)—A list of statements germane to the performance used by assessors to rate the performance by assigning a number that is anchored to a statement that describes the level of performance; best used for activities that have a multistage performance, such as target games.

range (chapter 11)—The difference between the highest and lowest scores; if the low is 10 and the high is 60, the range is 50.

rating scale (chapters 8 and 10)—Contains a list of important elements that are assigned a numerical level of achievement that corresponds with a verbal indicator to clarify the meaning associated with the number.

raw data (chapter 11)—A written record made up of assessment data consisting of numbers, check marks, tally marks, or words.

recording sheet (chapter 8)—Used for making a written record of assessment.

reflection (chapter 1)—The process of making inferences about learning using assessment data.

rubric (chapter 4)—Allows a performance to be judged by stated criteria divided into levels.

score sheet (chapter 8)—A form used to record the score in sports.

selected response (chapter 9)—Test items that require students to select the right answer from a list of options (e.g., multiple choice, true/false, matching).

self-assessment (chapter 5)—Type of formative assessment conducted and recorded by students on their own performance.

skill level (chapter 5)—Describes the psychomotor ability of students.

stable results (chapter 6)—An assessment produces similar data when it is repeated.

standardized test (chapter 6)—An assessment that has been validated by measurement experts.

standards (NASPE and state) (chapter 1)—These define what students should know, be like, and be able to do.

standards-based grade (chapter 13)—A grade that represents the degree to which the student met learning outcomes.

statistics (stat) sheet (chapter 8)—A form used to record product data about student performance.

subjective (chapter 6)—A teacher's personal bias influences the assessment.

summative assessment (chapters 5 and 7)—Used to determine a grade after students have experienced all the instructional lessons.

table of specifications (chapter 9)—Used to plan a balanced written test by computing the number of questions in each topic from the percentage of time spent on each topic.

tactics (chapters 7 and 9)—Offensive and defensive solutions to problems that arise during game play.

task orientation (chapter 14)—People with this orientation goal want to master a particular skill and they work toward self-improvement (ego-centered behavior is the other orientation).

teacher-directed assessment (chapter 5)—The teacher supervises and records the assessment task.

thinking like an assessor (chapter 1)—Teaching decisions are based on data about student learning.

unit goals (chapters 2 and 3)—Statements that define what students should accomplish during a unit of activity.

valid inferences (chapter 6)—Assessment yields accurate information about student learning and an accurate decision about the level or amount of learning is made.

Venn diagram (chapter 9)—Type of test item that allows students to demonstrate their ability to compare and contrast information or identify similarities and differences between two concepts.

weighting (chapter 13)—Giving more emphasis to a certain area.

written test (chapter 9)—Cognitive assessment that consists of open or selected response items.

zero (chapter 13)—Score used to represent a missing assignment.

REFERENCES

Berg, K. (2008). Are sports and games effective for fitness and weight control? *JOPERD, 79*(5), 13–17.

Black, P., & Wiliam, D. (1998a). Inside the black box: Raising standards through classroom assessment. *Phi Delta Kappan, 80*(2), 139–149.

Black, P., & Wiliam, D. (1998b). Assessment and classroom learning. *Assessment in Education, 5*(1), 7–75.

Black, P., Harrison, C., Lee, C., Marshall, B., & Wiliam, D. (2004). Working inside the black box: Assessment for learning in the classroom. *Phi Delta Kappan, 86*(1), 9–21.

Brookhart, S. (2011). Starting the conversation about grading. *Educational Leadership, 69* (3), 10–14.

Csikszentmihalyi, M. (1997). *Finding flow: The psychology of engagement with everyday life.* New York: Basic Books.

Cox, R.H. (2012). *Sport psychology: Concepts and applications* (7th ed.). New York: McGraw Hill.

FitnessGram. *Frequently asked questions for parents.* Retrieved November 15, 2011 from www.fitnessgram.net/faqparents.

French, K., Rink, J., Rikard, L., Mays, A., Lynn, S., & Werner, P. (1991). The effects of practice progressions on learning two volleyball skills. *Journal of Teaching Physical Education, 10,* 261–274.

Fronske, H. (1997). *Teaching cues for sport skills.* Boston: Allyn & Bacon.

Gardner, H. (1985). *Frames of mind: The theory of multiple intelligences.* New York: Basic Books.

Graham, G., Holt-Hale, S., & Parker, M. (2010). *Children moving: A reflective approach to teaching physical education* (8th ed.). St. Louis: McGraw-Hill.

Guskey, T. (2011). Five obstacles to grading reform. *Educational Leadership, 69*(3), 16–21.

Haywood, K., & Lewis, C. (1989). *Archery steps to success.* Champaign, IL: Human Kinetics.

Hastie, P., & Vlaisavljevic, N. (1999). The relationship between subject-matter expertise and accountability in instructional tasks, *Journal of Teaching in Physical Education, 19,* 22-33.

Hellison, D. (2011). *Teaching personal and social responsibility through physical activity* (3rd ed.). Champaign, IL: Human Kinetics

Lacy, A., & Hastad, D. (2006). *Measurement and evaluation in physical education and exercise science* (5th ed.). San Francisco: Benjamin Cummings.

Lambert, L. (2007). *Standards-based assessment of student learning: A comprehensive approach* (2nd ed.). Reston, VA: National Association for Sport and Physical Education.

Lee, A. (1997). Contributions of research on student thinking in physical education. *Journal of Teaching in Physical Education, 16,* 262–277.

Lund, J. (1992). Assessment and accountability in secondary physical education. *Quest, 44,* 352–360.

Lund, J., & Kirk, M. (2010). *Performance-based assessment for middle and high school physical education.* Champaign, IL: Human Kinetics.

Lund, J., & Shanklin, J. (2011). The impact of accountability on student response rate in a secondary physical education badminton unit. *Physical Educator, 68*(4), 210–220.

Lund, J., & Tannehill, D. (2010). *Standards-based physical education curriculum development.* Boston: Jones & Bartlett.

Lund, J., & Veal, M.L. (2008). Measuring pupil learning: How do student teachers assess within instructional models? *Journal of Teaching in Physical Education, 27,* 487–511.

Metzler, M. (2011). *Instructional models for physical education* (3rd ed.). Scottsdale, AZ: Holcomb Hathaway.

Mitchell, S., Oslin, J., & Griffin, L. (2006). *Teaching sport concepts and skills: A tactical games approach* (2nd ed.). Champaign, IL: Human Kinetics.

National Association for Sport and Physical Education (NASPE). (1992). *Outcomes of quality physical education programs.* Reston, VA: National Association for Sport and Physical Education.

NASPE. (1995). *Moving into the future: National standards for physical education.* Reston, VA: National Association for Sport and Physical Education.

NASPE. (2004). *Moving into the future: National standards for physical education* (2nd ed.). Reston, VA: National Association for Sport and Physical Education.

NASPE. (2009). *National standards and guidelines for physical education teacher education.* Reston, VA: National Association for Sport and Physical Education.

NASPE. (2010). *Position statement: Appropriate uses of fitness measurement.* Retrieved from http://AAHPERD.org/NASPE.

NASPE. (2011). *PE Metrics: Assessing national standards 1-6 in secondary school*. Reston, VA: National Association for Sport and Physical Education.

Popham, W. J. (2008). *Transformative assessment*. Alexandria, VA: Association for Supervision and Curriculum Development.

Popham, W.J. (2010). *Everything school leaders need to know about assessment*. Thousand Oaks, CA: Corwin.

Rink, J. (2000, July). *Physical education and the physically active lifestyle*. Keynote address presented at the NASPE 2000 standards conference: Linking Physical Activity and Fitness, Baltimore, MD.

Rink, J. (2010). *Teaching physical education for learning* (6th ed.). NewYork: McGraw-Hill.

San Diego County Office of Education (http://kms.sdcoe.net/differ/21-DSY/55-DSY.html).

Siedentop, D. (1991). *Developing teaching skills in physical education*. Mountain View, CA: Mayfield.

Siedentop, D., Hastie, P., & Van der Mars, H. (2004). *Complete guide to sport education*. Champaign, IL: Human Kinetics.

Siedentop, D., Mand, C., & Taggart, A. (1986). *Physical education: Teaching and curriculum strategies for grades 5-12*. Mountain View, CA: Mayfield.

Stiggins, R.J. (1997). *Student-centered classroom assessment*. Upper Saddle River, NJ: Prentice-Hall.

Stiggins, R.J. (2001). *Student-involved classroom assessment* (3rd ed.). Upper Saddle River, NJ: Merrill Prentice Hall.

Stiggins, R.J. (2002). Assessment crisis! The absence of assessment FOR learning. *Phi Delta Kappan, 83*(10), 758–765.

Stodden, D.F., Goodway, J.D., Langendorfer, S.J., Roberton, M.A., Rudisill, M.E., Garcia, C., & Garcia, L.E. (2008). A developmental perspective on the role of motor skill competence in physical activity: An emergent relationship. *Quest, 60,* 290–306.

Strand, B., & Wilson, R. (1993). *Assessing sport skills*. Champaign, IL: Human Kinetics.

Tritschler, K. (2000). *Barrow & McGee's practical measurement and assessment*. Baltimore: Lippincott, Williams & Wilkins.

Veal, M.L., & Anderson, W. (2011). *Analysis of teaching and learning in physical education*. Sudbury, MA: Jones & Bartlett.

Wiggins, G. (1998). *Educative assessment: Designing assessments to inform and improve student performance*. San Francisco: Jossey-Bass.

Wiggins, G., & McTighe, J. (1998). *Understanding by design*. Alexandria, VA: Association for Curriculum and Supervision Development.

Zimmerman, B.J., & Bamdura, A. (1994). Impact of self-regulatory influences on writing course attainment. *American Educational Research Journal, 31,* 845–862.

INDEX

ABOUT THE AUTHORS

Jacalyn Lea Lund, PhD, is a professor and chair in the department of kinesiology and health at Georgia State University in Atlanta. She taught for 16 years in public schools before entering the doctoral program at Ohio State University to prepare for a second career in teacher education. She received her PhD in 1990. Dr. Lund has presented on assessment at numerous workshops and has taught numerous classes on assessment in physical education.

Dr. Lund has been a member of the National Association for Sport and Physical Education (NASPE) for more than 40 years. She was on the committee that developed the 1995 NASPE content standards for physical education and has served as NASPE president. In 2009 she received a Service Award from the National Association of Kinesiology and Physical Education in Higher Education and was inducted into the NASPE Hall of Fame in 2013. She loves spending time with her family, dancing, reading, and, as she puts it, "having her dogs take her for a walk."

Mary Lou Veal, EdD, began her teaching career as an elementary physical education teacher in Dallas, Texas. She taught physical education for 16 years in elementary, middle, and senior high schools and along the way she coached volleyball and track in addition to serving as a curriculum coordinator in Denton, Texas. Since receiving her EdD, she has taught in physical education teacher education programs at the University of Houston, the University of North Carolina at Greensboro, and at Middle Tennessee State University.

Dr. Veal's research has focused primarily on teachers' assessment perceptions and practices. She is the coauthor of three books and numerous articles and book chapters. Dr. Veal served as president of the North Carolina Alliance for Coaching, Physical Education, Recreation and Dance and was a member of the 1995 NASPE Task Force to develop Teacher Education Standards. In her free time, Dr. Veal enjoys reading historical fiction, gardening, and genealogy. She serves as regent of the Captain William Lytle Chapter of the National Society of the Daughters of the American Revolution.

You'll find other outstanding
physical education resources at
www.HumanKinetics.com

In the U.S. call 1.800.747.4457
Australia 08 8372 0999
Canada. 1.800.465.7301
Europe . . . . . +44 (0) 113 255 5665
New Zealand 0800 222 062

HUMAN KINETICS
The Information Leader in Physical Activity
P.O. Box 5076 • Champaign, IL 61825-5076